Puer aeternus

SIGO PRESS

Marie-Louise von Franz

Puer aeternus

SECOND EDITION

SIGO PRESS, 2601 Ocean Park Blvd., 210, Santa Monica, CA 90405

Publisher and General Editor: Sisa Sternback-Scott

Library of Congress Cataloging in Publication Data

    Franz, Marie-Louise von, 1915-
      Puer aeternus

      Bibliography: p.295.
      1. Personality. 2. Psychology, Pathological.
    3. Jung, Carl Gustav, 1875-1961. 4. Saint-Exupéry,
    Antoine de, 1900-1944. The little prince. I. Title
    BF698.F7155 1980   155.2'32   80-28090
    ISBN 0-938434-01-2 (pbk.)   AACR1
    ISBN 0-938434-03-9

Typesetting in Caslon: Nancy Hope, Typesetting, Ltd.
Title page: Etching by B. A. Dunkere as it appeared in *Romische Riesen eines Kleinen Amors* by Johann Burkli, 1792.

Excerpts and illustrations from *The Little Prince* by Antoine de Saint-Exupéry are reprinted by permission of Harcourt Brace Jovanovich, Inc.,; copyright 1943, 1971 by Harcourt Brace Jovanovich, Inc.

Cover Design: John Coy
Cover: Photograph of Bronze Statue of Youth is reproduced by permission of Hirmer Verlag München.

ACKNOWLEDGEMENTS

The substance of these chapters was presented as twelve lectures at the C. G. Jung Institute Zürich during the Winter Semester 1959-60.

I wish to thank Una Thomas for her faithful transcript upon which the somewhat revised text has been based. I also wish to thank Patricia Berry and Valery Donleavy for the final form in which this seminar appears.

Marie-Louise von Franz
Zürich
January 1970

The Second Edition Produced and Edited: Sisa Sternback-Scott with the assistance of Becky Goodman and Rochelle Wallace.

CHAPTER ONE

Puer aeternus is the name of a god of antiquity. The words
themselves come from Ovid's *Metamorphoses*[1] and are there applied
to the child-god in the Eleusinian mysteries. Ovid speaks of the
child-god Iacchus, addressing him as *puer aeternus* and praising him
in his role in these mysteries. In later times, the child-god was
identified with Dionysus and the god Eros. He is the divine youth
who is born in the night in this typical mother-cult mystery of
Eleusis, and who is a redeemer. He is a god of life, death and
resurrection—the god of divine youth, corresponding to such oriental
gods as Tammuz, Attis, and Adonis. The title *puer aeternus* therefore
means "eternal youth," but we also use it to indicate a certain type
of young man who has an outstanding mother complex and who
therefore behaves in certain typical ways, which I would like to
characterize as follows.

In general, the man who is identified with the archetype of the
puer aeternus remains too long in adolescent psychology; that is, all
those characteristics that are normal in a youth of seventeen or
eighteen are continued into later life, coupled in most cases with too
great a dependence on the mother. The two typical disturbances of
a man who has an outstanding mother complex are, as Jung points
out,[2] homosexuality and Don Juanism. In the latter case, the image
of a mother—the image of the perfect woman who will give
everything to a man and who is without any shortcomings—is

[1]Ovid, *Metamorphoses* IV, 18-20.

[2]Carl Gustave Jung, *Symbols of Transformation*, Vol. 5, *Collected Works* (Princeton:
Princeton University Press, 1956; 2nd ed. 1967). par. 527.

sought in every woman. He is looking for a mother goddess, so that each time he is fascinated by a woman he has later to discover that she is an ordinary human being. Having lived with her sexually, the whole fascination vanishes and he turns away disappointed, only to project the image anew onto one woman after another. He eternally longs for the maternal woman who will enfold him in her arms and satisfy his every need. This is often accompanied by the romantic attitude of the adolescent.

Generally, great difficulty is experienced in adaptation to the social situation. In some cases, there is a kind of asocial individualism: being something special, one has no need to adapt, for that would be impossible for such a hidden genius, and so on. In addition, an arrogant attitude arises towards other people, due to both an inferiority complex and false feelings of superiority. Such people usually have great difficulty in finding the right kind of job, for whatever they find is never quite right or quite what they wanted. There is always "a hair in the soup." The woman is never quite the right woman; she is nice as a girl friend, but . . . There is always a "but" which prevents marriage or any kind of commitment.

This all leads to a form of neurosis which H. G. Baynes has described as the "provisional life"; that is, the strange attitude and feeling that the woman is *not yet* what is really wanted, and there is always the fantasy that sometime in the future the real thing will come about. If this attitude is prolonged, it means a constant inner refusal to commit oneself to the moment. Accompanying this neurosis is often, to a smaller or greater extent, a savior or Messiah complex, with the secret thought that one day one will be able to save the world; that the last word in philosophy, or religion, or politics, or art, or something else, will be found. This can progress to a typical pathological megalomania, or there may be minor traces of it in the idea that one's time "has not yet come." The one situation dreaded throughout by such a type of man is to be bound to anything whatsoever. There is a terrific fear of being pinned down, of entering space and time completely, and of being the specific human being that one is. There is always the fear of being caught in a situation from which it may be impossible to slip out again. Every just-so situation is hell. At the same time, there is something highly symbolic—namely, a fascination for dangerous sports, particularly flying and mountaineering—so as to get as high as possible, the symbolism of which is to get away from the mother; i.e., from the earth, from ordinary life. If this type of complex is very pronounced, many such men die at a young age in airplane crashes and mountaineering accidents. It is an exteriorized spiritual longing which expresses itself in this form.

A dramatic representation of what flying really means to the *puer* is given in John Magee's poem. Soon after the poem was written, Magee died in an airplane accident.

High Flight

Oh! I have slipped the surly bonds of Earth
    And danced the skies on laughter-silvered wings;
Sunward I've climbed, and joined the tumbling mirth
    Of sun-split clouds,—and done a hundred things
You have not dreamed of—wheeled and soared and swung
    High in the sunlit silence. Hov'ring there,
I've chased the shouting wind along, and flung
    My eager craft through footless halls of air . . .

Up, up the long, delirious, burning blue
    I've topped the wind-swept heights with easy grace,
Where never lark, or even eagle flew—
    And, while with silent, lifting mind I've trod
    The high untrespassed sanctity of space,
Put out my hand and touched the face of God.[3]

Pueri generally do not like sports which require patience and long training, for the *puer aeternus*—in the negative sense of the word—is usually very impatient by disposition. I know a young man, a classical example of the *puer aeternus*, who did a tremendous amount of mountaineering but so much hated carrying a rucksack that he preferred to train himself even to sleep in the rain or snow outdoors. He would make himself a hole in the snow and wrap himself up in a silk raincoat and, with a kind of yoga breathing, was able to sleep out-of-doors. He also trained himself to go practically without food, simply to avoid carrying any weight. He roamed about for years all over mountains in Europe and other continents, sleeping under trees or in the snow. In a way, he led a very heroic existence, just in order not to be bound to go to a hut or carry a rucksack. You might say that this was symbolic, for such a young man in real life does not want to be burdened with any kind of weight; the one thing he absolutely refuses is responsibility for anything, or to carry the weight of a situation.

In general, the positive quality of such youths is a certain kind of spirituality which comes from a relatively close contact with the collective unconscious. Many have the charm of youth and the stirring quality of a drink of champagne. *Pueri aeterni* are generally very agreeable to talk with; they usually have interesting subjects to talk about and have an invigorating effect upon the listener; they do not like conventional situations; they ask deep questions and go straight for the truth; usually they are searching for genuine religion, a search that is typical for people in their late teens. Usually the youthful charm of the *puer aeternus* is prolonged through later stages of life.

However, there is another type of *puer* that does not display the charm of eternal youth, nor does the archetype of the divine youth shine through him. On the contrary, he lives in a continual sleepy daze, and that, too, is a typical adolescent characteristic: the sleepy, undisciplined, long-legged youth who merely hangs around, his mind wandering indiscriminately, so that sometimes one feels inclined to pour a bucket of cold water over his head. The sleepy daze is only an outer aspect, however, and if you can penetrate it, you will find that a lively fantasy life is being cherished within.

The above is a short summary of the main characteristics of certain young men who are caught up in the mother complex and, with it, are identified with the archetype of the *puer*. I have given a mainly negative picture of these people because that is what they look like if viewed superficially, but, as you will see, we have not explained what is really the matter. The question to which my lecture is directed is why the problem of this type, of the mother-bound young man, has become so pronounced in our time. As you know, homosexuality—I do not think Don Juanism is so widely spread—is increasing more and more; even teenagers are involved, and it seems to me that the problem of the *puer aeternus* is becoming increasingly actual. Undoubtedly, mothers have always tried to keep their sons in the nest, and some sons have always had difficulty in getting free and have rather preferred to continue to enjoy the pleasures of the nest; still one does not quite see why this in itself, a natural problem, should now become such a serious time-problem. I think that is the important and deeper question we have to put to ourselves because the rest is more or less self-evident. A man who has a mother complex will always have to contend with his tendencies towards becoming a *puer aeternus*. What cure is there? you might ask. If a man discovers that he has a mother complex, which is something that happened to him—something that he did not cause himself—what can he do about it? In *Symbols of Transformation*, Dr. Jung spoke of one cure—work—and having said that, he hesitated for a minute and thought, "Is it really as simple as all that? Is that the only cure? Can I put it that way?" But work is the one disagreeable word which no *puer aeternus* likes to hear, and Dr. Jung came to the conclusion that it was the right answer. My experience also has been that it is through work that a man can pull out of this kind of youthful neurosis. There are, however, some misunderstandings in this connection, for the *puer aeternus* can work, as can all primitives or people with weak ego complexes, when fascinated or in a state of great enthusiasm. Then he can work twenty-four hours at a stretch or even longer, until he breaks down. But what he cannot do is to work on a dreary, rainy morning when work is boring and one has to kick oneself into it; that is the one thing the *puer aeternus* usually cannot manage and will use any kind of excuse to avoid. Analysis of a *puer aeternus* sooner or later always comes up against this problem. It is only when the ego has become sufficiently strengthened that the problem can be overcome, and the possibility of sticking to the work is given. Naturally, though one knows the goal, every individual case is different. Personally, I have not found that it is much good just preaching to people that they should work, for they simply get angry and walk off.

As far as I have seen, the unconscious generally tries to produce a compromise—namely, to indicate the direction in which there might be some enthusiasm or where the psychological energy would flow naturally, for it is, of course, easier to train oneself to work in a direction supported by one's instinct. That is not quite so hard as working completely uphill in opposition to your own flow of energy. Therefore, it is usually advisable to wait a while, find out where the natural flow of interest and energy lies and then try to get the man to work *there*. But in every field of work there always comes the time when routine must be faced. All work, even creative work, contains a certain amount of boring routine, which is where the *puer aeternus* escapes and comes to the conclusion again that "this is not it!" In such moments, if one is supported by the unconscious, dreams generally occur which show that one should push on through the obstacle. If that succeeds, then the battle is won.

In a letter[4] Jung says about the *puer*: "I consider the *puer aeternus* attitude an unavoidable evil. Identity with the *puer* signifies a psychological puerility that could do nothing better than outgrow itself. It always leads to external blows of fate which show the need for another attitude. But reason accomplishes nothing, because the *puer aeternus* is always an agent of destiny."

In order to get into the deeper background of the whole problem, I want first to interpret *The Little Prince* by Antoine de Saint Exupéry, because it throws much light on this situation. This man, as you know, died during World War II in an airplane crash. He displays all the typical features of the *puer aeternus*, which, however, does not alter the fact that he was also a great writer and poet. His life was at first, difficult to trace. In itself, this difficulty, is typical: when you try to follow the biography, you can only collect a very few facts here and there because, as is already clear, the *puer aeternus* never quite touches the earth. He never quite commits himself to any mundane situation but just hovers over the earth, touching it from time to time, alighting here and there, so that one has to follow such traces as there may be. More information became available only several years after his death. It is well summarized in Curtis Cate's *Antoine de Saint Exupéry, His Life and Times.*[5]

Saint Exupéry (born 1900) came from an old aristocratic French family and grew up in a beautiful country house with its traditional atmosphere. He chose to become a professional aviator and acted for a time as a pilot for the Compagnie Aero-postale, which ran a service between Europe and South America. About 1929, he flew over the Toulouse-Dakar-Buenos Aires line and was also a collaborator in establishing new lines in South America. Later, he was in command of a completely isolated aerodrome in the North-Africa

[4]Gerhard Adler and Aniela Jaffé, eds. *C. G. Jung: Letters*, 2 vols. (Princeton: Princeton University Press, 1973), vol. 1, p. 82. Letter dated February 23, 1931.

[5]Curtis Cate, *Antoine de Saint-Exupéry, His Life and Times* (New York: G. P. Putnam's Sons, 1970).

desert—Cap Julie—for a considerable amount of time. His main duty there was to rescue pilots who had crashed, from death in the desert or from falling into the hands of rebel Arab tribes. That was the kind of life such a man would like, and Saint Exupéry preferred this isolated desert post to any other. In 1939, at the beginning of the war, he fought for France as a captain in the air force. After the collapse of France he had intended to escape to Egypt, but for technical reasons that plan had to be abandoned. He was then demobilized and went to New York, where he finished his book *Flight to Arras*. Later when the Allies landed in Africa, he wanted to return to the air force, and though he was refused due to his age, he successfully used every conceivable ruse to fly again.

In July 1944, having left Algiers with his plane on a reconnoitering flight in France, he disappeared without leaving any trace either of his plane or of himself. Later—some time after the war had ended—a young German reported that he had been shot down over the sea by a German Fokker-Wolff plane. Out of a group of seven planes, one man said that a French machine had been shot down over the Mediterranean; from the indications given it would seem to have been Saint Exupéry's.

Saint Exupéry's marriage was not a very happy one. His wife seems to have been a very temperamental and sometimes difficult woman, and he usually did not stay with her for more than a week or two; then, for one reason or another, he would leave again. When he was not allowed to fly he always became depressed, walking up and down in his flat from morning till evening, desperate and irritated. Only when he could fly, he became his normal self again and felt all right. When he had to stay on the ground and be with his wife, or remain in some other situation, he fell back into these bad moods, so he always tried to get back into flying.

His other books show how much he was concerned with present-day problems and with the *Weltanschauung* of our time. Those of you who have read them will have noticed that like many French people, especially those of the French nobility, he has quite a bit of Nazi psychology. The French are Franks, something one forgets because they hate the Germans so much, but the upper layers of society are often of German stock which immigrated into France not so very long ago. From an historical point of view and therefore especially in military circles and among the nobility, they have quite an affinity with Prussian mentality. Undeniably, this comes out in the characters of Saint Exupéry's novels: for instance, in Riviere, he tries to outline a Führer type, the cold man who sends his young flyers to their death for a higher purpose. This is just a part of the local make-up in his milieu and not really relevant for his deeper problem, which is a search for . . .? But for what is he searching? That is a question which I will not answer now, but will try to find the answer to it with you.

One of his most popular works, as you know, is *The Little Prince*. The book was a tremendous success and many people made it their Bible and worship; if you talk to them about it, however, they generally adopt a slightly defiant attitude, insisting that they think it a marvelous book. I have wondered about this defiant attitude and I think the only explanation can be that even those who like it so very much have a small question mark in their minds. There is one question which I think one is allowed to put—even to its worshippers —and that is about the slightly sentimental style, a sentimental touch which, although it causes a certain malaise, does not detract from its value in other ways, even if one enjoys the book very much. Where there is sentimentality, in general, there is also a certain amount of brutality. Goering was a typical example, for without a qualm he could sign the death sentence for three hundred people, but if one of his birds died, then that old fat man would cry. He is a classic example! Cold brutality is very often covered up by sentimentality. You see this cold masculine brutality at work in the figures of Riviere and of the Sheikh in Saint Exupéry's books.

When we have interpreted *The Little Prince*, we shall examine some case material where this will become very clear: namely, in the shadow problem of the *puer aeternus*. Here, usually, is a very cold, brutal man somewhere in the background, which compensates the too idealistic attitude of consciousness and which the *puer aeternus* cannot voluntarily assimilate. For example, in the Don Juan type, that cold brutality comes out every time he leaves the woman. When his feeling has gone, out comes an ice-cold brutality with no human feeling in it, and the whole sentimental enthusiasm is projected onto another woman. This brutality, or the cold realistic attitude, very often appears also in matters related to money. Since he does not want to adapt socially, or take on some regular job and work, yet he must get money somehow, the *puer aeternus* generally achieves his purpose behind his own back—with his left hand, so to speak. He obtains the money, God knows from where, and in rather mean ways. If you touch the unconscious shadow problem, you get a complex—a reaction.

Remark: Many of the aspects which you ascribe to the puer aeternus *could also be ascribed to the psychopath. What distinction do you make between the two?*

Quite a lot. But I would not say that the above is typical for the psychopath. For instance, the case I shall bring afterwards, a schizoid borderline type, is another variety. My experience is that beside the *puer aeternus* there is the man who is either the psychopath or the schizoid or the hysteric, or just slightly neurotic, depending on the individual case and what additional form the problem takes on. Let's say somebody has a religious problem. That is a problem in itself, but, in addition, the person can be normal or be a psychopath, or a schizoid, or hysterical about it. The same applies to the problem of homosexuality, which can be combined with, or free from, other neurotic features and can be linked with the time-problem more or less closely. It seems to me to be a more paramount problem.

Dr. Jung had a very interesting idea about homosexuality: That perhaps it is an unconscious compensation for overpopulation; namely, that Nature pushes this tendency in order to compensate for overpopulation—so that a certain number of people refrain from producing children. Nature might possibly employ such a ruse, and overpopulation is just now our greatest problem. In former times there were no statistics, so it is difficult to prove anything by statistics here. We only know that homosexuality is now tremendously widespread. My father, who was an officer in the regular army in Austria and who spoke quite openly about such things, said that in his time, homosexuality was not a problem in the army and that there were very few cases; while nowadays, as you know, it is a real problem and very widespread, particularly among airmen.

I have been asked to say something about the *puer aeternus* problem as seen as the animus in women. I have no material on that except for some single dreams, but I can say that in its basic structure the problem is not different. It is just the same, but one layer deeper. You could say that with a woman the animus always anticipates what she has to do later in reality. So, the problem of the *puer aeternus* having to come down to earth is analogous to what the woman's mind had to do later; it is only one step removed from the ego. Naturally, the *puer aeternus* problem is always linked with the creative problem, and that is paramount in a woman's psychology. If she has a *puer aeternus* animus, she generally has a creative problem, and the cure for women is unfortunately exactly the same as for men: it is also work, or it can also be having children.

I remember the case of a woman who did not want to have children. She always dreamt about *puer aeternus* animi figures and Nature pinning her down to earth. The dreams wanted her to have children, which would be one of the main ways by which a woman comes down to earth. She is committed definitely to something and cannot toy around with this and that anymore. This applies especially to women who are more of the hetaera type, those who have a lot of affairs with a number of men and do not want to be pinned down. The child makes the relationship more definite. So that is one way which it takes with women, and it is a lot of work to have children—very regular, sometimes boring, work.

Now we will turn to the interpretation of *The Little Prince*. The story falls into two completely definite parts, beginning with an introduction which is told by Saint Exupéry in the first person, like part of a personal autobiographical account. It begins:

Once when I was six years old, I saw a magnificent picture in a book, called True Stories from Nature, *about the primeval forest. It was a picture of a boa constrictor in the act of swallowing an animal. Here is a copy of the drawing.*

In the book it said: "Boa constrictors swallow their prey whole, without chewing it. After that they are not able to move and they sleep through the six months that they need for digestion."

I pondered deeply, then, over the adventures of the jungle. And after

some work with a colored pencil I succeeded in making my first drawing.
My Drawing Number One. It looked like this:

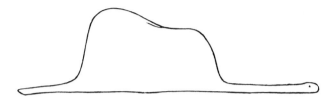

 I showed my masterpeice to the grown-ups, and asked them whether the
drawing frightened them.
 But they answered: "Frightened? Why should anyone be frightened by a
hat?"
 My drawing was not a picture of a hat. It was picture of a boa
constrictor digesting an elephant. But since the grown-ups were not able to
understand it, I made another drawing: I drew the inside of the boa
constrictor, so that the grown-ups could see it clearly. They always need to
have things explained. My Drawing Number Two looked like this:

 The grown-ups' response, this time, was to advise me to lay aside my
drawings of boa constrictors, whether from the inside or the outside, and
devote myself instead to geography, history, arithmetic and grammar.
That is why, at the age of six, I gave up what might have been a
magnificient career as a painter. I had been disheartened by the failure of
my Drawing Number One and my Drawing Number Two. Grown-ups
never understand anything by themselves, and it is tiresome for children to
be always and forever explaining things to them.

So then I chose another profession, and learned to pilot airplanes. I have flown a little over all parts of the world; and it is true that the geography has been very useful to me. At a glance I can distinguish China from Arizona. If one gets lost in the night, such knowledge is valuable.

In the course of this life I have had a great many encounters with a great many people who have been concerned with matters of consequence. I have lived a great deal among grown-ups. I have seen them intimately, close at hand. And that hasn't much improved my opinion of them.

Whenever I met one of them who seemed to me at all clearsighted, I tried the experiment of showing him my Drawing Number One, which I have always kept. I would try to find out, so, if this was a person of true understanding. But, whoever it was, he, or she, would always say:
"That is a hat."

Then I would never talk to that person about boa constrictors, or primeval forests, or stars. I would bring myself down to his level. I would talk to him about bridge, and golf, and politics, and neckties. And the grown-up would be greatly pleased to have met such a sensible man.

So I lived my life alone, without anyone that I could really talk to, until I had an accident with my plane in the Desert of Sahara, six years ago. Something was broken in my engine. And as I had with me neither a mechanic nor any passengers, I set myself to attempt the difficult repairs all alone. It was a question of life or death for me: I had scarcely enough drinking water to last a week.

The first night, then, I went to sleep on the sand, a thousand miles from any human habitation. I was more isolated than a ship-wrecked sailor on a raft in the middle of the ocean. Thus, you can imagine my amazement, at sunrise, when I was awakened by an odd little voice. It said:
"If you please—draw me a sheep!"
"What!"

Then he meets the little prince. Now we have to conclude from this first part. It contains the whole problem in a nutshell.

We see that he has never really gotten into the world of the adult. He speaks about its emptiness, its idiocy, and its meaninglessness. There is the talk about bridge and politics and neckties, it is true, but that is the kind of adult world one rightly rejects—it is persona-emptiness. But he omits other aspects of adult life as well. You see in the feeling-tone of this first part that he means that the childhood life is the fantasy life, the artist's life. He believes that this childhood life is the true life, and all the rest is empty persona running after money, making a prestige impression on other people, having lost one's true nature, so to speak. That is how he sees adult life, for he has not found a bridge by which he could take over what we call the true life into adult life. That is the great problem, I think, in a nutshell; namely, how can one pull out of this fantasy life of youth and youthfulness without losing its value? How can one grow up without losing the feeling of totality and the feeling of creativeness and of being really alive, which one had in youth? One can be cynical about it and say that one cannot have the penny and the cake—it has to be sacrificed—but from my experience I do not think that this is quite right. It is justifiable not to want to give up the childhood-world. The question is, how can one grow up and not lose it?

The great problem is that you can drive people out of this childhood paradise and fantasy life, in which they are in close connection with their true inner self on an infantile level, but then they are completely disillusioned and cynical. I remember once that I had an analysand who was a typical *puer aeternus* and wanted to become a writer, but he lived in a complete world of fantasy. He came over from the States with a friend, and the two decided that the friend should have a Freudian analysis and he, a Jungian analysis; after a year they would meet to compare notes. They went to different countries and met as arranged, and the young man who had had the Freudian analysis said that he was through with his problem and was cured and was going home. Everything was all right, and he understood his infantile attitude towards life; he had given up his mother complex and other nonsense. My analysand asked him what he was going to do, and the other said he did not know, but that he must earn some money and find a wife. My analysand said that *he* was not cured at all; he did not yet know where to go. He knew that he would become a writer and had started on that course, but he did not know where to settle, and so on. Then the one who had had the Freudian analysis said, "Well, it is strange; they have driven out my devils, but with them they have also driven out my angel!"

So you see, that is the problem! One can drive away devils *and* angels by saying that the problem is all infantile and part of the mother complex and, by a completely reductive analysis, reduce everything to the childhood sentimentality which has to be sacrificed. There is something to be said for that. This man was in a way more cured than my analysand; on the other hand, it seems to me that such a terrific disillusionment makes one ask whether it is worthwhile to go on living. Is it worthwhile just to make money for the rest of one's life and get small bourgeois pleasures? It doesn't seem to me very satisfactory. The sadness with which the man who was "cured" remarked that with his devils, his angels had also been driven out, made me feel that he himself did not feel quite happy about his own cure; it had the tone of cynical disillusionment, which to my mind is no cure.

It must not be forgotten that the atmosphere of a milieu in Paris, such as that in which Saint Exupéry lived, was partly very disillusioned and cynical. He usually moved in circles which looked at life as being important when one talked of bridge and money and such things. Therefore, he, in a way, rightly protests against it, clings to his inner artistic and total view of life, and is resentful and revolutionary against such adult life. One sees quite well how, in a subtle way, he mocks at the adult and how to the point that is. At the same time, however, he does not know how to pull out of his childhood world without falling into the disillusionment of what he sees as the only value in adult life. If you combine this with the symbolism of the picture, the implication becomes even worse. The boa constrictor obviously is an image of the unconscious, which suffocates life and prevents the human being from developing. It is the swallowing or the regressive aspect of the unconscious, the looking-backward tendency, which grips one when one is overcome by the unconscious. You could even say that the boa constrictor represents a pull towards death. The boa is the monster of the night-sea journey, but here, in contrast to most other mythological parallels, the swallowed hero does not come out of it again.

The animal that is swallowed is the elephant, so we should look into its symbolism. Since the elephant was not known in European countries until late antiquity, not much mythological material is available. However, in late antiquity the elephant had great significance. When Alexander the Great went to India, he saw elephants, and they were afterwards brought to Europe. The Romans later used elephants in the same manner as tanks are used in modern warfare. If we read what has been written about them, we see that a great deal of mythological fantasy was spun around the elephant. It is said that "they are very chaste, that they only mate once in a lifetime and very secretly in order to produce their young and therefore," according to a medieval reporter, "they are an allegory of marital chastity. Like the unicorn, the elephant also loves a virgin and can only be tamed by one, a motif which points to the incarnation of Christ." The elephant is said to represent invincible fortitude and to be an image of Christ. "In antiquity it was thought that elephants were terribly ambitious and that if they were not accorded the honour due to them they would die from disappointment, for their feeling of honour was so great. Snakes love to drink the cool blood, and suddenly the elephant collapses, which is why whenever an elephant sees a snake he goes for it and tries to trample it down. In the Middle Ages the elephant stood for a man who was generous but unstable and moody in character, for the elephant was said to be generous, intelligent, and therefore taciturn, but when he once gets into a rage he cannot be appeased by sensual pleasures but only by music." This all comes from the *Polyhistor Symbolicus* written by a Jesuit Father, Nikolaus Caussinus. He gives such funny stories about the elephant, having summed up what the antique idiom says and then adding a little of medieval fantasy. "Elephants wash very often," he continues, "and use flowers to perfume themselves. Hence they represent purification, chastity, and pious worship of God. This shows that the same thing happened to Europeans who met the elephant that happened long before to the Africans when they met it; namely, the hero archetype got projected. It is a great honor if a man is given the title of lion, but the highest title anyone can be given is that of elephant. It is considered to be far above the lion, which is the image of a courageous man of the Chief type, for the elephant is the archetype of the medicine man or wise man, who also has courage but, in addition, wisdom and secret knowledge.

So, in their hierarchy, the elephant represents the individuated personality. Strangely enough, the European automatically projected the same idea onto the elephant and took him as the image of the divine hero, the image of Christ, outstanding in virtue, except for being moody and inclined to fits of rage. That is amazing, but those were two outstanding qualities in Saint Exupéry, so that it could be said to be an exact picture of this character. He himself was subtle, chaste and—to a certain extent, in the sense of being sensitive in his feelings—very ambitious and very sensitive about everything affecting his own honor. He was continually on the search for religious meaning—he did not worship God, for he had not found Him—but he was always on the search. He was generous, intelligent and taciturn, but very irritable and inclined to terrible moods and fits of rage. So there is an amazing self-portrait in the elephant, and one sees the archetypal pattern illustrated in a single individual, without even much difference.

It can be said that the elephant is the model fantasy of the grown-up hero. Already, this model fantasy—the image in his soul of what he wanted to become—is swallowed by the boa, the devouring mother, and this first picture shows the whole tragedy. Very often, childhood dreams anticipate the inner fate twenty or thirty years ahead. This first picture shows that Saint Exupéry had a hero aspect, alive and constellated, and that this aspect would never quite come through but would be swallowed back by the regressive tendencies of the unconscious and, as we know from later events, by death.

The devouring-mother myth should naturally also be pinned down in connection with Saint Exupéry's mother, but, since she is in a conspicuous position, I hesitate to comment on her too much. She certainly is a very powerful personage. She is a big, stout woman, about whom we hear that she has a tremendous amount of energy, is interested in all kinds of activities, and tries her hand at drawing, painting and writing. She is a very dynamic person and, in spite of the fact that she is now pretty old, is still going strong. Obviously, it must have been very difficult for a sensitive boy to pull away from the influence of such a mother. It is also said that she always anticipated her son's death. Several times she thought he was dead and dressed herself in large black veils such as French women like to wear when they become widows, and then she had to take them off again, for he was not yet dead. So the archetypal pattern of what we call the death-mother was alive in her psyche.

In our layers of society, the death-mother is something not openly acknowledged, but I got the shock of my life when I had the following experience. I had to go somewhere to meet someone, and at that place the house-owner had a *puer aeternus* son whom she had quite eaten up. They were very simple people. They had a bakery and the son did no work at all, but went about in riding outfit. He was a typical Don Juan type, very elegant and having a new girl about every four days. This young man once went bathing and carried his girl friend out into the Lake of Zurich and, in a classic situation, *halb zog sie ihn, halb sank er hin* ("Half drew she him, half sank he down")—as Goethe would have put it—both went under.

The girl was saved, but when he was brought out he was already dead. This I read in the paper, but when I came back to this house, I bumped into the mother, who was a widow, and condoled with her, saying how sorry I was when I heard of the terrible accident. She invited me in and took me to the sitting-room where there was a very big photograph of the son on his death-bed, surrounded by flowers, set up like a hero's tomb, and she remarked, "Look at him! How beautiful he looks in death." I agreed, and then she smiled and said, "Well, I'd rather have him like that than give him away to another woman."

The Great Mother makes a religious cult out of her son and then he becomes the dead Tammuz, Adonis, Attis; he replaces the image of God. He is really also the crucified Christ and she is the Virgin Mary crying beside the Cross. The great satisfaction is that one has an archetypal meaning in one's life. One is not just Mrs. So-and-So who has lost her son in an accident, but the Great Mother, the Virgin Mary who weeps at the foot of the cross—and that elevates the mother herself and gives her sorrow some deeper meaning. If she turns to it in the wrong way, then it is like that. I was terribly shocked by what the woman said, but then I told myself that this woman had had the naiveté to say what many others have thought. Being a simple woman, she said it right out: "It was better that way than to give him away to another woman." *She* was his wife! It seems to me that there must have been something similar in Saint Exupéry's mother; otherwise why should she always anticipate his death and wear black veils ahead of time? It was as if she knew all along that it would end like that. We only know that this terrible impersonal pattern seems to have penetrated her personal life, too. Consciously, Saint Exupéry certainly had a positive mother complex, which always includes the danger of being eaten up by the unconscious.

It is interesting that Saint Exupéry says that he always goes round with this picture and tries it out on people to make them understand. It looks as though he were not definitely doomed, as though there was still a hope and an attempt in him to find some understanding. If only he could find somebody who would ask him what on earth he was drawing, that it was dangerous and meant such and such a thing. He wanted understanding, but he did not receive it. I think that if he had gotten in touch—perhaps it is awfully optimistic—but if he had come into touch with psychology, something might have been done about his problem, because he was very near to finding the solution himself. But somehow, tragically enough, he lived in this kind of light French milieu where there was absolutely no psychological understanding yet at work, and in such an atmosphere it is very difficult to get near the unconscious. Modern French civilization, for different local and national reasons, is particularly cut off from the unconscious, so that he probably never met anyone who could give him a hint as to what was happening in his psyche.

The story then transfers to the little prince. We have heard the part where Saint Exupéry's airplane crashes in the Sahara, where he meets the little prince. I will go on with the text. The voice said:

"Draw me a sheep!"

I jumped to my feet, completely thunderstruck. I blinked my eyes hard. I looked carefully all around me. And I saw a most extraordinary small person, who stood there examining me with great seriousness. Here you may see the best portrait that, later, I was able to make of him. [He drew him like a little Napoleon, by the way, which was an unusual idea and typically French! It means that he is seen as a potential hero, a great conqueror and not as the childlike genius he really should be.] *But my drawing is certainly very much less charming than its model. That, however, is not my fault. The grown-ups discouraged me. . .* [Then he goes off in the old way.]

Now I stared at this sudden apparition with my eyes fairly starting out of my head in astonishment. Remember, I had crashed in the desert a

thousand miles from any inhabited region. And yet my little man seemed neither to be straying uncertainly among the sands, nor to be fainting from fatigue or hunger or thirst or fear. Nothing about him gave any suggestion of a child lost in the middle of a desert, a thousand miles from any human habitation. When at last I was able to speak, I said to him:

"But—what are you doing here?"

And in answer he repeated, very slowly, as if he were speaking of a matter of great consequence:

"If you please—draw me a sheep!"

When a mystery is too overpowering, one dare not disobey. Absurd as it might seem to me, a thousand miles from any human habitation and in danger of death, I took out of my pocket a sheet of paper and my fountain pen. But then I remembered how my studies had been concentrated on geography, history, arithmetic and grammar, and I told the little chap (a little crossly too) that I did not know how to draw. He answered me:

"That doesn't matter. Draw me a sheep . . ."

But I had never drawn a sheep. So I drew for him one of the two pictures I had drawn so often. It was that of the boa constrictor from the outside. And I was astounded to hear the little fellow greet it with,

"No, no, no! I do not want an elephant inside a boa constrictor. A boa constrictor is a very dangerous creature, and an elephant is very cumbersome. Where I live, everything is very small. What I need is a sheep. Draw me a sheep."

So then I made a drawing.

He looked at it carefully, then he said:

"No. This sheep is already very sickly. Make me another."

So I made another drawing.

My friend smiled gently and indulgently.
"You see yourself," he said, "that this is not a sheep. This is a ram. It has horns."
So then I did my drawing over once more.
But it was rejected too, just like the others.

"This one is too old. I want a sheep that will live a long time."
By this time my patience was exhausted, because I was in a hurry to start taking my engine apart. So I tossed off this drawing:

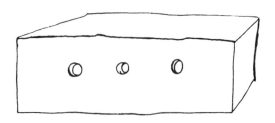

And I threw out an explanation with it.
"This is only his box. The sheep you asked for is inside."

I was very surprised to see a light break over the face of my young judge.

"That is exactly the way I wanted it! Do you think that this sheep will have to have a great deal of grass?"

"Why?"

"Because where I live everything is very small . . "

"There will surely be enough grass for him," I said. "It is a very small sheep that I have given you."

He bent his head over the drawing.

"Not so small that—Look! He has gone to sleep . . . "

And that is how I made the acquaintance of the little prince.

Then Saint Exupéry says that it took him a long time to learn where the prince came from because he always asked questions and did not answer them. Slowly, he finds out that the little man has come down from the stars and that he lives on a very small planet.

The miraculous encounter in the desert is in one way linked up with Saint Exupéry's personal life. Once he had had an airplane crash in the Sahara desert but was not then alone, as in this book, but with his mechanic, Prevost, and they had had to walk endlessly and nearly died of thirst. They already experienced hallucinations, saw mirages and were practically dying when an Arab found them and gave them some water out of his gourd. Later they were rescued. Naturally, therefore, he uses this recollection in the story, but changes it very typically; namely his shadow, the mechanic, is not with him and he is not rescued for the moment. But something supernatural happens, and there you see how the archetypal fantasy comes into the memory of the real life; that is, the hopeless and impossible situation which in all myths and fairy tales is the beginning situation where supernatural beings appear. In many fairy tales, a man gets lost in the woods and then find a little dwarf, and so on. It is typical that when someone is lost in the woods or on the sea, something numinous appears. It shows the psychologically typical situation where the conscious personality has come to the end of its wits and does not know how to go on any more consciously. One feels completely disorientated, with neither goal nor outlook in life. In those moments, energy, blocked from a further flow into life, piles up and generally constellates something from the unconscious, which is why this is the moment of supernatural apparitions such as we have here. It often happens in concrete situations that people have hallucinations of some kind if the conflict and the blockage go far enough. On a minor scale, the dream life becomes very much activated, people are forced into paying attention to it—then come the apparitions within the dreams. Generally, that happens when the previous form of life has broken down.

When he experienced this crash with his mechanic, Saint Exupéry was already in the crisis of his life. He was in his thirties, and his flying was no longer quite satisfactory, but he could not switch over to any other occupation. He already had these spells of irritability and nervousness, which he broke through by taking on another flying job. Originally, flying had been a real vocation for him, but slowly it became an escape from something new to which he did not know how to adapt. Very often, one chooses some activity in life which for the time being is absolutely right and could not be called an escape from life; then suddenly the water of life recedes from it, and slowly one feels that the libido wants to be reoriented to another goal. One perseveres in the old activity because one cannot change to the new one. In such situations, perseverance in the old activity means regression, or flight, and escape from one's own inner feeling, which says that one should now change to something else. But because one does not know and does not want to go in a different direction, one perseveres. When Saint Exupéry had this airplane crash, he was already in the beginning crisis of his aviator's life. Here the apparition shows what is meant.

There is a marked parallel to the meeting of the star prince in Islamic tradition. I think it is even possible that, having lived so long in the Sahara and having made friends with a number of Bedouins, Saint Exupéry might have heard about it. The famous story is found in the 18th Sura of the Koran, which Jung has interpreted in detail,[6] of Moses in the desert with his servant Josua, the son of Nun, who is carrying a basket with a fish in it for their meal. At a certain place the fish disappears, and Moses says that they will stay there because something will happen, and suddenly Khidr appears. (Khidr means the Verdant One.) He is supposed to be the first angel, or the first servant of Allah. He is a kind of immortal

[6]Carl Gustav Jung, *The Archetypes and the Collective Unconscious*, vol. 9, part i *Collected Works* (Princeton: Princeton University Press, 1959), par. 200.

companion who then goes along with Moses for some time, but tells him that he (Moses) will not be able to stand him and will doubt his deeds. Moses assures him that he will have enough confidence to go with him, but he fails miserably. Most of you know the story of how Khidr first comes to a little village where there are boats on the water and of how he drills a hole in each so that they sink, and Moses remonstrates Khidr asking, how he could do such a thing. Khidr says that he had said that Moses would not understand. Then he explains that robbers would have stolen the boats and that by his bringing about this minor calamity the fisherman will be able to repair their boats and still have them, whereas otherwise, they would have been lost. Therefore, Khidr was doing them a service, but Moses naturally, being too stupid, had not understood. Again, Moses promises that he will not doubt again and will not have rational reactions. Next, they meet a young man and Khidr kills him. Again, Moses explodes and asks how he could do that; Khidr smiles, then explains that the young man was on his way to murder his parents and that it was better for him to die before he became a criminal, and thereby save his soul. This time, Moses is really willing to accept the explanations. However, when a third similar event happens when Khidr causes a wall to collapse, only to uncover the hidden treasure of two orphans, Moses rebels again. Finally, Khidr has to leave him.

The story illustrates the incompatibility of the conscious rational ego with the figure of the Self and its purposes. The rational ego, with its well-meaning intentions and thoughts, is absolutely off the track in relation to the greater inner personality, Khidr. Naturally, this famous story serves to tell people that they should be able to doubt their conscious attitude and should always expect the miraculous thing from the unconscious to happen. This is the same situation, for something happens here that is absolutely contrary to Saint Exupéry's conscious ideas, which tell him that he wants to repair his engine and has no time. He wants to save himself with the old airplane and is not willing to go on with the childish play with the little star prince. On the other hand, it is very significant that the little star prince is the only one who immediately understands the drawing. He should be very pleased and see that it is his other side which really understands him, the first companion who belongs to *his* world, the childhood world he missed so much. He is impatient, however; he thinks it is a nuisance and that he must get his engine into working order. And then something absolutely classical happens —the gesture of impatience that is typical for the *puer aeternus*! When he has to take something seriously, either in the outer or in the inner world, he makes a few poor attempts and then impatiently gives up. My experience is that it does not matter, if you analyze a man of this type, whether you force him to take the outer or the inner world seriously; that is really unimportant, though perhaps it depends on the type. The important thing is that he should stick something out. If it is analysis, then analyze seriously, take the dreams seriously, live according to them; or, if not, then take a job and really live the outer life. The important thing is to do something thoroughly, whatever it is. But the great danger, or the neurotic problem, is that the *puer aeternus* man caught in this problem tends to do what Saint Exupéry does here: just put it in a box and shut the lid on it in a gesture of impatience. That is why such people tell you suddenly that they have another plan, that this is not what they were looking for. And they always do it at the moment when things become difficult. It is this everlasting switching which is the dangerous thing, not what they do. Unfortunately, but typically, Saint Exupéry switches at this crucial moment.

CHAPTER TWO

Last time, we spoke of the boa constrictor which ate up the elephant, and of how Saint Exupéry had made the drawing as a boy. Always looking for somebody to understand it, he never found anyone, and we said that this short introduction foreshadowed the tragic end of the book and of Saint Exupéry's life, since there was no lysis. In the hero myth, if the hero is swallowed by the dragon, or the big snake, or the sea monster, or the whale, he must cut the heart or the stomach from the inside, or he dances inside the whale until the monster either dies or vomits the hero out. In our story, the hero animal—we interpreted the elephant as a kind of symbolic anticipation of the hero on the animal level—is swallowed and does not come out again. We can, therefore, take this introduction, which has no lysis, symbolically. As a childhood dream, this would mean that the childhood fantasy of Saint Exupéry has no lysis and shows that there is something basically weak, basically broken, in him from the very beginning. There is something which cannot escape the fatal aspect of the unconscious.

Saint Exupéry, in a slightly ironical manner, speaks mockingly of the grown-up world and grown-up people who take themselves so seriously and are occupied with such trifles. That he himself had such attributes is shown quite clearly in the biographies. General Davet, one of his military superiors, says of him: "He was a man of integrity with a taste for childish pleasures which were sometimes surprising and he had unaccountable fits of shyness when faced with administrative stubbornness; the latter always remained his *bête noire.*" Other biographies state that he was a little bit disappointing to people who met him because he was a bit of a poseur: he gave the impression of always acting and not being of a completely genuine personality. This tendency to go off into surprisingly childish pleasures is not only a symptom of the *puer aeternus* problem, but it also belongs to the creative personality. Creativeness presupposes a great capacity for being genuine and for letting go, for being spontaneous—for if one cannot be spontaneous, one cannot really be creative—and therefore most artists and other creative people have a normal and genuine tendency to playfulness. That is also *the* great relaxation and means of recovery from an exhausting creative effort. Therefore, we cannot ascribe this trait only to Saint Exupéry's *puer aeternus* nature; it might also belong to the fact that he was an artist.

The remark made by General Davet that Saint Exupéry never overcame his rage over administrative obstinacy, either of the State or the Military, and that, on the other hand, he was shy and afraid of those in administrative positions, is important in connection with the motif of the sheep, which we will now discuss.

To the man in an office, other people are sheep; as soon as we are faced with somebody in an official position we become sheep and he, the shepherd. We are just number so-and-so to him, and naturally, officials will make one feel like that. It is the modern problem of the overwhelming power of the State, of the devaluation of the individual. On a minor scale, this is the problem of every *puer aeternus* whenever he has difficulty adapting, but it is also the problem of our time. The revolt which most people feel at being reduced to the level of a sheep of the flock is not confined to the *puer aeternus*, for there is something genuine and justifiable in it. Everyone who has not settled that problem within himself—namely, how far one has to accept the fact of being just one of a number and how much one is an individual with the right to individual treatment —experiences this complex reaction against what Davet describes as military stubbornness.

The problem is not only Saint Exupéry's, but it is also the great problem of the whole Christian civilization. In France, however, it takes a specific turn, for the French tend to display exaggerated individualism, a kind of protest against all administration. Since World War I, there has been a tendency in France to revolt and be negative in connection with everything having to do with the pressure of the State, even to the extent that numbers of people voted for Communism not because they were really Communists in their *Weltanschauung*, but simply as a demonstration against the existing order. Such people would proclaim that since they did not like the lawyers and clowns in Paris who constituted the Government, they intended to vote Communist. This shows an infantile attitude towards the problem of social and collective responsibility. It is the attitude which we now see exploding in the behavior of the teenagers who challenge the police or overturn a row of cars or do some such thing as a protest against collectivity. That, however, is understandable on the part of very young people who explode without any reflection. But when grown-ups behave similarly, when they vote for Communism simply because they do not like those in the Government—that seems very immature. But this is a very general complex and one which we all have in some form, for we have not decided how far we must accept being sheep shepherded by the State and how far we can reject such collective pressure and revolt against it. The *puer aeternus* naturally has this problem in an even more pronounced form.

Before we go into the symbolism of the sheep, we should ask ourselves why Saint Exupéry meets the little prince in the desert. In interpreting the story, we have taken the airplane crash as illustrating, in one way, an incident of Saint Exupéry's personal life and, on the other hand, a symbolic or archetypal situation with which every encounter with the unconscious begins: namely, the complete breakdown of the former activities, the goal in life and, in some form, the flow of the life energy. Suddenly, everything gets stuck; we are blocked and stuck in a neurotic situation, and in this moment the life energy is dammed up and then generally breaks through in the revelation of an archetypal image.

In the last lecture, I quoted the Islamic story of the 18th Sura of the Koran where, after having lost his only nourishment, the fish, Moses took Khidr, Allah's first angel, with him into the desert. It is not self-evident that after such a collapse a child would be found; any other kind of archetypal figure might turn up. We must therefore go into the problem of the child-god. I want to subdivide this discussion of the greatest symbol there is in the book, because part of what the little prince really represents only becomes clearer much later when we know more of the story. Now I will only read, as a general outline, what Jung says about the child-god:

The archetype of the "child-god" is extremely widespread and intimately bound up with all the other mythological aspects of the child motif. It is hardly necessary to allude to

28

the still living "Christ Child," who in the legend of Saint Christopher also has the typical feature of being "smaller than small and bigger than big." In folklore the child motif appears in the guise of the dwarf *or the* elf *as personifications of the hidden forces of nature. To this sphere belongs the little metal man of late antiquity . . . who until far into the Middle Ages inhabited the mine-shafts and represented the alchemical metals, above all, Mercurius reborn in perfect form (as the hermaphrodite,* filius sapientiae, *or* infans noster*). Thanks to the religious interpretation of the "child," a fair amount of evidence has come down to us from the Middle Ages showing that the "child" was not merely a traditional figure but a vision spontaneously experienced (as so-called "irruption of the unconscious"). I would mention Meister Eckhart's vision of the "naked boy" and the dream of Brother Eustachius. Interesting accounts of these spontaneous experiences are also found in English ghost-stories, where we read of the vision of a "Radiant Boy" said to have been seen in a place where there are Roman remains. This apparition was supposed to be of evil omen. It almost looks as though we were dealing with the figure of a* puer aeternus *who had become inauspicious through "metamorphosis," or in other words had shared the fate of the classical and the Germanic gods who have all become bugbears. The mystical character of the experience is also confirmed in Part II of Goethe's* Faust, *where Faust himself is transformed into a boy and admitted into the "choir of blessed youths," this being the "larval stage" of Doctor Marianus.*[7]

. . . I do not know whether Goethe was referring with this peculiar idea, to the cupids *on antique gravestones. It is not unthinkable. The figure of the* cucullatus *points to the hooded, that is, the* invisible *one, the genius of the departed, who reappears in the childlike frolics of a new life, surrounded by the sea-forms of dolphins and tritons.* [If I may interrupt Dr. Jung's quotation, *cucullatus* means "one who wears a hood," who has a coat with a hood, and I think it highly symbolic that Jean Cocteau, who wore this sort of coat, thereby instituted the fashion of youths wearing these hooded coats. They are mostly *pueri aeterni* and even wear that costume! I wonder that Cocteau knew about that.] *The sea, the mother of all that lives, is the favorite symbol of the unconscious. Just as the "child" is in certain circumstances (e.g., in the case of Hermes and Dactyles) closely related to the phallus, symbol of the begetter, so it comes up again in the sepulchral phallis, symbol of the renewed begetting.*[8]

[7]Ibid., pars. 268 ff.   [8]Ibid., par. 298f.

The great problem with which we are confronted in this general outline by Jung is the double aspect of the child archetype. Just as it means a renewal of life, spontaneity, and a new possibility suddenly appearing within or without and changing the whole life situation in a positive way, so also does the child-god have a negative aspect, a destructive one; namely, where Jung alludes to the apparitions of a "radiant boy" and says that this must have to do with a pagan child-god who has been condemned to appear only in a negative form. The negative child-god leads us into very deep waters, but it is safe to say that whenever the child-motif appears, we are almost always confronted with the following problem.

When the child motif turns up, it represents a bit of spontaneity, and the great problem—in each case an ethical individual one—is to decide whether it is now an infantile shadow which must be cut off and repressed, or something creative that is moving towards a future possibility of life. The child is always behind and ahead of us. Behind us, it is the infantile shadow which we leave behind, and infantility which must be sacrificed—that which always pulls us backwards into being infantile and dependent, being lazy, playful, escaping problems, responsibility and life. On the other hand, if the child appears ahead of us it means renewal, the possibility of eternal youth, of spontaneity and of new possibilities—the life flow towards the creative future. The great problem always is to make up one's mind in every situation whether there is now an infantile impulse which only pulls backwards, or an impulse which seems infantile to one's own consciousness but which really should be accepted and lived because it leads forward.

Sometimes, the answer to this dilemma is quite obvious, for the context of the dreams may show very clearly which is meant. Let us say a *puer aeternus* type of man dreams about a little boy; then we can tell from the story of the dream if the apparition of the child has a fatal effect, in which case I treat it as the infantile shadow still pulling backwards. If the same figure appears positively, however, then you can say that it is something which looks very childish and silly but which must be accepted because there is a possibility of life in it. If it were always like that, then the analysis of this kind of problem would be very simple. Unfortunately, like all products of the unconscious, the destructive side and the constructive side, the pull backward and the pull forward, are very closely intertwined and are completely enmeshed in each other. That is why if such figures appear, it is very difficult to decide between them; sometimes, it is practically impossible. That seems to me a part of the fatal situation with which we are confronted in this book and in Saint Exupéry's problem. One cannot (or at least, I cannot) make up one's mind whether to treat the figure of the little prince as a destructive infantile shadow whose apparition is fatal and announces Saint Exupéry's death, or to treat it as the divine spark of his creative genius.

One of our students, Dr. Robert Stein, has evolved the idea that there is something like a defective Self; that in certain people whose fate is very unfortunate, the symbol of the Self appears defective. This would mean that such people have no chance in life because the nucleus of their psyche is incomplete and defective, and therefore the whole process of individuation cannot develop from this kernel. I do *not* agree with this idea because I have never seen such symbols of a defective Self without an accompanying defective attitude of the ego. Wherever you find such a defective Self symbol, where it is ambiguous and incomplete and morbid, there is always at the same time an incomplete and morbid attitude of the ego. Therefore, it could not be scientifically asserted that the cause of the whole problem lies in a defective Self. It could just as well be said that it was because the ego had such a wrong attitude that the Self cannot come into play in a positive manner. If you eat completely wrong and your stomach consequently does not react properly, you can say one of two things: either that there is something wrong with your stomach and go to many doctors about it without telling them that you are eating all wrong. The doctors will conclude that it is very tragic, but that the person in question has a defective stomach, and it is not possible to discover the cause. On the other hand, it can just as well be said that if you eat all the wrong things, or do not eat, or eat irregularly, then it is not the stomach which is at fault. Thus, the defective Self always accompanies an ego which does not function properly and therefore, naturally, the Self cannot function properly either. If the ego is lazy, inflated, not conscientious, does not perform the duties of the ego-complex, then it is clear that the Self cannot appear positively. If Dr. Stein were here today, he would certainly object and say, "No, it is the other way around. The ego cannot function because the Self is defective." There we are practically confronted with the age-old philosphical problem of free will: Can I want the right thing? That is the problem which the *puer aeternus* man will generally present to you. He will say that he knows that everything goes wrong because he is lazy, but that he cannot want not to be lazy! He will say that perhaps *that* is his neurosis: that he is unable to fight his laziness. Therefore, it is useless to treat him as a rascal for whom everything would go right if he were not so lazy. That is an argument which I have heard I don't know how many times! It is to a certain extent true, for the *puer aeternus* man cannot make up his mind to work, so you can possibly say that it is the defective Self; that something is wrong in the whole structure and he cannot be saved.

This is a problem which comes up in many neuroses, not only in that of the *puer aeternus*. It goes very deep, and my attitude toward it is paradoxical: as long as I can, I behave as if the person could make up his or her mind because that is the only chance of salvation. If the case goes wrong, nevertheless, then I turn around and say that it was not possible for things to have gone differently. Otherwise, one falls into an incorrect psychological superiority; namely, that if a person goes wrong, or dies as the result of a disease or an accident, one might conclude that this occurred because he did not realize his problem—that it is his fault that he has this fate—that I consider disgusting. One does not have the right to decide that. Nature has her own revenge. If an individual cannot solve his problems, he generally gets horribly punished with hellish diseases or accidents. It is not the business of others to point that out and make it a moral issue. There, I think one should stop short and take the other hypothesis—that the person could not do it, that the structure was defective and therefore it was not possible. However, as long as the catastrophe has not taken place, it is better to take the other attitude: to try to create a hopeful atmosphere and believe in the possibility of a certain amount of free will. Empirically, there are many cases where suddenly people can make up their minds to fight their neuroses and can pull out. Then you can call it a miracle or that person's good deed, whichever you like, but it is also that which in theology is spoken of as an act of grace. Is it your good deeds which lead to salvation, or is it the grace of God? In my experience, you can only stay in the contradiction and stick to the paradox. We are confronted with that problem in a specific form here because throughout the story there is this tragic question in our minds. Something constantly goes wrong through the book and one does not know whether it is Saint Exupéry's fault or whether he could not do it. Was there some reason from the very beginning which prevented him from solving his problem?

Remark: But Jung says that there is no sickness in the collective unconscious and so, since the Self is an archetype, it does not seem to me that there can be anything defective.

I quite agree. I think that if it appears defective, it is because of the wrong ego attitude. Objectively, in itself, it cannot be defective, which is why I cannot accept the idea of the defective Self. If the ego is able to change, something else changes; if the ego-attitude changes, then the symbols of the Self become positive. That is something that we experience again and again; namely, that if the person can achieve a certain amount of insight, then the whole unconscious constellation changes. But my philosophical adversaries would say that the fact that one man can change and the other cannot is due to the Self—and then one walks in a circle.

In this specific story I shall therefore try to interpret the child figure in a double way—as the infantile shadow and as the Self. Then we will attempt to discover which is which, which means that we shall interpret the whole material on a double rail to try to find out more about this problem. The thesis that the star child whom Saint Exupéry meets is the infantile shadow can very easily be proved, since he is the only one who understands the story of the boa constrictor and the elephant. That is a remnant of childhood, and we have a letter from Saint Exupéry to his mother written in 1935, shortly before his death, in which he says that the only refreshing source he finds is in certain memories of his childhood, such as the smell of Christmas candles. His soul nowadays is completely dried up and he is dying of thirst. There is his nostalgia for his childhood, and one can say that the little prince represents this world of childhood and therefore is the infantile shadow. It is typical that he writes like that to his mother; one really sees that he is still involved in his mother complex.

On the other hand, it can be said that the fact that this child appears on earth is not *only* negative; it is not the apparition of just the infantile shadow, because, as we shall hear later, the little prince comes down from a star. One could say that an interesting parallel has taken place. Saint Exupéry crashed, and from the stars above something else has come down, for the little prince comes from a planet. So, for the first time, two things meet on earth which hitherto were in the air: the star prince, who was far away in the cosmos, and Saint Exupéry, who was constantly flying in the air. From the moment the little prince lands on the earth, he is not quite the infantile shadow anymore because something has touched reality. He is therefore now in an ambiguous position. If it could be realized, then it would become a part of the future, instead of a pull backwards. It is no longer only an infantile shadow but also a form of realization which goes on all the time. To become more conscious means, practically, to grow more and more into the reality of things—it means disillusionment.

The greatest difficulty we drag along with us from our childhood is the sack of illusions which we carry on our backs into adult life. The subtle problem consists in giving up certain illusions without becoming cynical. There are people who become disillusioned early in life; you see it if you have to analyze neglected orphans from either very low or very high layers of society, those who are nowadays called "neglected children," which means either that they are just poor children who have grown up in slums and had a terrible family life and fate, or very rich children who had all the same miseries except the lack of money—divorced parents, a bad atmosphere at home and so on—that is, where the feeling atmosphere has been neglected, which is so important for children. Such people very often grow up more quickly than others because they become very realistic, disillusioned, self-contained, and independent at a very early age. The hardships of life have forced them to this, but you can generally tell from a rather bitter and falsely mature expression that something went wrong. They were pushed out of the childhood world too soon and crashed into reality.

If you analyze such people, you find that they have not worked out the problem of childish illusions but have just cut it off. Having assured themselves that their desire for love and their ideals simply hamper them like a sack of stone carried on their backs. They believe that must all be done away with. But that is an ego decision which does not help at all, and a deeper analysis shows that they remain completely caught up in childhood illusions: their childish longing for a loving mother or for happiness is there just the same, but in a repressed state. They are really much less grown-up than other people, the problem having simply been pushed into a corner. One has then the horrible task of reviving those illusions because life has stuck there. So the person must be pushed back into them, and then one tries to get him out again properly. That is the problem which one meets within people who say that they can neither love nor trust anybody. For anyone stuck in that situation, life no longer has any meaning. Through the transference they begin to hope that perhaps they might trust or love again, but you can be sure that the love which first comes up is completely childish. The analysand very often knows what will happen—that it will mean disappointment again and be of no use. This is quite true, for such people bring out something so childish that it has to be rebuffed either by the analyst or by life itself. Such people are so childish in their feelings that should, for instance, the analyst be in bed with flu, they experience that as a personal insult and a terrible letdown and disappointment. Quite grown-up people say that they know it to be absolutely unreasonable and idiotic, but that that is how they feel, and they ask quite rightly, "What does one do if one has such a child, such incorrigible infantilism, within oneself?" Preaching does no more good than it would to a small furious child, who just does not listen.

How can a person meet this tremendous problem? If he shelves it as something hampering in life, as a source of illusion and of making trouble for himself, then he is no longer spontaneous, but disillusioned and grown-up in a wrong way; but if he lives it, he is just impossible and reality hits him over the head all the time. That is the problem. People who have shelved their feelings, or their demands on other people, or their capacity for trust, always feel not quite real, not quite spontaneous or really themselves. They feel only half alive and they generally do not take themselves as quite real. To shelve the divine child means not taking oneself completely serious. One acts! A person can adapt throughout life, but if he is honest with himself, he knows that it is acting. Otherwise, he would behave in such an infantile way that nobody could stand him. So what can he do?

That is the problem of the divine child when it appears in this state of being between true personality and childishness, and one just does not know what to do. Theoretically, the situation is clear: one should be able to cut away the childishness and leave the true personality. One should somehow be able to disentangle the two, and if an analysis goes right, that is what slowly goes on. One succeeds in disentangling and definitely destroying what is really childish and in saving the creativity and the future life. But, practically, this is something which is immensely subtle and difficult to accomplish.

The divine child, or star prince, whom Saint Exupéry meets in the desert, asks for a sheep, and we learn that he has come down to fetch a sheep to take back with him. Later in the story it is said that on the planet there is an overgrowth of baobab trees which are continually sprouting. The star prince wants a sheep to eat the shoots as they appear so that he has not constantly to work at cutting them off. But he does not explain this to Saint Exupéry, and the real reason only comes out later.

At first, we have to look at the symbolism of the sheep in the personal life of Saint Exupéry, and then in general mythology. In one of his books, Saint Exupéry says himself: "There is no bad outer fate, only an inner one. There comes a moment when you are vulnerable and your own mistakes seize you and pull you down like a sort of whirlpool. [He naturally must be speaking with reference to flying. He means that there is no such thing as a chance crash: the one day you have an accident is the result of a whole inner and outer process.] It is not the big obstacles that count so much, but the little ones: three orange trees on the edge of an airfield, or thirty sheep which you fail to see in the grass and which suddenly emerge between the wheels of your plane." At one time, flocks of sheep were used to keep down the grass on the airfields in many places, and it could happen that your plane by some mistake ran into them. One could say that he projects onto the sheep that fateful thing which one day kills the *puer aeternus*, or in this case, himself. It is the fatal enemy.

The sheep has a very revealing name in Greek. It is called *probaton*, which comes from the verb "to walk forward animal." This is a marvelous name: the animal has no other choice and no other function than the capacity to walk forward! That is all it can do! The Greeks are even more witty, for they make the animal a neuter and call it "The walking forward thing." That illustrates that most negative aspect of the sheep, which always follows the leading ram wherever it goes. You can read again and again in the paper that if a wolf or a dog chases the leading ram over the precipice, two or three hundred sheep will jump over after him. This happened about ten years ago at Lenzerheide on an Alp when a wolfhound chased the leading ram over the precipice; afterwards, men had to go with their guns and knives and kill about two hundred sheep. They were not all dead, but they had just piled up one on top of the other. That is why one talks of a person as a "silly sheep." The instinct of walking and sticking together in the flock is so much developed in the sheep that they cannot pull out even to save their lives. Those who have seen Walt Disney's film, *The White Wilderness*, have seen the same thing with the lemmings, who wander into the sea. Once caught in such an instinctive move, the single animal cannot pull out again.

The sheep tends to a similar instinctual behavior and therefore stands—when it appears in a negative connection in dreams—for the same thing in us, mass psychology, our tendency to be infected by mass movements and not to stand up for our own judgment and impulses. The sheep is the crowd animal, par excellence. Naturally, there is the crowd-man in us. For instance, you may hear that there are a lot of people at a lecture and you say, "then it must be good." Or you hear that someone has an exhibition at the Kunsthaus and you go, but have not the courage to say that you think the pictures are horrible. You first look round and see others whom you think you ought to know, admiring them, and you daren't express your own opinion. Many first look at the name of the artist before expressing an opinion. Such people are all sheep.

The sheep in mythology has a strange relationship to the world of the divine child. You all remember representations of the Madonna, very often together with her own mother and Christ and St. John the Baptist (these are mainly from the 16th century on) playing with the little lamb, or there is the Christ-child with a lamb, holding a cross, and so on. Naturally, the lamb is a representation of Christ himself, but in art it is exteriorized as something separate. He himself is the sacrificed lamb, holding a cross, and so on. The lamb is a representation of Christ himself, but in art it is exteriorized as something separate. He himself is the sacrificed lamb, the *agnus dei*. In art, the sheep is shown as the playmate, which naturally means (as always, when a god is depicted with an animal) that it is his totem animal, his animal-appearance. In German folklore, there is a belief that the souls of children, before they are born live as sheep in the realm of Mother Holle—a kind of earth-mother goddess—and those souls of unborn children are identical with what the Germans call *Lämmerwölkchen* (lamb-clouds)—in English, "fleecy clouds." The peasants thought these "little sheep clouds" were the souls of innocent children. If on Innocents' Day there were many such clouds in the sky, it was thought to predict the death of many male chidren. Further, if you look up the traditional beliefs about sheep, you will find that they carry the symbolism of innocence and that they are specially easily influenced and easily affected by the evil eye and witchcraft. They can more easily be bewitched than almost any other animal, and they can be killed by the evil eye. A sixth sense is also attributed to the sheep, for by their behavior they are supposed to be able to predict. That sort of thing is projected onto many domestic animals: horses are also supposed to have a sixth sense, as are bees. Prediction is not something confined to sheep, but to be easily bewitched and persecuted by witches and wolves is specific in folklore tradition about sheep.

Milk, another white substance, is also a symbol of innocence and purity, but it can be bewitched at any time. One of the chief activities of wizards and witches in peasant countries is to spoil the neighbor's milk. Therefore, innumerable precautions have to be taken: milk must not be carried across the street after seven o'clock in the evening; the bucket must be turned round before the cow is milked; three "Ave's" have to be said, and so on. Our hygienic precautions are not compared with the precautions against witchcraft made in earlier times; they were infinitely more complicated, because if a witch even walks past in the street, the milk in the bucket will turn sour, or blue, at once; if an evil eye is cast onto the cowshed, the milk will be bluish from then on and an exorcist must be found. It is interesting that symbols of something especially pure and especially innocent are particularly exposed to infection or to attack by evil; this is because the opposites attract each other, for that is a challenge to the powers of darkness.

In the practical life of the *puer aeternus*, that is of the man who has not disentangled himself from the eternal-youth archetype, one sees the same thing; i.e., a tendency to be believing, naive and idealistic. Therefore, he automatically attracts people who will deceive and cheat such a man. I have often noticed in analyzing men of that kind how they, in a fatal way, are attracted to rather dubious women or pick up friends about whom one does not have a good feeling. It is as though their inexperienced naiveté and their wrong kind of idealism automatically call forth the opposite, and it is no use warning such people against such relationships. You will only be suspected of jealousy, or something similar, and not listened to. Such naiveté or childish innocence can only be cured of these illusions by passing through disappointment and bad experiences. Warnings are no good—such men must learn by experience, without which they will never be awakened from their innocence. It is as if the wolves—namely, the crooks and destructive people—instinctively see such lambs as their legal prey. This naturally leads much deeper into the whole problem of our religious tradition.

As you know, Christ is the Shepherd and we are the sheep. This is a paramount relevant image in our religious tradition and one which has created something very destructive; namely, that, because Christ is the shepherd and we, the sheep, we have been taught by the Church that we should not think or have our own opinions, but just believe. If we cannot believe in the resurrection of the body—such a mystery that nobody can understand it—then one must just believe it. Our whole religious tradition has worked in that direction, with the result that if now another system comes along, say

Communism or Nazism, we are so taught that we should shut our eyes and not think ourselves, that we are trained to just believe the Führer or the people in the Kremlin. We are really trained to be sheep! As long as the leader is a responsible person, or the leading ideal is something good, then it is okay. The drawback of this religious education is now coming out in our civilization very badly, for the western man of Christian civilization is much more easily infected by mass epidemics than the eastern man. He is predisposed to belief in slogans, having always been told that there are many things he cannot understand and must just believe; then he will be saved. So we are trained in sheep psychology, and that is a terrific shadow of the Christian education for which we are now paying.

Saint Exupéry's work shows that he was possessed by this idea. He says in *Citadel*: "To build the peace is to build a stable big enough to embrace the whole flock, so that the whole flock can sleep in it. [What an ideal! Just to put mankind to sleep!] To build the peace is to borrow from God his shepherd's cloak so that all people can be accepted under it, under the divine cloak." You can see that he identifies with God. He is the godhead who accepts mankind under his cloak, the religious megalomania of the *puer aeternus*.

And now comes another complex: "It is just like a mother who loves her sons, and one son is timid and full of tenderness, another burning to live, and another is perhaps a hunchback, another perhaps delicate, but all of them in all their differences move the heart of the mother, and all in the difference of their love serve the glory." (In French, it is even more sentimental and more impressive: *Bâtir la paix, c'est bâtir l'étable assez grand pour que le troupeau entier s'y endors. Bâtir la paix, c'est obtenir de Dieu qu'il prête son manteau de berger pour recevoir les hommes dans tout l'entendu de leur désir. Ainsi de la mère qui aime ses fils et celui là timide et tendre et l'autre ardent à vivre, et l'autre peut-être bossu, chétif et malvenu, mais tous, dans leurs diversités, émouvent son coeur, et tous dans la diversité de leur amour servent la gloire.*)

There you see how the religious image of the divine shepherd and the sheep is mixed up with the mother-complex sentimentality in a very dangerous way. Suddenly, it is the mother who is the shepherd and children are the sheep. A wolf comes, eats the shepherd and takes the cloak, and then you see what happens to the sheep! It is just the opportunity for a wolf! In the religious situation, the wolf can be the great dictators and leaders we have now, or any kind of person who lies and cheats in public life. In private life, it is the animus of the devouring mother who takes the lead for the sheep-son. And there are such decent, devoted sons who believe that they have to honor and be chivalrous to their mother, the elderly lady; they do not see that the animus of the mother has eaten them and just feeds on their innocence. The devouring animus of the mother sometimes feeds on the innocence and the best and most devoted feelings of the son; there, too, the sheep have been eaten by the shepherd.

So the little star boy in our story wants a sheep. We learn that it is needed to eat the over-prolific trees, which are obviously a symbol of the devouring mother, so that wanting the sheep seems at first sight to have a positive meaning; namely, that the asteroid is threatened by an overgrowth, which is the mother complex. I have just illustrated it the other way round, with the sheep as part of the mother complex which it helps, and not as the right remedy against the overgrowth. So here again it seems to me that we are confronted with complete ambiguity. In what way does the sheep help combat the mother complex? Afterwards, we can see how it cooperates. The story says that it bites off the new shoots, which are the overgrowth of the mother complex, but what does that mean, psychologically? How far can the crowd-man within us help against the mother complex?

Answer: The mother does not seem to be so devouring when he surrenders to her.

You mean that if the sheep walks into the wolf's mouth, then the wolf becomes less dangerous because he is well fed. In a way, I don't think that a son who gives in to his mother's devouring desire has ever succeeded in improving matters; that has not been my experience, for the devouring complex generally fattens and grows on every bite it gets.

Answer: I would say that everybody has to get free of the mother.

Yes, and what can help to free the man from the mother?

Answer: If a man follows his pattern—namely, frees himself from his mother—then he is doing the right thing.

You mean he hears a psychological saying that everybody has to free himself from his mother. If he does that, he really follows the sheep mentality; he does it because "one says so," and by that he frees himself from the mother. That is quite correct. Normally, very few young men have a strong enough individuality to pull away from the mother of their own accord; they do it via collectivity. For instance, in our country it is military service which helps young men fight against their mother complexes. Many are improved or even cured of their attachment to the mother by military service. It is the sheep mentality, the crowd-man, which drives them into military service, but this collective adaptation can be—and is sometimes temporarily—a help to pull away, especially here in Switzerland. In the simpler layers of the population, military service still functions to a great extent like the male initiation rituals in primitive tribes: it is the moment to pull away from the mother.

You can say that all kinds of very humble, unindividualistic, collective adaptations help against the mother complex; namely, as I mentioned before, doing one's work, going to military service, trying to behave like everybody else, not having that kind of fancied individuality which is typical for the mother-complex man—and giving up the idea of being somebody special, someone who does not need to make all such low kinds of adaptations—for that is a poison of the mother complex. Therefore, to give that up and to accept being just somebody or nobody, in the crowd, is to a certain extent a cure, although only a temporary one and not the whole cure. Still, it is the first step in pulling away from the personal mother.

You see—*similia similibus curantur* ("like cures like")—how dangerous situations are generally cured by dangerous situations. To become a crowd-man is psychologically a very dangerous thing, but it helps against the danger of the false individuality which the man develops within a mother complex. But he is then up against another danger: the medicine used in such a case is dangerous. Therefore, the fact that the star prince wants a sheep could be interpreted positively. He wants in his ideal, divine isolation the company of the crowd-soul. That would enlarge his asteroid and his world. There are no animals in his star world; if he brings one up there, it is a bit of an earthly instinct which seems extremely positive. But you could also interpret it negatively, for it is not a conscious realization but only pitting one instinct against another, which is what is expressed in the story. I think from that you can arrive at a definite judgment and say that the sheep is completely negative.

Remark: The sheep is in the box!

That adds to it. I would say rather that he wants to take the sheep up instead of going down to it; he wants to pull the sheep up into the stars. A sheep is something which walks on the earth. So if, in order to have it, he would stay on the earth, then it would be the thing which pulled him down into reality. In the same way, a man gets pulled down onto the earth if he goes through military service and a lot of other painful adaptations. But if you take the sheep up into the fantasy world of childhood, then it is not an adaptation to reality; rather it is a pseudo-adaptation. That is something very subtle and specific for Saint Exupéry, and not very widespread in other cases. It is for him a specific danger, but one to which he reacted very strangely. He praises clinging to the earth, social adaptation, submittance to the earthly principle, acceptance of the bonds of love, and so on, but all that he praises he himself, does not stand by. He assimilates the whole thing intellectually and takes it back into his imaginary world. It is a trick which many *pueri aeterni* perform: the realization that they should adapt to reality is an intellectual idea to them which they fulfill in fantasy but not in reality. The idea is executed only in reflection and on a philosophical level, but not on the level of action. It looks as though they had quite understood, as if they had not the wrong attitude, as if they knew what was important and right. But they do not *do* it. If you read Saint Exupéry's work, you could attack me and say that he is not a *puer aeternus*: look at the Sheikh in *The Citadel*, a mature man who would take responsibility on earth; look at Riviere in *Vol de Nuit*: he is not a *puer aeternus*, but a man who accepts his responsibilities; he is a grown-up, masculine man, not a mother-complex fellow. It is all there in his ideas, but Saint Exupéry never lived either the Sheikh or Riviere; he fantasied them, and the idea of the down-to-earth, grown-up man, but he never lived his fantasy. That, I think, is one of the trickiest problems in that specific neurotic constellation. The *puer aeternus* always tends to grasp at everything which would be the right thing to do and then to draw it back into his fantasy-theory world. He cannot cross the very simple border from fantasy to action. It is also the dangerous curve in the analysis of such people, for unless the analyst constantly watches this problem like an alert fox, the analysis will progress marvelously, the *puer aeternus* will understand everything, will integrate the shadow and the fact that he had to work and come down to earth, but, unless you are like a devil's watchdog behind it, it is all a sham. The whole integration takes place up in the sky and not on the earth, not in reality. It comes down to having to play the governess and ask what time he gets up in the morning, how many hours have been worked in the day, and so on. It is a very tedious job, but that is what it boils down to, because otherwise a fantastic self-deception goes on in which one can very easily be caught oneself.

We should now consider the sheep in the box. When you assimilate something intellectually, you put it into a box. A concept is a box. When Saint Exupéry impatiently puts the sheep in a box, he accepts the idea, but *as an idea*. It exists, but only in his brain-box. The little prince thinks the design is as good as a real sheep. Everything remains in the world of reflection.

Question: If Saint Exupéry had been cured of his puer aeternus *personality, would he have continued to be an artist?*

Being "cured" of being a *puer* does not imply being "cured of being an artist." If we consider Goethe, we can see that in his early writing there is evidence of a mother complex, and he too felt that there would be nothing left if he gave up the *puer* mentality. But he pulled through this crisis, and although the *puer* in his book, *The Sorrows of Young Werther*, shot himself, Goethe himself survived.

In the really great artist there is always a *puer* at first, but it can go further. It is a question of the feeling-judgment. If a man ceases to be an artist when he ceases to be a *puer*, then he was never really an artist. If analysis saves such pseudo-artists from being artists, then thank God! We must not forget that Saint Exupéry does not only express his problem; he describes a collective neurosis. He has displayed in literature such a *puer* situation, and so beautifully; he has raised the question. There is a type of artist who cannot make the switch that Goethe made, and these have to die. One cannot say they have not been artists, but they did not grow beyond that switch-over. In *The Sorrows of Young Werther*, Goethe did not deal with the problem of the *puer* in a final way, and it went on into other works. In the next step, his drama *Torquato Tasso*, Goethe represented it as a problem within himself; at the same time, by objectifying the *puer* in Tasso and Antonio, the man who wants to live on earth, he detached from the problem. It then became a conflict that went even further in *Faust*. One's feeling tells one when the writer does—or does not—extricate himself from this problem. Objectifying the *puer* is only the first step.

Question: Can you qualify the statement that laziness is characteristic of the puer aeternus? *Goethe and Saint Exupéry both worked hard in their lives.*

The *puer aeternus* has to learn to carry on with the work he does not like, rather than only with the work where he is carried away by great enthusiasm, which is something that everybody can do. Primitive people who are said to be lazy can do that. As soon as they are gripped by something, they work, even to the point of exhaustion, but I would not evaluate that as work but as being carried away by a festival of work. The work which is the cure for the *puer aeternus* is where he has to kick himself out of bed on a dreary morning and again and again take up the boring job—through sheer will power. Goethe took on a political position and served in Weimar, sitting in his office and reading little requests concerning taxation, and so on. That is what he experienced in his work as Antonio; that somehow all belonged in his life. Goethe lived what he wrote. He stayed in his office and gave his mind to the most boring questions when often he would have preferred to ride off somewhere. Somehow, he had a deep insight into the necessity of that part of life. Being a feeling type, he thus developed his inferior thinking, which showed very much in the rather boring and unexciting side of his maxims (his conversations with Eckermann are most disappointing).

Remark: Perhaps that throws a light on Rousseau's statement that the greatest fault in his character was his laziness, but it is well known that he worked from morning to night and read a great many books.

Yes, but he must have escaped some other kind of work. People can cheat themselves by working themselves to death in order to avoid doing the work they should do. Rousseau had to keep his feet in a tub of hot water in order to get himself to work; he worked in a kind of trance with footbaths. His *Confessions* might have been more to the point and less sentimental without these baths!

Remark: To go back to the idea of an author writing out his neurosis—many people are celebrated for that and such an activity is taken for talent.

I do not think that it is mistaken for talent; I think it is something we would all like to be able to do. I would like very much to make money out of my neurotic spots. I think the problem comes after the thing has been written. I think that what one writes does concern one's own problem—otherwise the writing dries up—

but when you have written out the problem, or while you are writing it, you have to live it. Whenever I have lectured on a problem, it has always come back on me afterwards. I have observed that with sensation types it goes the other way round; they live it first, and then write it. When you are writing on a problem, synchronistic events often happen to you at the same time, so that you have to live it concurrently. Dr. Jung told me that when he was writing on special problems he would get letters from all sorts of places, Australia and elsewhere, which put to him the question he was then addressing. If you touch on an important and vital problem of your own, it generally happens that way, sometimes behind and sometimes ahead of you, and that is the difference between only writing of your neurosis or going further. The problem will always tie in with you, and if you live it at the same time, then afterwards what you next write will be a step further on; otherwise, you will again write of the same problem. Some writers always turn on the same gramophone record, whereas if you live it, the next thing will show progress. Goethe lived what he wrote, and what he wrote next was always a step further on. The romantic poets repeated themselves much more, for they went round in a circle because they did not, or could not, live it at the same time. I do not mean to make accusations, but one should be prepared for what one writes to be constellated. So many artists do not want their work to be analyzed because they are afraid that then they would have to live it. That is the resistance which many of them have against psychoanalysis, for they say that their creativity would be analyzed away. But genuine creativity is so terribly strong that not even the most gifted analyst in the world could wipe it out. This resistance to putting their work to the test is therefore very suspect.

CHAPTER THREE

I have been asked privately by somebody about the problem of the sheep being put in a box. This listener thought that I had been too hard on Saint Exupéry, who had shown courage and the capacity for substantial reaction in his life, and that one could not accuse him of trying to escape reality in any way, or at least not in this way. I think this simply shows that I have not made myself clear.

Placing the sheep in the box is not a gesture of escape; rather, it springs from what one might call a certain vital strength in order to be able to stand a conflict. Saint Exupéry wants to get back to work on his engine. Instead of letting him quickly draw a sheep, the star prince bothers him, saying this drawing is not right, nor this, nor this, so that Saint Exupéry is torn between the engine and the child, whose importance he competely realizes, and who, in a typically childlike way, bothers him. He feels sure that even if he draws another sheep it won't be right, or there will be a lot of questions, and in reality there is the urgent situation of getting his engine in order. If you take that symbolically, it means a conflict between the demands of the outer and the inner life, which establishes a tremendous tension. How can you comply with the demands of outer reality, which reason tells you is right, and those of the inner life at the same time? The difficulty is that the demands of the inner life need time. You cannot do active imagination for five minutes and then go off and do other things! If, for instance, one is in analysis, dreams have to be written down. This may mean two hours' work to just write them down, which is only the beginning, for one has not yet done any work. One should also meditate on them. It is a full-time job, but very often there are also the urgent necessities of outer life. This is one of the worst and most difficult tensions to stand—to be capable as far as possible of giving each claim what it needs. The weak personality—and I don't mean "weak" as a moral criticism—would imply not being born physically strong. The weak personality reacts with a short-cut response, making a definite decision to do the one and put the other aside. Here, there is an incapacity for standing the tension beyond a certain point. A weak personality has an impatient reaction, whereas a strong personality can continue in the tension for longer. In this case, one sees that Saint Exupéry, after the third attempt to draw the sheep, gives up and makes a short-cut solution in order to get back to his engine. This is an indication of a weakness that shows in certain other features; for instance, the star prince's planet is very tiny, he himself is very delicate, or, to take the first dream, the hero does not come out of the devouring snake; i.e., the mother. Also, if you look at the photographs of Saint Exupéry, you will see that he has a very strange "split" face: the lower part of it is like that of a boy of seven, the expression of the mouth is completely immature; it is a naive, little child's mouth, and there is a thin little chin, whereas the upper part of the face gives the impression of a very intelligent and mature man. Something is weak and just like a child; therefore, there are certain tensions which he cannot stand. I had not meant my comments as a criticism, but a statement such as a doctor might make, saying that the person is not strong and probably would not survive pneumonia. There is no criticism, but the statement of a tragic fact.

There are other men swallowed by the *puer aeternus* problem who would have the strength to stand more conflict, but who also react out of sheer impatience rather than from a tragic weakness. In the mother complex, it is so often the sufferer who does not want to stick out a situation. For instance, in *Aion*, Dr. Jung says: "A mother's son always only makes impatient and half-hearted attempts to touch reality. The secret memory that he could be given the world and happiness through the mother, lames his impetus and his perseverance. That piece of reality with which he gets in touch never seems the right one because it does not give itself to him, is not compliant but unyielding and has to be conquered, but for that he would need virility and a faithless Eros to make him forget the mother."[9]

[9]Carl Gustave Jung, *Aion: Research into the Phenomenology of Self*, vol. 9, part ii, *Collected Works* (Princeton: Princeton University Press, 1959; 2d ed., 1968), par. 22.

So you see, impatience is sometimes an effect of the mother complex. In the case of Saint Exupéry, I think it is that too. But on the top of it, there is something tragic; namely, an inborn weakness for which he cannot be held responsible. That means that his vitality was crushed somehow, and that is a tragic fate where nothing can be done.

Question: Did you say "a faithless Eros"?

Yes. That would mean the capacity to turn away from time to time from a relationship. That would lead to another problem— namely, that the *puer aeternus*, in the negative sense of the word, very often tends to be too impressed, too weak, and too much of a "good boy" in his relationships, without a quick self-defense reaction where required. For instance, he takes much too much from the animi of the women around him: if one of them makes a scene, finding fault with him about this or that, he accepts too much of it at first; then suddenly, one day he has had enough, and just walks out of the whole situation in a completely cruel and reckless manner. You could say that consciously he is too weak and yielding, and the unconscious shadow is too cruel, reckless, and unfaithful. I have seen some who have taken from their girlfriends practically everything (where one would have expected a woman to flare up long before), and then one day the *puer aeternus* simply walks out of the situation and turns to another woman, not even answering. There is no transition stage. The yielding "good boy," the man who gives in too much, is suddenly replaced by the cold gangster shadow without any human relatedness whatsoever. The same thing happens in analysis: they take everything, never coming out with resistances or asserting their own standpoint against that of the analyst; suddenly, out of the blue, they say that they are going to another analyst, or are giving up analysis altogether, and you fall out of the sky if you have not happened to notice that this was on the way. There are no thanks, nothing at all. It is just finished. At first there was insufficient coldness and independence, or masculine aggressiveness, and afterwards too much in a negative, inhuman and unrelated form. That is typical for many *pueri aeterni*. Much more strength would be required to work the problem out patiently with someone than just to give in, and then walk out.

To continue with our story, there now comes a long conversation in which Saint Exupéry learns that the little prince has fallen from heaven, from Asteroid B-612, and that he wants the sheep so that it may eat up the planet's baobab trees. I have never discovered what the association is for the number of the asteroid—612. One can imagine from the way in which it is described that Saint Exupéry is playing with his astronomical and mathematical knowledge and wants to express the idea of a little star X–Y. If there is a symbolic meaning, I don't know what it might be, or at least I could not make a definite assertion.

The great danger comes from the baobab sprouts which grow into huge trees and whose roots, if allowed to grow, would split the planet, so that the little prince is kept constantly busy pulling up the plants before they grow too big. That is his constant worry, and his idea is to get a sheep from earth which would eat the shoots to relieve him of the constant fight with the baobab tree. (In German, the trees are called Affenbrotbaum, the ape-bread-tree. They are big trees which grow in Africa.)

Saint Exupéry says that it would take a great many elephants to eat such trees. The little prince says that if he needs a lot of elephants, he would have to put them one upon the other; they would not have space otherwise, and from such remarks Saint Exupéry constructs the situation. He makes a drawing to illustrate this idea of what it would look like if the elephants were put one on top of the other, since there is not sufficient space on the asteroid for enough elephants to eat enough of the trees. His sketch shows three elephants on one side, two on two other sides, standing upon each other, but the two elephants on the fourth side he draws from the back, indicating the fourth function is turned in another direction.

It is interesting that without knowing anything about Jungian psychology, he makes three alike and the fourth function turning the other way. The three elephants—the main and the auxiliaries—have a bit of overweight, and the fourth function is turned and looks in the other direction. Saint Exupéry says:

So, as the little prince described it to me, I have made a drawing of that planet. I do not like to take the tone of a moralist. But the danger of the baobabs is so little understood, and such considerable risks would be run by anyone who might be lost on an asteroid, that for once I am breaking through my reserve. "Children," I say plaintively, "watch out for the baobabs!"

My friends, like myself, have been skirting this danger for a long time, without ever knowing it; and so it is for them that I have worked so hard over this drawing. The lesson which I pass on by this means is worth all the trouble it has cost me. Perhaps you will ask me: "Why are there no other drawings in this book as magnificent and impressive as this drawing of the baobabs?"

The drawings in the book, which are by Saint Exupéry himself, are very light both in color and drawing, but the one of the baobab trees has much deeper colors and is done with much more care and accuracy. He says himself that he has worked on it, and you see that at once, for not only are the colors strong, but a lot of trouble has been taken to draw the details of the tree.

The reply is simple. I have tried. But with the others I have not been successful. When I made the drawing of the baobabs I was carried beyond myself by the inspiring force of urgent necessity.

Here we touch the main problem. Saint Exupéry says that when he made this drawing of the baobabs, he felt the terrific danger. There are three big trees, but there is also a fourth figure, namely a small boy dressed in red with an axe in his hand. The little prince tells Saint Exupéry that he had a neighbor on another asteroid who was too lazy to pull up the little roots of the baobab, so they grew to the size shown in the picture and then it was too late; standing with his axe, he cannot cut down the trees, and his asteroid perishes. The drawing shows the big trees and the helpless boy; from the little axe and the size of the large trunks of the trees you see that there is no chance of cutting the trees down anymore. That is the "urgent" drawing, the one which Saint Exupéry drew with an enormous effort.

If we take the problem of the elephants which have to be piled on top of each other on the asteroid, you will see what I was driving at before. What would you say was the trouble in that picture?

Answer: The mother trouble is piling up more and more.

Yes, but the elephant is not the mother problem. The problem is the hero, the male hero-substance, the thing which is eaten up by the snake; that is, he himself. The trouble is not that the elephants are too big, but the earth is not strong enough to carry them. The elephants are okay, but there is not enough space for them. What would that mean?

Answer: The ego is not strong enough.

No, I am not sure that you could say the ego. Perhaps, that is the result. Well, we often say of people that they have not enough earth—that is a kind of intuitive way of talking—but what do we mean when we say that?

Answer: That they are not in touch with reality.

Yes. They can have earth, but they fly off it, though that is not so bad. Some people have a lot but are not in touch with it, while others have no earth, or not enough, even if they are in touch with it—which would mean that there is not enough vitality. It is naturally an irrational concept, an intuitive concept. You could call earth psychological substance. You see that again and again. One of the great problems in psychotherapy is: how much substance does that person have? How much can he or she carry? You can only guess that with your feeling; you have a feeling impression about it. It cannot be weighed scientifically, and sometimes one can misjudge the situation. Sometimes you think that a peron does not have much substance, but when it comes to a vital conflict, suddenly and surprisingly a lot appears. You have the feeling that other people carry a lot, but then, out of the blue, they break down. They have no strength, so it is something which is only proved by results. But if one has some experience of people, then one has a certain possibility of guessing more or less correctly how much carrying-substance there is.

As you know, in his theory of schizophrenia, Dr. Jung describes a difference between what he calls the asthenic type and the strong type. In the strong type, the problem is that there is an overwhelming wealth of strength and fantasy in the unconscious, confronted with a relatively weak ego; because of that, the person can split. But in the strong type, really it is a plus which makes them ill. In the asthenic type, the minus makes the person ill. Somewhere, neither the ego nor the unconscious has quite enough impetus. People in such a situation have no dreams. Where, in the greatest conflict, you would expect a vital reaction from the unconscious, the dreams are small and petty, or there are none. It is as though Nature does not react. It is very important to know that, because naturally, in the strong type one can risk a kind of reckless therapy. For instance, one can just confront the person with the problem and risk a terrific crisis—a healing crisis—and then they come through.

With the asthenic type, you can never do that. There, one must adopt a nursing attitude, making constant blood transfusions, so to speak, never forcing the problem or pushing the person up against the wall, because that would break him. One does not have to decide that oneself; in general, the unconscious decides. In the asthenic type, the dreams themselves do not push the problem. I have often been amazed when people of the type who have the most urgent problem have dreams which only talk about this or that detail and do not delve into the main problem. Then I say to myself: "Well, it is not meant; the confrontation would *not* be possible. The unconscious knows better than I do and says that this problem cannot be touched. It is too hot; it would explode the person." One must go along with the seemingly little dreams there are and take the advice contained in them.

With the strong type, you generally see that the dreams hit directly at the core of the problem, with great dramatic structure. Then you see that the whole thing is driving to a climax and a healing crisis and terrific fighting situation, and then the problem decides itself, either on the good or the bad side. The same thing occurs to certain people, who, if they get pneumonia, have a tremendous reaction. There is a life-and-death fight with very high fever, but they get through and are cured. Others, and this is much more uncanny, don't get any fever, only a little increased temperature. The illness drags on and does not come to a climax because the vital reaction in the body is not strong enough; there is not sufficient vitality. Sometimes there are combined cases. For instance, there may be strong people who are weak in one corner, so the situation is mixed. Someone may have a vital make-up, belong to the plus type with which risks can be taken, but somewhere there is a minus, a split in the make-up. Here, the situation becomes even more difficult because one has to follow two lines, putting a lot of weight where it can be carried but never pressing on the weak point which needs endless nursing, care, and patience. That is a combination often to be found in very split personalities: on the one side there is an unusual capacity for life, but extreme vulnerability in one corner, which has to be fenced off and especially cared for. Such mixed types are not really difficult, for if one can only get them to realize the situation themselves, they can take care of their weak spots. It simply means making them realize their dangerous corner, but you have to do the nursing with patience—no forcing—and constant vital attention to the weakness, so that the weak spot may slowly recover.

I think Saint Exupéry is a mixed type, neither weak nor strong. He has tremendous strength, courage, vitality, and the capacity to swing difficult situations on the one side, but one corner of his personality is extremely weak and lacking vitality—and that is what this planet personifies. Naturally, that one corner is the essential corner in his case, and these symptoms of having no vital reactions where they are important go through the whole book. So, you can say that the will to live is too small in comparison with his genius and capacities. The earth signifies the will to live and the acceptance of life, and this is the weak spot. The incongruity of the personality is the problem. This does not so much illustrate the *puer aeternus* problem in general, but is a specific problem in Saint Exupéry; however, one situation is often found combined with the other. While the person who has too little earth may be able to assimilate everything psychologically, he will have great difficulty realizing things in reality. Such people take everything in analysis with honesty and strength, but when you press them to do something about it in outer reality, a terrific panic comes up. At the moment when the inner realization has to be put into life, strength collapses, and you are confronted with a trembling child, who exclaims, "Oh, no! That I cannot do!" This is an exaggerated illustration of the introvert's attitude in which there is great strength in accepting the inner truths but very little when it comes to real life. Then the trembling child appears.

We have now had the only two elephant drawings in the whole book, and it is interesting to compare them with each other. They represent reverse situations: in the first, the elephant is overwhelmed by the snake; in the second the elephant is the overwhelming thing, and it has not enough earth, which shows that the situation can be regarded from two angles: namely, either that the greater personality, the hero, in Saint Exupéry has been overwhelmed by the devouring unconscious—by the mother complex—or you can say that the hero personality in Saint Exupéry did not have enough foundation in order to become real. They are the two aspects of the same tragedy. It is interesting that the little prince himself says that "a boa constrictor is a very dangerous creature and an elephant is very cumbersome." Saint Exupéry is between the devil and the deep blue sea, for he does not know either how to accept his greatness or his weakness. He does not know how to get on with either of them.

The baobab trees in the drawing are enormous and give the impression of overrunning the whole star with their luxuriant growth, so you can say that Mother Nature is overwhelming the field of human culture and consciousness. If you look at the picture, you will see that the roots of the trees are drawn exactly like snakes. I think also that it is not by chance that he chooses in the first drawing a *boa* and calls these trees *bao*bab trees. There seems to be a play on the words. He seems to have associated the two factors: both boa constrictor and trees are overwhelming. We should therefore amplify the trees rather on the negative side. How would you interpret them in this drawing?

Answer: Gilgamesh had to cut down the cedar tree.

Yes, Gilgamesh had to cut down the cedar tree in Ishtar's forest. There, the tree represents the power of Ishtar, who, among other things, is the tree goddess who has appointed Chumbaba as guardian to defend the tree. Here again the tree is linked up with the negative mother. What are other amplifications?

Answer: The tree is a symbol of life itself.

Yes. If you read Dr. Jung's chapter of the tree in *The Philosophical Tree*, there the tree is generally interpreted as the symbol of life, of inner growth, of the process of individuation and of maturing. But that does not fit here.[10]

Remark: The tree is very often connected with mother goddesses—not only Ishtar but Idun in German mythology, and with Demeter and others in Greek mythology.

Yes, the tree is frequently connected with the mother-goddess, who is often even worshipped as a tree. But there is an even closer relationship: for instance, Attis in the tree, or Osiris hung up in his coffin in a tree. There, the tree is what one generally calls the death-mother in mythology; the coffin in the tree, and the dead person being put in the coffin were interpreted as being given back to the mother, put back into the tree, the death-mother. At the Festival of Attis in Rome, a fir tree was carried with an image of Attis at the top of the tree, generally only the torso, and Dr. Jung, in *Symbols of Transformation*, quotes an old poem which says that the Christian cross has been looked upon as being the terrible stepmother who killed Christ.[11] That would be the first association; namely, that the tree is the mother, the coffin, and has to do with the death of the *puer-aeternus*-god. How can you interpret that? We get into a contradiction: the tree being clearly in so many symbolic connections the process of individuation, and here that same symbol is identified with death, a destructive factor.

[10]Carl Gustav Jung, *Psychology and Religion: West and East*, vol. 13, *Collected Works*, pars. 304ff.

[11]Carl Gustav Jung, *Symbols of Transformation*, pars. 661ff.

Remark: In the drawing, the tree is monstrous. It is too big for the star, which would indicate that the mother problem is too large and too devouring.

Yes, but how do you connect it with the process of individuation? The process of individuation is a process of inner growth to which one is tied—one cannot get away from it. If you say no to it and do not accept it, then, since you are not in it, *it grows against you*, and then it is your own inner growth which kills you. If you refuse the growth, then it kills you, which means that if a person is completely infantile and has no other possibility, then not much will happen. But if the person has a greater personality within—that is, a possibility of growth—then a psychological disturbance will come. That is why we say that a neurosis is a positive symptom in a way. It shows that something wants to grow; it shows that that person is not right in his or her present state. If the growth is not accepted, then it grows against you, at your expense, and then there is what might be called a negative individuation. The process of individuation, of inner maturing and growth, goes on unconsciously and ruins the personality instead of healing it. That is how the death-tree, the death-mother tree and the life-tree are essentially connected. The inner possibility of growth in a person is a dangerous thing because either you say yes to it and go ahead, or you are killed by it. There is no other choice. It is a destiny which has to be accepted.

If you look at the *puer aeternus* in the negative sense, you can say that he does not want to outgrow the mother problem; he does not want to outgrow his youth or his youthful stage, but the growth goes on all the same, until it destroys him; he is killed by the very factor in his soul through which he could have outgrown his problem. If you have to contend with such a problem in actual life, then you see how people refuse to grow, become mature and tackle the problem, and more and more a destructive unconscious piles up. Then you have to say, "For God's sake, do something, for the thing is growing against you and you will be hit over the head by it." But the moment may come, as the star prince says in the book, when it is too late, for the destructive growth has sucked up all the energy.

The luxuriant growth is also an image of a rich fantasy life, of an inner creative richness. Very often, you find in the *puer aeternus* such a rich fantasy life, but that wealth of fantasy is dammed back and cannot flow into life because the *puer* refuses to accept reality as it is, and thereby piles up life. He dams up his inner life. In actuality, for instance, he gets up at 10:30 a.m., hangs around till lunch time with a cigarette in his mouth, giving way to his emotions and fantasies. In the afternoon he means to do some work but first he goes out with friends and then with a girl, and the evening is spent in long discussion about the meaning of life. He then goes to bed at one, and the next day is a repetition of the one before. In that way, the capacity for life and the inner riches are wasted, for they cannot get into something meaningful but slowly overgrow the real personality. The individual walks about in a cloud of fantasies, fantasies which in themselves are interesting and full of rich possibilities, full of unlived life. You feel that such a person has a tremendous wealth and capacity, but there is no possibility of finding a means of realization. Then the tree—the inner wealth—becomes negative, and in the end kills the personality. That is why the tree is frequently linked up with the negative mother symbol, for the mother complex has that danger; because of it, the process of individuation can become negative in this sense.

There is a parallel in the Finnish epic *Kalevala*, which describes the fight of divine child and the tree. "A man rose out of the sea, a hero from the waves. He was not the hugest of the huge nor yet the smallest of the small: he was as big as a man's thumb, the span of a woman. His helmet was of copper, copper the boots on his feet, copper the gauntlets on his hands. . ." Vainamoinen asked the hero from the sea what he intended to do, and he replied: "I am a man as you see—small, but a mighty water-hero. I have come to fell the oak-tree and splinter it to fragments!" Vainamoinen, old and wily, scoffed, "Why, you haven't the strength, you'll never be able to fell the magic oak-tree and splinter it to fragments!" But the little man took his axe. "He struck the tree with his axe and smote it with the polished blade, once, twice, and a third time. Sparks flew from the axe and flame from the oak as he tried to bend the magic tree to his will. At the third stroke the oak-tree was shattered; the hundred boughs had fallen. The trunk stretched to the east, the top to the west, the leaves were scattered to the south and the branches to the north. . . Now that the oak-tree was felled and the proud trunk levelled (now comes the important part), the sun shone again and the dear moon glimmered pleasantly, the clouds sailed far and wide and a rainbow spanned the heavens."[12]

---

[12] Carl Gustav Jung and Carl Kerényi, *Essays on a Science of Mythology*, trans. R.F.C. Hull (Princeton: Princeton University Press, 1949), pp. 137ff.

There you see that when the wrong inner overgrowth of fantasy is pulled down and recognized as being simply the mother complex, then another dimension of consciousness appears: the sky is seen again, the clouds can sail far and the sun and moon can shine. It is not a narrowing of the horizon, for pulling down that wrong growth of fantasy means a widening of the human horizon. I think that is an infinitely important text because one of the objections which the *puer aeternus* always brings up when you want to encourage him to fell the tree is that he does not want such a narrowing of the horizon. What would be left if he had to give up his wishful fantasies, his masturbating, and such stuff? He would be just a petty little bourgeois who goes to his office, and so on. He could not stand such narrowing! But it is not true! If one has the courage to cut down this wrong kind of inner greatness, it comes again, but then in a better form—the horizon and life are widened and not narrowed as was thought. I think this myth should always be told because that is what the hero, when he has to cut the tree, always does not want to realize, or does not believe. If he only knew how much wider life would be if he could give up that wrong kind of inner life, then he might perhaps do it.

The little prince's asteroid has not yet been destroyed by the baobab tree, whose shoots he wants the sheep to eat up, but his neighbor's asteroid has been. How would you interpret this fact? The only drawing by which Saint Exupéry admits that he was carried beyond himself "by the inspiring force of urgent necessity" is the one which describes the lost situation, where there is no more hope. Into that drawing he put his whole love and energy. How would you psychologically interpret the doubling of the asteroids? The one which is not yet lost and the other which is?

Answer: The one is the shadow's star.

Yes, you could say that. The lazy fellow who let the trees grow too big is a shadow of our little prince, which is why the latter speaks of him so negatively, calling him the lazy neighbor who did not cut the trees. And now see what has happened! But what does that mean for Saint Exupéry psychologically, if the divine child's motif doubles and falls apart into a divine child and his shadow?

Answer: One part has already been swallowed up by the mother complex.

Yes, that's right. It is already half eaten, but that would not yet be hopeless. On the contrary, it could also turn out well.

Remark: It is a very serious warning if he could understand it. He puts himself into the drawing.

Yes, but I am driving at something slightly different. First, a general question. What does it mean if a motif doubles into a yes and a no?

Answer: That something is on the edge of consciousness.

Yes. You can say that doubling is a symptom that something is beginning to touch the rim of consciousness. But why does it then fall apart into the opposites?

Answer: We are unable to perceive the opposites united—as one—(the state they are in the unconscious), so when we see them simultaneously, we see them as two. Then, as they come closer to consciousness, it seems as if one part recedes into the unconscious and the other side comes forward.

Yes, it comes forward if things go right. In what way can you now prove that theory? How would you apply it to the material? In what way is the star prince a yes and a no, before he falls apart? What is the yes and no in this divine child?

Answer: One side of the child is infantile and the other a symbol of the Self.

Yes, exactly. You could say the star prince figure is the infantile shadow, or a symbol of the Self, and up till now that figure appeared double; you could never quite know which way to take it; whether negatively, and call it the infantile shadow, or positively, and call it the Self. Hitherto, we were always in trouble as to how to interpret the child figure: was it infantilism or was it the future life? It was, and is, both, and that is the terrible difficulty. I want to remind you briefly of what Dr. Jung says in his essay on "The Psychology of the Child Archetype":

> *The "child" is . . . renatus in novam infantiam* [reborn into a new childhood]. *It is thus both beginning and end, an initial and a terminal creature. The initial creature existed before man was, and the terminal creature will be when man is not. Psychologically speaking, this means that the "child" symbolizes the pre-conscious and the post-conscious essence of man. His pre-conscious essence is the unconscious state of earliest chidhood; his post-conscious essence is an anticipation by analogy of life after death. In this idea the all-embracing nature of psychic wholeness is expressed. Wholeness is never comprised within the compass of the conscious mind—it includes the indefinite and indefinable extent of the unconscious as well . . . .* [And now comes the really important

sentence.] *The "eternal child" in man is an indescribable experience, an incongruity, a handicap, and divine prerogative* [in more potential and better language that expresses what we are driving at: the incongruity or the handicap is the childish shadow and a divine prerogative]; *an imponderable that determines the ultimate worth or worthlessness of a personality.* [13]

It is quite clear that Saint Exupéry's genius is that divine child in him. He would not be such a genius or artist if he had not that capacity of being absolutely naive and absolutely spontaneous; that is the source of his creativeness and at the same time it is a little close to being something worthless, something which devaluates his personality. This is why I am always skating between a negative and a positive evaluation in my interpretation, for it is both combined, and one does not quite know how to judge it. One cannot judge it, but must simply take it as a contradictory factor, an imponderable thing. Here, one could say that there is an attempt by the unconscious to disentangle the two motifs. The one definitely would be the infantile shadow, the lazy one who just misses fighting the mother complex until it is too late; the other, the star prince, would be the Self, something which tries to flow toward the future, toward the possibility of being reborn, of finding a new possibility of life after a crisis, of finding a renewal. Here, the unconscious attempts to show the two aspects separately so that consciousness can realize it, because consciousness is too stupid to realize a *mixtum compositum*. It generally needs to have it taken apart first so that it can be put together again, because our consciousness is made in such a way that it wants to separate things.

In my first lecture, I spoke of the problem of the neurosis of the provisional life; namely, that people live in the expectation of being able *one* day (not yet—but one day), which is often linked up with the savior complex. Mr. Malamoud has given me a copy of a paper by Erich Fromm, *Vom Gefuhl der Ohnmacht (The Feeling of being Incapable of Doing Anything)*, in which he speaks of this problem in detail. I am taking only an extract. He says: "If one believes in Time, then one has no possibility of sudden change; there is a constant expectation that 'in time' everything will come out all right. If one is not capable of solving a conflict, one expects that 'in time'

<hr>

[13] Ibid., pp. 134, 135.

the conflicts will solve themselves, without having to risk a decision. You find that very often, especially in believing in Time as far as one's own achievements are concerned. People comfort themselves, not only because they do not really do something but also for not making any preparation for what they have to do, because for such things there is plenty of time and therefore there is no need to hurry. Such a mechanism is illustrated by the case of a very gifted writer who wanted to write a book which he thought would be the most important book in world literature, but he did not do more than have a few ideas as to what he would write and enjoy in fantasy what the effect of his book would be and tell his friends that he had not nearly finished it. In reality he had not even written a single line, nor a single word; though, according to him, he had already worked for seven years on it. The older such people get, the more they cling to the illusion that *one day* they will do it. In certain people, the reaching of a certain age, generally at the beginning of the forties, brings a sobering effect so that they then begin to use their own forces, or there is a neurotic breakdown which is based upon the fact that one cannot live if one does not have the comforting time illusion."

That is a vivid description of what I tried to express. H. G. Baynes wrote about this long ago in his paper on the problem of the provisional life.

The next part of the book I am going to read in detail.

Oh, little prince! Bit by bit I came to understand the secrets of your sad little life . . . For a long time you had found your only entertainment in the quiet pleasure of looking at the sunset. I learned that new detail on the morning of the fourth day, when you said to me:

"I am very fond of sunsets. Come, let us go look at a sunset now."

"But we must wait," I said.

"Wait? For what?"

"For the sunset. We must wait until it is time."

At first you seemed to be very much surprised. And then you laughed to yourself. You said to me:

"I am always thinking that I am at home!"

Just so. Everybody knows that when it is noon in the United States the sun is setting over France. If you could fly to France in one minute, you could go straight into the sunset, right from noon. Unfortunately, France is too far away for that. But on your tiny planet, my little prince, all you

need do is move your chair a few steps. You can see the day end and the
twilight falling whenever you like . . .
  "One day," you said to me, "I saw the sunset forty-four times!"
And a little later you added:
  "You know—one loves the sunset, when one is so sad . . ."
  "Were you so sad, then?" I asked, "on the day of the forty-four
sunsets?"
  But the little prince made no reply.

How would you interpret that?
Answer: Is it a preview of his own early death?
Yes, you could say so—with the symbolic forty-four sunsets. It
might be a foreboding of his own death, and what else? It is the
romantic way of always thinking of death which is to be found in
early youth. How does that connect up with the rest of the
problem?
Answer: There is nothing realistic about it. The thing keeps receding; he
sees the sunset over and over again.
Yes, it is a form of egotism, of narcissism, and that is the kind of
mood people get into when life is not flowing, when time is not
filled out. When you are involved in inner or outer adventure, you
have no time to look at the sunset, which might, however, be a
restful momentary, beautiful experience, after a full day—the moment
when the peace of the evening comes to you. But then one does not
generally feel sad; then the sunset is something beautiful and
restful. If it makes you sad, it is because it has not been preceded
by enough adventure.
  It has again, I think, to do with this tragedy of youth that people,
especially when they are young, are very much tortured by a kind of
boredom. I remember myself that between fourteen and eighteen I
was very often bored, since then, never. Outwardly, it was because I
had to stay for hours and hours in school instead of doing what I
liked. As soon as I was able to do what I liked, the boredom
disappeared. I have seen that, strangely enough, very often it is a
neurotic disease among young people which lessens as they grow
older. It has to do with the fact that they cannot yet do what they
would really like to do, but always a lot of things that they don't
want to do, and therefore they do not feel that they are in life.
Boredom is simply a subjective feeling of not being in life. Actually,
there is no real boredom. I still had to follow boring courses at the

University, but then I learned how to amuse myself at the same time. If you are inventive enough, you can always avoid boredom if you know how to put yourself into reality. One puts one's spontaneous fantasy into reality, and then boredom is gone forever. Then life can be agreeable or disagreeable, exciting or not, but it is certainly not boring anymore. So boredom is a symptom of life being dammed up—that one does not know how to get what one has within oneself into reality. If one knows how to play, boredom goes. But there are children, and adults also, who don't know what to do, who don't know how to draw on their inner resources. In youth, this is not so much a negative symptom because, to some extent, it is a part of the situation, for they cannot yet fulfill themselves.

The suffering of normal young people consists partly in the fact that inwardly they are already very efficient, intelligent and grown-up, but outwardly, they are not given the possibility of using these capacities. They are held back by society, with the result that they are bored. I have taught in schools myself, with pupils mainly between fourteen and eighteen years old, and have often seen that many of their problems were due to the fact that many pupils were capable of reasonable judgment and were inwardly rich and intelligent; in the outer situation, however, both at home and in school, they were treated as children and did not have a chance. Naturally, then, life was dammed up. Then there comes a kind of bored resistance against everything, with bad moods and poor work. Generally, if one succeeded in getting those students onto a higher level by giving them more and more intelligent work and more responsibility, the problem righted itself. They were artificially kept below their level, which resulted in a sulky boredom. So one should always say, "Just because you are bored, and just because you are lazy, now you have to do a double amount of work, but good stuff!" That puts an end to the boredom!

You know that between the ages of sixeteen and twenty, suicide is very frequent; it is less so afterwards. People at that age have very often that strange kind of melancholy sadness, and they feel like old people and have an expression in their faces as if they knew all about it, all about life and felt very, very old. What would be the use of playing about with the others, of dancing with girls or with boys? So they retire in a kind of grandfatherly and grandmotherly attitude towards life. This is only a symptom and simply means that they have not found the clue to the water of life, where they could find an issue for themselves, so they drift on in this way. At that age it is technically difficult for people who are a bit specific and different from others to find out which would be their possibility of life, and then life gets dammed up. Obviously, we have the same situation here with the child who constantly and sadly looks at the sunset.

Next, we learn that life on B-612 was not quite as boring as we had imagined, for Saint Exupéry hears from the little prince that there is a rose on the planet; that one day the seed of a rose came through space and landed on the little planet and has slowly grown, until a lovely rose has unfolded its beauty. Saint Exupéry discovers this because the little prince is suddenly terribly upset and constantly asks him if a sheep will eat roses. If it does, then he can't have a sheep, because it must eat the baobab trees but not the rose! So, through his anxiety, the little prince indirectly gives away the fact that he has such a rose on his planet. Then the description goes on:

But the shrub soon stopped growing, and began to get ready to produce a flower. The little prince, who was present at the first appearance of a huge bud, felt at once that some sort of miraculous apparition must emerge from it. But the flower was not satisfied to complete the preparations for her beauty in the shelter of her green chamber. She chose her colors with the greatest care. She dressed herself slowly. She adjusted her petals one by one. She did not wish to go out into the world all rumpled, like the field poppies. It was only in the full radiance of her beauty that she wished to appear. Oh, yes! She was a coquettish creature! And her mysterious adornment lasted for days and days.

Then one morning, exactly at sunrise, she suddenly showed herself.

And, after working with all this painstaking precision, she yawned and said:

"Ah! I am scarcely awake. I beg that you will excuse me. My petals are still all disarranged . . ."

But the little prince could not restrain his admiration:

"Oh! How beautiful you are!"

"Am I not?" the flower responded, sweetly. "And I was born at the same moment as the sun . . ."

The little prince could guess easily enough that she was not any too modest—but how moving—and how exciting—she was!

"I think it is time for breakfast," she added an instant later. "If you would have the kindness to think of my needs—"

And the little prince, completely abashed, went to look for a sprinkling-can of fresh water. So, he tended the flower.

So, too, she began very quickly to torment him with her vanity— which was, if the truth be known, a little difficult to deal with. One day, for instance, when she was speaking of her four thorns, she said to the little prince:

"Let the tigers come with their claws!"

"There are no tigers on my planet," the little prince objected. "And anyway, tigers do not eat weeds."

"I am not a weed," the flower replied, sweetly.

"Please excuse me . . ."

"I am not at all afraid of tigers," she went on, "but I have a horror of drafts. I suppose you wouldn't have a screen for me?"

"At night I want you to put me under a glass globe. It is very cold where you live. In the place where I came from— "

But she interrupted herself at that point. She had come in the form of a seed. She could not have known anything of any other worlds. Embarrassed over having let herself be caught on the verge of such a naive untruth, she coughed two or three times, in order to put the little prince in the wrong.

"The screen?"

"I was just going to look for it when you spoke to me . . ."

Then she forced her cough a little more so that he should suffer from remorse just the same.

So the little prince, in spite of all the good will that was inseparable from his love, had soon come to doubt her. He had taken seriously words which were without importance, and it made him very unhappy.

"I ought not to have listened to her," he confided to me one day. "One never ought to listen to the flowers. One should simply look at them and breathe their fragrance. Mine perfumed all my planet. But I did not know how to take pleasure in all her grace. This tale of claws, which disturbed me so much, should only have filled my heart with tenderness and pity."

And he continued his confidences:

"The fact is that I did not know how to understand anything! I ought to have judged by deeds and not by words. She cast her fragrance and her radiance over me. I ought never to have run away from her . . . I ought to have guessed all the affection that lay behind her poor little stratagems. Flowers are so inconsistent! But I was too young to know how to love her . . . ."

You see very clearly that he alludes here to his experience of woman and of the first anima projection and how difficult it was for him. He gives away the fact that he was not up to the vanity and moods as well as the charm and beauty of the rose. One of his wife's names was Rosa, and he married her in a very romantic mood himself. Because he suffers too much from the moodiness of the rose, he decides to leave the planet, and seeing the migration of a flock of wild birds, he decides to catch hold of one and let himself be carried away, which is how he came to earth. So now we learn suddenly that he came to earth because he could not stand the flower any longer. The moodiness and all the difficulties with the haughty princess in this rose drove him away from his planet. The rose is a bit sad, too, when he leaves, but she does not show it. The book says:

On the morning of his departure he put his planet in perfect order. He carefully cleaned out his active volcanoes. He possessed two active volcanoes; and they were very convenient for heating his breakfast in the morning. He also had one volcano that was extinct. But, as he said, "One never knows!" So he cleaned out the extinct volcano, too. If they are well cleaned out, volcanoes burn slowly and steadily, without any eruptions. Volcanic eruptions are like fires in a chimney.

On our earth we are obviously much too small to clean out our volcanoes. That is why they bring no end of trouble upon us.

The little prince also pulled up, with a certain sense of dejection, the last little shoots of the baobabs. He believed that he would never want to return. But on this last morning all these familiar tasks seemed very precious to him. And when he watered the flower for the last time, and prepared to place her under the shelter of her glass globe, he realized that he was very close to tears.

"Goodbye," he said to the flower.

But she made no answer.

"Goodbye," he said again.

The flower coughed. But it was not because she had a cold.

"I have been silly," she said to him, at last. "I ask your forgiveness. Try to be happy . . ."

He was surprised by this absence of reproaches. He stood there all bewildered, the glass globe held arrested in mid-air. He did not understand this quiet sweetness.

"Of course I love you," the flower said to him. "It is my fault that you have not known it all the while. That is of no importance. But you— you have been just as foolish as I. Try to be happy . . . Let the glass globe be. I don't want it any more."

"But the wind—"

"My cold is not so bad as all that . . . The cool night air will do me good. I am a flower."

"But the animals—"

"Well, I must endure the presence of two or three caterpillars if I wish to become acquainted with the butterflies. It seems that they are very beautiful. And if not the butterflies—and the caterpillars—who will call upon me? You will be far away . . . As for the large animals—I am not at all afraid of any of them. I have my claws."

And, naïvely, she showed her four thorns. Then she added:

"Don't linger like this. You have decided to go away. Now go!"

For she did not want him to see her crying. She was such a proud flower . . .

That is an absolutely perfect description of a lovers' relationship where each tortures the other. Both suffer in their inner hearts and are too proud to make a gesture of conciliation, or don't know how to—negatively, animus and anima are opposed to each other. Due to lack of human feeling and lack of life experience, such young people often don't know how to bridge the momentary difficulty, but run apart because of a momentary quarrel. That is the fate of many early love affairs. It is also a magnificent description of the vanity and moodiness of the typical anima. The anima woman generally has a certain amount of infantile moodiness, that kind of irrational behavior, and especially male men like this type of woman; she is a compensation for the continuity of their conscious life, but there is an intolerable kind of childishness in such behavior. The rose here is, in other ways, as infantile as the little prince, and therefore they have to be separated.

In antiquity, the rose belonged to the cult of the goddess Venus and of her divine child Eros (Cupid). Roses were also used in the Dionysian mysteries, for Dionysus too is naturally an image of the early dying youth, and in the cult of Isis, and Venus and Isis, roses also play a role. In Christianity, the symbol of the rose became split into two aspects: it became a symbol of the Virgin Mary and heavenly love and, on the other hand, of earthly lust—the Venus aspect. There is one medieval author who says of the thorns "thus the pleasures of love never lack a bitter sting." The Christian assimilation of antique symbolism generally goes this way: it is cut into two, one part being ascribed to the devil and the negative aspect, and the other the positive aspect. Where, as in antiquity and in pre-Christian times, the positive and negative aspects were more closely linked together, in the light of Christian consciousness the two have been separated. This is why most symbols in medieval symbolic books are contradictory: The lion is the symbol of the devil, the lion is a symbol of Christ; the rose is symbol of the Virgin Mary, the rose is the symbol of earthly lust; the dove is a symbol of the Holy Ghost, the dove is a symbol of lust, etc. You can go through the whole list of symbols and find the opposite in them all. The rose has four thorns and is in the form of a mandala; therefore, it is also a symbol of the Self and very often, in mythological symbolism, the place of an inner mystical transformation. But here, like the star child, the rose represents a too undeveloped and too infantile aspect of the anima, and therefore the two have to be separated from each other in order to become mature. Presently, they are only an anticipation of the inner totality, not yet the realization.

There are many fairy tales in which a pair of children, usually called Little Brother and Little Sister, are persecuted by a stepmother. This occurs in"Little Red Riding-Hood," the fairy tale entitled "Little Brother and Little Sister," and others. Generally, one of the two gets killed and is then transformed by a spell and redeemed by the other partner. This same type of child-myth can also be found in classical Greek mythology, as in the story of the two children of Nephele (cloud). Mrs. Cloud has two children, Phrixos and Helle. Cloud's two children are persecuted by their stepmother, and they fly away through the air on a golden ram, but Helle falls into the sea and dies. The brother, Phrixos, escapes and later sacrifices the ram, whose fleece is fastened to a tree. This is the original myth of the Golden Fleece, which nowadays members of the Order of the Golden Vliess carry a golden chain around their necks. The golden ram whose fleece was nailed to a tree was compared to Christ sacrificed and nailed to the cross, which explains why the Golden Fleece was looked on as a symbol of Christ and why it came to play such a special role in the Maltese Order. One could say that all these motifs of two children, a little brother and sister, who are always partly killed and partly restored to life, are images of the inner totality of man which in its infantile preformation has to be cut away so that ego consciousness can mature. The two are later reunited in a higher form, which explains why the rose drives the little prince away from the planet. If we look at it from the side of Saint Exupéry, it can be said that his inner genius (that would be the little prince) was tormented by his anima moods and that the aim of this suffering is to mature the too infantile nucleus of his personality. It could be expressed even more simply by saying that if someone is infantile, then he will suffer from terrific emotional moods —ups and downs—being constantly hurt. That is correct, because as long as one is childish there is only one cure, that of suffering. When one has suffered long enough, one develops; there is no way around this problem. The childish nucleus is inevitably tortured.

Question: If the rose had cried, instead of trying to hide her tears from him, would there then have been a possibility of both maturing?

Yes. If they could have talked over the trouble and exchanged their sorrow and not hidden it by a wrong kind of pride, then they could have matured together. But if you are not mature, then you cannot talk about it. Again and again, one sees that every time the childish spot is touched, people begin to cry. For years, people hide their childish spot in analysis. This is not due to dishonesty or repression, but when it comes out in the end, they say that they knew they would start to cry, so what was the good of mentioning it, because crying would end every conversation. Because they know this, they shelve the problem all the time, but that means it does not develop. That is the great difficulty, for the sore spot must come out and must be tortured—that is the only way by which it can mature.

Something even more dangerous is where the childish side is cut off. Such people do not show it, but you always have the feeling when you are with them that they are not quite genuine. When you have established sufficient contact to talk to them and can tell them that they are never really quite themselves, that there is something not quite genuine, then come the tears! They don't know what to do about it because such people would be genuine only if they cried, and they naturally do not want to cry. That is a form in which infantilism comes up, or the infantile shadow always makes exaggerated feeling demands on the partner. Repression does not solve the problem, for the repressed child continues to cry or be angry in the corner, so it must be split off. One should keep close to it and not lose contact with it, for that would be losing contact with one's genuine personality, but one cannot let it out either. In my experience, it must simply be tortured, it must suffer on and on, until suddenly it grows up. If a man has an infantile anima, he has to go through a tremendous amount of feeling trouble and feeling disappointments. When he has gone through them, he begins to know women and himself, and then he is really emotionally grown up. But if he *pretends* to be reasonable and represses his childish feelings, then there is no development. So it is even better to expose one's childishness so that it may be tortured than to be too reasonable and hide it away, because then it only gets stuck. Therefore, it is better to behave like a child and be hit over the head by the surroundings and those people with whom one is in touch all the time, because then one suffers and then the *prima materia* slowly transforms. That is the great problem which the infantile shadow—the divine child—puts upon a person.

Remark: In the "Visions," Dr. Jung expressed the same thing when he said that people who have difficulty in getting near their center only really experience themselves when they suffer, when they come to the experience of their real self, and that it does not seem possible for them to get there any other way.

Yes. I would therefore say that the child in the grown-up person is the source of suffering; it is that which suffers because with the grown-up part of oneself one can take life as it is and therefore one does not suffer so much. The sufferings of childhood are the worst—that is the real suffering—though they may be over minor trifles, perhaps because the child has to go to bed just when it wants to go on playing. We can all remember the catastrophic disappointments we had as children. Looking back, they appear to be trifles, but in childhood—in that moment—it was an agony of suffering. This is because a child is whole, and whole in its reactions; therefore, even if only a toy is taken away from him, it is as though the world were going down. Thank God, there is the compensation that five minutes later he can be distracted and laugh again and has forgotten it all. But in childhood there are such terrific tragedies, which shows that the child within one is the genuine part, and the genuine part within one is that which suffers, that which cannot take reality, or which still reacts in the grown-up person like a child, saying, "I want it all, and if I don't get it, then it is the end of the world. Everything is lost." That is what the genuine kernel of the person remains like and that is the source of suffering. One could say that what is genuine in a person and what is naive like a child in them is the source of suffering. Many grown-ups split off this part and thereby miss individuation, for only if one accepts it and the suffering it imposes on one, can the process of individuation go on.

Saint Exupéry's wife seems to have been a bit of an hysterical person with tremendous moods. He quarrelled with her so badly that he left her for quite a while and lived with another woman who taught him how to take opium. It is also remarkable, and sheds some light from the personal angle on the tragedy expressed in the book, that Saint Exupéry's mother seems to have disliked his wife and took a tremendous liking to the woman who had taught him to smoke opium. She lost him less than when he had to cope with his wife's moods. This, however, we know only from his wife, and it must therefore be taken with a grain of salt.

CHAPTER FOUR

A little intermezzo in the book gives us further information about Asteroid B-612: two active volcanoes and one extinct volcano exist on the planet. Every morning when the little prince gets up, he cleans the three because, as he says, "One never knows." In the drawing he is just cleaning one of the volcanoes, while on another volcano, where a pan with a handle sits, he is cooking his breakfast. We see the flower under its glass, and a little cap on the extinct volcano, because it does not work. Thus, there are four landmarks on his asteroid: three volcanoes and a flower. It is a mandala.

How would you interpret the extinct volcano? One speaks of people sometimes as being like a volcano. That would be someone inclined to have emotional eruptions, someone with a hot temperament and a lot of emotion which bursts out at any time. If one of the volcanoes is extinct, how would you interpret that?

Answer: Perhaps he has overcome one corner of his emotions.

You are an optimist! I think if he had overcome it, it would not look like that. When a volcano becomes extinct, crust upon crust has formed within, so that the fiery kernel of the earth is covered over with material and its activity does not burst out any longer; therefore, this does not look to me as though something had been overcome, but as if the possibility of expression of the inner fire were closed up; the central fire of the asteroid has faded out in that particular corner. What would that mean in reality? It is a rather catastrophic picture.

Answer: The libido has gone!

Yes. There is no way for the energy to come out, not even by a negative eruption. You could also say that if the volcano dies out on a heavenly body, it would mean that the central fire was slowly burning down and fading away; that the earth was in a process of dying or getting colder; and that the inner process of transformation of the material which is within is slowing down, thereby becoming less intense. We must look at it in conjunction with the planet's small size—the smallness of the earth on which the elephants cannot stand. Again there is a hint of vital weakness; the vitality is giving out in some corner, and with that, the capacity for a direct emotional reaction.

In psychiatric material, the image of an extinct volcano very often appears, illustrating what might be described as a post-psychotic state. People in a psychosis have tremendous emotional explosions, after which there comes the regressive restoration of the persona,[14] when such people are literally comparable to a burnt-out volcano. They are reasonable, adapted, back in life, but the fire has gone out—something has been burnt out by the previous destructive explosion. If you treat such post-psychotic cases, you notice that no reaction occurs when certain important problems are touched upon. Usually, if one gets close to a person's vital problem, things get hot: people get excited and nervous, and they begin to lie, to blush, or to become aggressive—there is some sort of emotional reaction. This is not so with a post-psychotic stage, for just when one might expect things to get really hot, there is a matter of fact: "Yes, yes, I know!" No reaction occurs exactly when it might be expected to be really painful. That could be expressed by the simile of the burnt-out fire. The destruction has been so great that the fire has disappeared. The dreams may show the burnt-out volcano as a picture of the post-destruction condition. You have probably experienced the awful comedown one feels after expressing a very strong affect: fatigue and indifference. All reaction has been exhausted and one is burnt out. Here, the destruction is only partial, for only one of the four landmarks, one of the three volcanoes, is extinct. We might compare these four with the functions, which would mean that one function has given out. The flower would probably stand for feeling, in which case the opposite of the flower, where the volcano is the biggest and is well drawn, would be thinking. Then we have to find out which of the others is burnt out. From this type, I would say that it is probably sensation and the touch with reality. However, I

14Jung, *Two Essays*, pars. 252ff., 461ff.

do not think that an explanation through the functions is very relevant. Probably, it alludes to another problem.

Saint Exupéry had a younger brother of whom he was very fond and who died at the age of fourteen. His brother's death was a great shock to him from which he never quite recovered. This child is mirrored in the whole story of the little prince, and I think that Saint Exupéry consciously had him in mind when he wrote the story. For him, the child who came to earth and then left it, was associated with the trauma of the death of this little brother, with whom he had a very good relationship. That, I think, is probably related to the shock which burnt out a part of his personality and from which he did not quite recover. It is as though a part of his infantile personality had died at the same time as the child who died in real life. Afterwards Saint Exupéry was only a half, so that the dead little brother is a picture, probably, of a part of his own being; of his capacity for reaction. The little prince would thus be an exterior image of what happened within himself—a projection of something which is dead and split off in Saint Exupéry himself.

Question: How old was he when his brother died?

Saint Exupéry died at the age of forty-four, and François was three years younger than his brother. He died in 1917, when he was fourteen years old.[15] He was still a boy, but old enough to fully realize the catastrophe of the child's death. The brother probably succumbed under the pressure of the unfavorable family situation, and from Saint Exupéry's standpoint, he would be the one who could not stand the atmosphere and had to leave the earth because he could not come down into this world. The fact that the little prince always cleans the dead volcano because "one never knows" shows a faint hope that it might become active again. I think this confirms our idea that there is a basic vital weakness, or destruction, in the deeper layers of the psychological earth in Saint Exupéry, which ultimately was responsible for the fact that he could not survive the mid-life crisis—a tragedy which is so frequent for the *puer aeternus.*

The little prince leaves Asteroid B-612 and, holding onto a flock of birds, travels through space. He does not come to earth directly, but visits and explores six neighboring asteroids. This does not seem to be a very important part, so I will only address it briefly. On the

---

[15]Cate, *Saint-Exupéry*, pp. 19-47.

first asteroid is a king who gives silly and completely ineffectual orders which nobody obeys. To save face, he finds out what is about to happen, such as when the sun is about to set, and then orders the sun to set. (I do the same thing with my dog, who never obeys me. If I want to show how obedient he is, I tell him to do something which he is going to do anyway. Then I say, "See how well he obeys me!") This king is very clever in doing this. Obviously, Saint Exupéry is making fun of the inefficiency of the power complex and of those false pretensions which are up against reality as it is. These six figures which the little prince meets could be called shadow figures, or some of Saint Exupéry's inner possibilities of adaptation to his reality, but we will go into that later.

A man who only wants admiration—he is a personification of vanity—is on the next planet. On the third planet is a drunkard who drinks to drown his sorrow because he is ashamed of being a drunkard. On the fourth asteroid is a businessman who does nothing but count his star coins: the stars represent coins to him and he counts them all night long. The fifth is, to my mind, the most interesting. This asteroid is very small, and on it is a lamplighter who must light his lamp every evening and extinguish it in the morning, as was formerly the case in big cities. By some unfortunate development, this particular planet has become much smaller and rotates much more quickly, so that when the little prince sees him, he must light and extinguish his lamp once every minute. On the sixth planet is a geographer who tells the little prince about the earth and says he should visit it.

The idea that the little prince should visit a number of planets before he descends to the earth is an interesting variation of an archetypal motif. In some gnostic philosophical systems influenced by Platonic ideas, it was believed that the soul was a spark which lived in heaven. When born, it descended through all the spheres of the planets, each of which invested it with some quality. Afterwards, the soul was in a human body on earth, where it lived an earthly life with the fortunate and unfortunate inherited dispositions which it had received from the planets on the way down. The idea was linked with astrology, for in heaven the soul spark was beyond astrological influences. It was only during the descent from heaven to earth that the human soul acquired its horoscope: from Venus, an attribute in a certain constellation; from Mars, a quality of that planet in a certain constellation; and so on. As a result, each human being had a specific horoscope upon reaching the earth. When returning upwards, the dying person's soul gave back the qualities (sometimes symbolized as clothes) which it had received on the way down, and thus arrived naked at the heavenly gates to return into the eternal light. After death, therefore, the soul had to rid itself of the planetarian influences. It can be said that the soul spark is a symbol of the Self, and the different planetarian qualities are the inherited psychological and instinctual dispositions with which the human being is born, having received, for example, aggressive instincts from Mars and sexual instincts from Venus, in all their aspects, as well as psychological and spiritual qualities. Later on, I shall present material in which the same idea is seen in the dreams of a typical *puer aeternus*, who must descend to earth and who first goes through the region of the stars. This illustrates the idea that Saint Exupéry has not yet entered the just-so-ness of his own earthly disposition, but keeps away from his own body and his own inner earth. In that way, he is not really himself; in some respects, it is as if he were not completely born.

One could take the king, the vain man, the drunkard, and the businessman in a parallel manner and call all of them different possibilities of the future grown man. Saint Exupéry describes them all in a rather mocking way, again making fun of adult life. He says that one prays to money, the other to nonexistent power, and another indulges in a Don Quixotic activity in keeping up past values which are no longer valid. The king could be said to represent something which Saint Exupéry could have lived. This is also true of the vain man, for Saint Exupéry was very vain, as has been confirmed by several reporters who met him and who said he was a bit of a poseur—he had a certain amount of self-reflecting vanity. He could also have taken to drink. I cannot quite imagine the businessman, but perhaps that was possible too. So, with the exception of the lamplighter, the different planet dwellers represent ordinary possibilities of becoming grownup in a wrong way, or an endeavor to find a pseudo-style of grown-up existence.

I think the lamplighter is most interesting because, if Saint Exupéry had followed the family tradition, he would have turned into a Don Quixote personality. There are many such persons in the higher French nobility; they simply live on the past glories of France, having gotten stuck in the 18th century with all the ideals of the gentlemen and chivalry, and with a solid Catholic background.

They are peculiarly out of time in regards to present-day life. The poet Lavarande, a contemporary and colleague of Saint Exupéry, obviously took on such a fate. He wrote novels in praise of the "good old times," the times of chivalry and nobility. But Saint Exupéry was, I think, too sensitive and intelligent and, in a way, too much of a modern man to accept such a regressive form of life: as he says of the lamplighter, the pace of life has accelerated too much and does not allow for the gentlemen-farmer or the nobility-officer ideal anymore; such roles have become ridiculous illusions. This shows the difficult position in which the poet finds himself for he cannot discover any given form of life which would suit him and offer him a collective pattern for fulfillment.

The geographer is a more positive figure. Saint Exupéry was very fond of geography, something which a pilot must know very well. This geographer could be interpreted as a psychological function of orientation—a capacity for finding and mapping out the way on earth. Power, money, public applause and drink symbolize four elements which he cannot make his god, or to which he cannot pray. There remains the lamplighter, of whom he says, "That man is the only one of them all whom I could have made my friend. But his planet is indeed too small. There is no room on it for two people. . ." That was something which tempted him for a minute, but he rejected it. Then comes the relatively positive figure of the geographer. The story goes on:

So then the seventh planet was the Earth.

The Earth is not just an ordinary planet! One can count, there, 111 kings (not forgetting, to be sure, the Negro kings among them), 7,000 geographers, 900,000 businessmen, 7,500,000 tipplers, 311,000,000 conceited men. That is to say about 2,000,000,000 grown-ups.

He states quite clearly what he thinks about grown-up people on the earth, where he now arrives. The first thing he meets there is a snake.

When the little prince arrived on the Earth, he was very surprised not to see any people. He was beginning to be afraid he had come to the wrong planet, when a coil of gold, the color of the moonlight, flashed across the sand.

"Good evening," said the little prince courteously.

"*Good evening,*" *said the snake.*

"*What planet is this on which I have come down?*" *asked the little prince.*

"*This is the Earth; this is Africa,*" *the snake answered.*

"*Ah! Then there are no people on the Earth?*"

"*This is the desert. There are no people in the desert. The Earth is large,*" *said the snake.*

The little prince sat down on a stone, and raised his eyes toward the sky.

"*I wonder,*" *he said,* "*whether the stars are set alight in heaven so that one day each one of us may find his own again . . . Look at my planet. It is right there above us. But how far away it is!*"

"*It is beautiful,*" *the snake said.* "*What has brought you here?*"

"*I have been having some trouble with a flower,*" *said the little prince.*

"*Ah!*" *said the snake.*

And they were both silent.

"*Where are the men?*" *the little prince at last took up the conversation again.* "*It is a little lonely in the desert . . .*"

"*It is also lonely among men,*" *the snake said.*

The little prince gazed at him for a long time.

"*You are a funny animal,*" *he said at last.* "*You are no thicker than a finger . . .*"

"*But I am more powerful than the finger of a king,*" *said the snake.*

The little prince smiled.

"*You are not very powerful. You haven't even any feet. You cannot even travel . . .*"

"*I can carry you farther than any ship could take you.*" *said the snake.* *He twined himself round the little prince's ankle, like a golden bracelet.*

"*Whomever I touch, I send back to the earth from whence he came,*" *the snake spoke again.* "*But you are innocent and true, and you come from a star . . .*"

The little prince made no reply.

"*You move me to pity—you are so weak on this Earth made of granite,*" *the snake said.* "*I can help you, someday, if you grow too homesick for your own planet. I can—*"

"*Oh! I understand you very well.*" *said the little prince.* "*But why do you always speak in riddles?*"

"*I solve them all,*" *said the snake.*

And they were both silent.

How would you interpret the golden snake? What does it offer the little prince?

Answer: Help.

Yes, and in what form?

Answer: Death.

Yes. It is the temptation to die; it offers help in the form of a way in which to commit suicide. The snake says that he can send people back to the place from whence they came. He suggests that the earth is too hard for the little prince, that he will not be able to stand it, but that he, the snake, can help, meaning that the snake can send him back. The snake says that he can solve all riddles, for death solves all problems. It is a death temptation; it offers a way to escape from life, an ultimate solution of an insoluble problem. The offer is quite clear: the snake would kill with its poison, which is what happens at the end of the book. Before we go into the specific quality of the snake here—namely, as the temptation or the helpfulness of death—we should see what it represents in general.

Like all animals, the snake represents a part of the instinctive psyche, but it is an instinct far removed from consciousness. Jung says about the snake:

The lower vertebrates have from earliest times been favorite symbols of the collective psychic substratum, which is localized anatomically in the sub-cortical centres, and cerebellum and the spinal cord. These organs constitute the snake. Snake-dreams usually occur, therefore, when the conscious mind is deviating from its instinctual basis.[16]

When a snake dream occurs, it is a signal that consciousness is especially far away from instinct; it shows that the conscious attitude is not natural and that there is an artificial dual personality which appears to be, in some ways, too well adapted and too much fascinated by the outer world and, at the same time, inclined to fail hopelessly in decisive moments. In such a case, Jung continues, we find that there always exists a sort of secret attraction to the missing inner double, which one both fears and loves as that which could make one whole. That is why the snake is essentially double in mythology. It arouses fear, brings death, and poisons; it is an enemy of light and at the same time a savior in animal form—a symbol of the logos and of Christ. When it appears in the latter form, it represents the possibility of becoming conscious and whole. Instead

[16]Jung, *Archetypes and the Collective Unconscious*, vol. 9, part i, pars. 282ff.

of intellectual understanding, it promises knowledge born from immediate inner experience: insight and secret wisdom—gnosis.

You can see that the snake in our story has the same double role. It offers to kill the little prince, freeing him from the weight of the earth, but the offer can be understood in two ways: as suicide, or as the good fortune of getting rid of life. It is this ultimate philosophical attitude which says that death is not a catastrophe or a misfortune, but a means of escape at last from an intolerable reality situation, which may be looked upon as something unimportant and which hampers one in one's innermost being.

Very often, the snake appears in ancient mythology combined with the motif of the child. For instance, the mythical god of the Athenians was King Erechteus, who was the son of Athene and who was kept as a little child in a basket into which one should not look, for one would see a child surrounded by snakes. One cannot be sure exactly what it means, but *coffrets gnostiques* have been found in Southern France (probably material from the Middle Ages and not earlier), in which naked children are playing with snakes. The child-god and the snake-god are very often combined like that.

The child-god is also the archetype of the poisoner, so to speak. The Cupid of antiquity has a very poisonous arrow with which he can even subdue—as the poets say—the great god Zeus, for if Cupid shoots an arrow at him, Zeus may have to hopelessly pursue an earthly woman, though he may not even like the situation. Many late poems of antiquity, so-called *anakreontika*, lightly poke fun at this little boy who, with his poisonous arrow, can subdue the whole world to his will. If Cupid shoots an arrow at you, which means that you fall in love involuntarily, whether or not you like it depends to a certain extent on your own reaction. If you do like it, you will be happy and say that you have fallen in love. If you do not like it, you will say that you have been poisoned; you are bound to do something you do not like and are forced into a situation which feels like subjection or poison to the ego.

So a secret connection exists between the snake and the eternal child. The snake is the shadow of the little prince himself; it is his dark side. Therefore, if the snake offers to poison him, it could mean an integration of the shadow. Unfortunately, it takes place in the Self and not in Saint Exupéry, and that means that the whole thing happens in the unconscious and removes the psychological nucleus away from reality again. It is really Saint Exupéry who should have been poisoned, which would have detached him from the little prince. It is likely that when his brother died, he was told that François was now an angel in heaven and quite happy not to have to live on this earth, and so on. Saint Exupéry probably believed this more than others might have done. He realized that death was only partly a misfortune, which could have created his very detached and philosophical attitude towards life.

The *puer aeternus* often possesses this mature, detached attitude towards life, which is normal for old people but which he has acquired prematurely: the idea that life is not everything; that the other side is valid too; that life is only a relative half of another part of existence. Here, the death temptation prevents the little prince from going right to the earth. Before he has even touched it, the snake appears and says, "If you don't like it, you know a way out." Even before he has descended to earth, he has already had the offer of death. I have met many people with a similarly difficult constellation who do the same thing: they live only "on condition"; secretly, they flirt with the idea of suicide. At every step of their lives, they think that they will try something or other, and that if it does not work, they will kill themselves. The *puer aeternus* always keeps his revolver in his pocket and constantly plays with the idea of getting out of life if things get too hard. The disadvantage of this is that he is never quite committed to the situation as a whole human being; there is a constant Jesuitical mental reservation: "I will go into this, but I reserve my right as a human being to kill myself if I can't stand it anymore. I shall not go through the whole experience to the bitter end if it becomes too insufferable." If one cuts off the wholeness of the experience, one cuts oneself into bits and remains split. Transformation can only take place if one gives oneself completely to the situation.

On a minor scale, this is very often to be found when people have been analyzed for years, but still have a lot of mental reservations tucked away in some overcoat pocket which are never brought into the analytical process. Therefore, it is always slightly conditioned and not quite "it." You wonder why it does not go further. If such a sticking place exists you generally find that it is made by the animus in a woman and by the anima in a man. They just leave something out. For example, "Oh well, this is just analysis, but *life* is something different," or "This is an analytical relationship. One has to stand by one's transference, but it does not quite count; it is something different from another relationship,"— and so on. Such secret detaching thoughts prevent the process from ever being quite whole. One plays the role of the analysand and goes through the process in a seemingly honest manner. But the secret is not given up, and with some people it is actually the idea of suicide. Until this idea is blocked through some inner process, nothing is quite real. If you live with the idea that you might escape life, then the possibility of total living is lamed, for one needs to be totally involved with all one's feelings.

The snake is very clever, for just when the little prince arrives on earth and might get involved with reality, it sneaks up and says, "Oh you see, life is hard and it is very lonely on earth. I have a secret, I can help you out of it." It is very ambiguous. I think the most poisonous aspect of this problem is that a person does not notice that he has such a mental reservation: it has hold of him; he is possessed by it. Sometimes, he can only notice it if he asks himself why he is not living completely. "Why am I cut off from life? Why is everything not quite real all the time?" Then you can be fairly sure that either the animus or the anima has put something between you and the reality in a very clever way. In a man, it is generally through the mother complex, for that is like a plastic envelope between him and reality so that he is never quite in touch. There is always a transparent plastic envelope separating him; nothing quite counts at the present moment. With a woman, it is the animus who whispers something at the back of her mind, some kind of "nothing-but" remark.

Question: How does the animus work in a woman?

Suppose you get into touch with a woman towards whom you feel warmly, to which she seems to respond, but you always have the feeling that you cannot quite get through to her feeling. It might be your fault, but perhaps—I am a woman myself, so I am not in the situation of a man who is wooing a woman. But it may happen that a woman comes to me in analysis who seems to have a positive attitude, who does not appear to lie but to hand me her whole material, and who seems to have confidence in me. But I have a constant and uncanny impression that the thing is not sticking together somehow. I feel that if a catastrophe happened, if there should be a chance of this woman snapping or committing suicide, that—to express it symbolically—we are not attached to each other.

Such a person might suddenly write to say that she was interrupting the analysis for some reason—because she was going away, or for lack of money, or some other reason, or pseudo-reason—and then you are just left completely nonplussed.

Question: But how do you account for that?

It is the father complex causing an animus possession. I remember the case of a young girl with whom I had a very good contact, but one day she attacked me in a most horrible way. When I broke through it, she collapsed, and it came out that she had made up her mind to commit suicide and this was to be a goodbye quarrel. She wanted to kill her feeling for me so that she could commit suicide. That came absolutely out of the blue. The contact of the day before had been very good; nothing had happened in our relationship, but for some other reason she had had enough of her difficulties in life and secretly made up her mind to commit suicide. When she thought that her feeling for me was something which stood between her and suicide, she made up her mind to behave so nastily to me that I would have enough of her; then she would be free to go. That was an idea which had suddenly stung her like a snakebite.

Question: But would that have been conscious to her?

I had warned her. She had had a dream which said that an old man was rattling around autonomously on a child's red bicycle. This old man was a suicidal drunkard. So I knew she had a father-animus figure who was linked up with childish emotion—the child's red bicycle—and that was rattling around autonomously at the back of her psyche. Though I interpreted the dream and told her that something in her was like that, she could not get it; she looked at me blankly, but then one day it broke through. That is what happens when snake dreams occur. Then one has to expect that people will act out of the blue.

A man who had a lot of snake dreams, after fifteen years of marriage, suddenly made up his mind from one minute to another to divorce his wife without even talking to her about it first. He might have done such a thing after one year's marriage, perhaps, but not after fifteen! I had met him the week before when everything was okay, and the next week the whole thing was done and the lawyer was in charge! He had lived with her for fifteen years, and apart from animus-anima trouble, which was not worse than in many cases, it had been all right. But there was the snake in him! I had always warned him to watch out either of committing suicide or something else when such sudden ideas got hold of him. The snake indicates the capacity for cold fits in which some instinctive action can be made. I think that in that case, the divorce was not wrong in itself, or possibly not, or at least it was something to be seriously considered—but what was absolutely inhuman was the sudden cold fit. The idea had not occurred to him before, and then he made up his mind and arranged the whole thing with his lawyer in twenty-four hours! Naturally, his wife could rightly complain that this was inhuman, for it was. He could have discussed it with her, saying that their marriage had become a habit without any meaning in it, or something like that, to prepare her emotionally for the shock. But he did not even do as much as that.

The girl who wanted to commit suicide did do something more, for she had at least wanted a goodbye quarrel. She was more related, for she did not just go and commit suicide, but tried to ruin our relationship first; that was a gesture of relatedness. If someone even rings up and says, "I am going to commit suicide, but I just wanted to say goodbye," that is human; it means that one part of the human personality is still outside the snake. What really had affected her was the old man on the child's bicycle; that is why I said that with a woman it was connected with the animus—in this instance with the father image, which was very negative. The old man showed the unrelatedness. He ran along autonomously and that caught her, for she was doing the same thing. I told her I thought that if she committed suicide, her ghost would hover over her corpse and be very sorry! It would have been a suicide motivated by an affect.

Remark: Such a situation would bring the problem of life and death into consciousness, and the committal would have to take place in order to resolve that, would it not?

Yes, if that comes up, then one must consciously make up one's mind. I did not tell her not to commit suicide; I told her not to do it so rashly and under the compulsion of an affect. It was not a mature decision. She should think it over, and if she had really made up her mind to commit suicide, then it would not matter if she waited another week when she could do it after having come to a definite decision. That would be a reasonable, mature decision, but she should not do it in the middle of an affect and then afterwards regret it—if that is possible! The immaturity of the sudden decision for self-destruction was wrong; a week's delay would have caused her to question whether she really wanted to die or not. Many people live involuntarily and have never made up their mind about that question. That is very dangerous. When you get in touch with such people, you realize a constant secret mental reservation. If you tell them, they do not understand and just shake their heads, for it is completely autonomous. The person never seems to be quite present. There is always something evasive. In the case of the girl, when the crisis came, she and I then caught the man on the bicycle. He had always worked at the back of her mind, always making everything not quite true.

With man, it is the mother complex which has exactly the same effect, except that in a way it is even more difficult to catch, because it does not form itself in the man's mind as an idea. The girl had the definite idea of killing herself and that life was not worthwhile; it was a kind of reflection. But the mother-complex form of that is manifested in a depressive mood, a "nothing-but" mood, something completely vague and intangible. Men with a negative mother complex especially have it in the form that, particularly when something goes well (say that they find a girlfriend who suits them or they are successful in their professional life), you might expect them to look a bit happier. Instead, they look pale and say, "Yes, but . . .," but they cannot express that mood in words. A childish state of constant dissatisfaction exists with themselves and with the whole of reality. That is something very difficult to catch, and it is very infectious; one gets depresssed by it oneself, and one cannot even react. It is like a wet blanket over everything.

Saint Exupéry is an example of the irritated bad mood. He had moods where he paced up and down his flat the whole day, smoking one cigarette after another and feeling annoyed—annoyed with himself and everything else in the world. That is how the mother complex comes out in a man; in those snarling disagreeable moods, or in flat depression. It is an anti-life reaction and it has to do with the mother. Saint Exupéry also had a tendency to take opium. As a member of the class has just pointed out to me, the whole psychology of the drug taker is connected with the idea of flirting with death, getting away from reality and its hardships. Generally, people who take drugs have quite a lot of snake dreams; the poisonous snakes make them poison themselves, because they do not know, or do not see, how to get out of their conflicts in some other way. Alcohol sometimes goes along with this problem, for that also acts as a kind of drug. To Saint Exupéry, flying and drugs represented the two possibilities of getting rid of those irritated depressive moods. The problem was that he never worked through the mood. He tried to switch out of it by flying again, but he never got to the bottom of the trouble; namely, a suicidal tendency due to this deepest weakness which he could not overcome.

When the little prince goes on, he meets with a number of astonishing things. The first discovery he makes on earth is that there are hundreds of roses exactly like his own.

And he was overcome with sadness. His flower had told him that she was the only one of her kind in all the universe. And here were five thousand of them, all alike, in one single garden!

"She would be very much annoyed," he said to himself, "if she could see that . . . She would cough most dreadfully, and she would pretend that she was dying, to avoid being laughed at. And I should be obliged to pretend that I was nursing her back to life—for if I did not do that, to humble myself also, she would really allow herself to die . . ."

Then he went on with his reflections: "I thought that I was rich, with a flower that was unique in all the world; and all I had was a common rose. A common rose, and three volcanoes that come up to my knees—and one of them perhaps extinct forever . . That doesn't make me a very great prince . . ."

And he lay down in the grass and cried.

You probably all know examples among the Romantic writers, such as E. T. A. Hoffmann's *The Golden Pot*, about which Mrs. Aniela Jaffé has written a very good paper, or the novel *Aurelia*, by Gerard de Nerval, which shows what a great problem it was, especially for the Romantic authors, to accept the paradox that the anima could be a goddess and an ordinary person of our time simultaneously. Actually, Gerard de Nerval fell in love with a little midinette in Paris. Perhaps his having some German blood was responsible for the fact that he was carried away by deep and overwhelming romantic feelings when he fell in love. That girl seemed to him to be the goddess herself and at least meant as much to him as Beatrice had to Dante. He was completely overwhelmed by his feelings of romantic love. But the French cynical side, the Gaulois side in him, could not stand it, and spoke of her as *une femme ordinaire de notre siècle*—an ordinary woman of our time! As a result, he ran away from her and then had a very catastrophic dream. In the dream, he came into a garden where there was the statue of a beautiful woman which had fallen from its pedestal and broken into two parts. The dream says: if you judge her like that, you break your soul-image into two—an upper and a lower part. The upper part is the romantic goddess and the other part is just an ordinary woman—any other girl would do—and she is a statue and no longer alive. Afterwards came the whole catastrophic development of his schizophrenia, which he ended by hanging himself in the canals of Paris.

The catastrophe was that he could not stand the paradox that this woman was to him divine and unique and that his reasonable personality said she was just one pretty little midinette among hundreds in Paris; that he was a young man who had fallen in love with her, and there were hundreds of others like him too! It is the paradox of being human—that we are one specimen among three billion other specimens of the same kind, plus the fact that each one of us is unique.

To think of oneself in a statistical way is, as Dr. Jung points out, most destructive to the process of individuation, because it makes everything relative. Jung says that communism is less dangerous than the fact that we are all more and more penetrated by our habit of thinking statistically about ourselves. We believe in the scientific statistics which say that in Switzerland so many couples marry per year and find no flat, or that there are so many people in each town, etc. You do not realize what it does to you when you read statistics. It is a completely destructive poison, and what is worse is that it is not true; it is a falsified image of reality. If we begin to think statistically, we begin to think against our own uniqueness. It is not only thinking, but also a way of feeling. If you go up and down the Bahnhofstrasse, you see all those stupid faces and then look into a window yourself and say that you look just as stupid as the others, if not worse! And then comes the thought that if an atom bomb destroyed all that, who would regret it? Thank God, those lives have come to an end, incuding my own! In the statistical mood, one is overwhelmed by the ordinariness of life. This is wrong, because statistics are built on probability. Probability is only one way of explaining reality, and as we know, there is just as much uniqueness and irregularity. The fact that this table does not levitate, but remains where it is, is only because the billions of electrons which constitute the table statistically tend to behave like that. But each electron in itself could do something else. Or, suppose you confronted one human being with a lion. Suppose you put a lion into a room, into which you introduced individuals. You would see that each individual would behave differently. One would stand petrified and exclaim, "Oh!" Another would dash out of the room. The third might not be frightened at all; he might have a delayed reaction and at first laugh, and afterwards say he had not believed in it. Each action would be unique. Taken as a test, it would be revealing, for each person would react typically and differently. But if you brought a lion into this room now, I would bet that everyone would retire to the back of the room, for then the collective reaction prevails. That is why statistics are only half right. They give a completely falsified picture because they only give the average probability. When we walk through the woods, we step on a certain number of ants and snails and kill them, but if we could write the life history of each ant and snail, we would see that when it was killed, it was a very meaningful end at a typical moment of the ant's life.

That was really the basic philosophical problem Thornton Wilder raised when he wrote *The Bridge of San Luis Rey*. The bridge collapsed at a certain moment and a few people were drowned—you read of such things every day in the newspaper. But Thornton Wilder asked whether that was just chance, and he tried to show that those five people had a typical inner development in their lives and that being drowned when the bridge collapsed was the finale to a very meaningful moment in the lives of each of those five people. The statistician would say that it was quite probable; that every day, two hundred people crossed the bridge, so that when it fell at a certain moment, there would probably be about five who would be drowned, and they would be there by chance. That is a falsified view of reality, but we are all poisoned through and through by it. It is something that has to be faced. Gerard de Nerval, for instance, could not face the problem that the woman he loved was absolutely unique to him, for his statistical reasoning told him that she was just one of the many thousands—which in a way was true, too. But it was a half-truth, which as Toynbee says, is worse than an absolute lie. This is what causes so much difficulty for the *puer aeternus*. This is why he does not want to go to an office and do some ordinary work, or to be with a woman. He is always inwardly toying with a thousand possibilities of life and cannot choose a definite one; it seems to him that that would mean a statistical-average situation. Recognition of the fact that one is among thousands and that there is nothing special about that is an intellectual insight against which there stands the feeling function.

The inner battle between the feeling of uniqueness and statistical thinking is generally a battle between intellectualism and allowing feeling its own right in life. Feeling evaluates what is important to me, and my own importance is the counterbalance. If you have real feeling, you can say that this is an ordinary woman (for if you see her walking along the street, she is not very different from any other), but to *me*, she is of the highest value. That would mean that the ego makes up its mind to defend and stand up for its own feeling without denying the other aspect. The solution would be to say, "Yes, that may be so from the statistical point of view, but within my life there are certain values, and within my life this woman has this value." For that, an act of loyalty is required toward one's own feeling; otherwise, one is split off from it by statistical thinking, which is why intellectual people tend towards communism and such ways of thought. They cut themselves off from the feeling function. The feeling function makes your life and your relationships and your deeds feel unique; it gives them a definite value.

When the statistical way of thinking gets people, it always means that they have either no feeling, or weak feeling, or that they tend to betray their own feeling. You can say that the man who does not stand up for his feelings is weak on the Eros side. He is the intellectual type with a weak Eros, for he cannot take his own feelings, stand by them, and say, "That is how I intend to live, for that is the way I feel." Admittedly, that is more difficult for a man than for a woman, which is expressed when we say that the man is weak on the Eros side. For example, if you say to a mother that her children are not unique, that there are such brats all over the place, she will reply that to *her* they are unique, for they are her children. A woman tends to have a more personal attitude. The man must think impersonally and objectively and, if he is a modern type, also statistically, and then it turns like a poison against him. This is especially true for men who have a military career and who must decide the life and death of many people. A high-ranking officer must decide what battalion to send to a certain place, knowing that those men will probably not come back, but that some have to be sacrificed. He must detach his feeling to be able to act, for if he were to think personally and with feeling about those men whom he is sending to their death, he would not be able to do it. The same applies to a surgeon who, when he has to perform an operation, must not reflect that this is such-and-such person. He must perform a technical operation which will result in life or death. This is why most surgeons do not operate on members of their own families. Experience has proved that it is much better not to do so. I know of many accidents which have happened (just an awkwardness on the part of a surgeon who never makes a mistake, but if it is his own wife or daughter, he may), so it is better that the operation should be performed by the colleague in whom he has the most confidence. To be able to detach from his feelings is an essential part of a man's life, for he needs a cold, scientific, objective standpoint. But if he does not relate to the anima and try to deal with his Eros problems, then he cuts his soul in two. That is why men, in general, have more trouble accepting Jungian psychology than women. Because of our insistence on the acceptance of the unconscious, men have to accept feeling and relatedness—Eros—and to a man, this is often disgusting; it is as if he must nurse babies from now on. It feels like that to him—it is against nature—but if men wish to develop further, just as women must learn to share the man's world by becoming more objective and less personal, they must make the counter-gesture of taking their own feelings and their own Eros problems more seriously. It is an unavoidable part of human development that we must integrate the other side—the undeveloped side—and if we do not, it will catch us against our will. Therefore, the more the man takes his Eros problems seriously, the *less* effeminate he becomes, although it may look to him as if it would be the opposite; whereas if he stiffens and does not take his feeling problem seriously, then he will involuntarily become effeminate. In general, it can be said the *puer* who has a tendency to become effeminate has a *better chance if only he will take his feelings seriously and not fall into the pitfall of statistical thinking*—if he does not suddenly think, "Oh Lord! hundreds and thousands!—and me too!"

The story continues very logically, and the next creature the little prince meets is a fox, who tells him that he wants the little prince to tame him.

It was then that the fox appeared.
"Good morning," said the fox.

"Good morning," the little prince responded politely, although when he turned around he saw nothing.

"I am right here," the voice said, "under the apple tree."

"Who are you?" asked the little prince, and added, "You are very pretty to look at."

"I am a fox," the fox said.

"Come and play with me," proposed the little prince. "I am so unhappy."

"I cannot play with you," the fox said. "I am not tamed."

"Ah! Please excuse me," said the little prince.

But, after some thought, he added:

"What does that mean—'tame'?"

"You do not live here," said the fox. "What is it that you are looking for?"

"I am looking for men," said the little prince. "What does that mean—'tame'?"

"Men," said the fox. "They have guns, and they hunt. It is very disturbing. They also raise chickens. These are their only interests. Are you looking for chickens?"

"No," said the little prince. "I am looking for friends."

So you see Saint Exupéry knows what projection is!

"What does that mean—'tame'?"

"It is an act too often neglected," said the fox. It means to establish ties."

" 'To establish ties'?"

"Just that," said the fox. "To me, you are still nothing more than a little boy who is just like a hundred thousand other little boys."

Now he is going to say how you get out of statistical thinking.

"And I have no need of you. And you, on your part, have no need of me. To you, I am nothing more than a fox like a hundred thousand other foxes. But if you tame me, then we shall need each other. To me, you will be unique in all the world. To you, I shall be unique in all the world . . ."

"I am beginning to understand," said the little prince. "There is a flower . . . I think she has tamed me . . ."

"It is possible," said the fox. "On the Earth one sees all sorts of things."

"Oh, but this is not on the Earth!" said the little prince.
The fox seemed perplexed, and very curious.
"On another planet?"
"Yes."
"Are there hunters on that planet?"
"No."
"Ah, that is interesting! Are there chickens?"
"No."
"Nothing is perfect." sighed the fox.
But he came back to his idea.
"My life is very monotonous," he said. "I hunt chickens; men hunt me.
All the chickens are just alike, and all men are just alike. And, in
consequence, I am a little bored. But if you tame me, it will be as if the
sun came to shine on my life. I shall know the sound of a step that will be
different from all the others. Other steps send me hurrying back
underneath the ground. Yours will call me, like music, out of my burrow.
And then look: you see the grain-fields down yonder? I do not eat bread.
Wheat is of no use to me. The wheat fields have nothing to say to me.
And that is sad. But you have hair that is the color of gold. Think how
wonderful that will be when you have tamed me! The grain, which is also
golden, will bring me back the thought of you. And I shall love to listen
to the wind in the wheat . . ."
The fox gazed at the little prince, for a long time.
"Please—tame me!" he said.
"I want to, very much," the little prince replied. "But I have not
much time."

A little later he says:
"What must I do to tame you?"
"You must be very patient," replied the fox, "First you will sit down
at a little distance from me—like that—in the grass. I shall look at you
out of the corner of my eye, and you will say nothing. Words are the
source of misunderstandings. But you will sit a little closer to me, every
day . . ."

So they became closer friends. When the hour for the little
prince's departure comes, the fox tells his secret, as he had
promised he would.

"And now here is my secret, a very simple secret: It is only with the
heart that one can see rightly; what is essential is invisible to the eye."

"What is essential is invisible to the eye," the little prince repeated, so that he would be sure to remember.

"It is the time you have wasted for your rose that makes your rose so important."

"It is the time I have wasted for my rose—" said the little prince, so that he would be sure to remember.

"Men have forgotten this truth," said the fox. "But you must not forget it. You become responsible, forever, for what you have tamed. You are responsible for your rose . . ."

"I am responsible for my rose," the little prince repeated, so that he would be sure to remember.

It can be said that the fox teaches the little prince the important value of the here-and-now and, with it, of feeling. Feeling gives value to the present, for without it, one has no relationship to the here-and-now situation; with it comes responsibility, and through that, a realization of one's individuality.

Here again, we have the frequent motif of the helpful animal which teaches man how to become human or, in other words, teaches the process of individuation.

In his article, *The Primordial Child in Primordial Times*, Karl Kerényi gives a Tatar poem which runs:

> Once upon a time, long ago
> There lived an orphan boy,
> Created of God
> Created of Pajana
> Without food to eat,
> Without clothes to wear:
> So he lived.
> No woman to marry him.
> A fox came;
> The fox said to the youth:
> "How will you get to be a man?" he said.
> And the boy said:
> "I don't know myself
> How I shall get to be a man!"[17]

And then, exactly like the fox in our story, this fox teaches the orphan boy how to become human. Like the snake, the fox

---

[17]Jung and Kerényi, *Essays on a Science of Mythology*, p. 41.

represents an instinctual power in man himself which, though it is represented as an animal, really belongs to humanity. In mythology and in medieval allegories, the fox plays a very paradoxical role. For instance, Picinellus says in his *Mundus Symbolicus*: "The fox represents sly cruelty; he is a bad flatterer. He represents lust. He is extremely cautious and moves along in crooked paths." Gregory the Great says, "Foxes are false animals, they always use crooked ways and therefore represent cunning sly demons." This fits with the fact that in Southern Germany, Austria, and Switzerland, foxes are supposed to be the souls of witches. In our local stories, it is believed that when a witch goes out, her body lies in bed, half-dead, and her soul goes out as a fox and causes damage. There are a lot of stories where a hunter meets a fox who causes a storm, so that the hay which has just been heaped up gets blown away—or something of that kind. Or a fox is seen near an avalanche and the avalanche comes down. The hunter then shoots the fox but only wounds him; the next morning when he goes through the village, he sees an old woman limping, or with a bandaged arm, and he says, "Aha! That was the fox!"

Strangely enough, in China and Japan there is the same belief that a fox is the exteriorized soul of the witch or the hysterical woman and is also the cause of hysteria and psychological trouble in women. A man called Erwin Baelz, a German psychiatrist, was in Tokyo about 1910. He saw such a fox case and described it, without knowing any of the mythology which I have been telling you about. A Japanese peasant woman was brought in who had fits. When she was normal, she was absolutely stupid; a fat, unintelligent woman. Then she got what could be called "fox fits" and became quite different. She herself said that she felt a pain in her chest; then she had a nervous need to bark and would bark like a fox. Afterwards, as Baelz relates, she fell into a trance-like state and became clairvoyant, telling the psychiatrists in the ward all about their private lives, their marriage problems, and everything else. She was highly witty and intelligent at such times, and very cunning. After a while, she would grow tired and pale and would bark a little again, and then fall asleep. When she woke up, she would be the stupid woman with whom you could not do much. It was a typical case of a dual personality: she was either the fox-witch or the stupid peasant. In conjunction with the belief in this country that foxes are witch souls, it is a very interesting story.

In medieval symbolism, the fox not only has this negative meaning, but is also an animal of the god Dionysus, who has, among others, the name Bassareus, which is derived from the Greek word for *fox*. This idea continued in Christian allegory. As Picinellus says, "The fox is a symbol of faith and foresight because a fox investigates things by his hearing, and thus also the Christian can perceive the divine mysteries only with his ears and not penetrate them with his eyes." Here, the fox is the one who knows about the invisible. This is interesting, because in our story (quite independently, for I do not think Saint Exupéry read anything as strange as Picinellus) the fox also says, "Only the things seen by the heart which are invisible outwardly are the real things." The fox believes in that which is not obvious but is known to feeling—that which is opposed to statistical reality.

If the little prince had understood what the fox said, if he had really understood it and had not just repeated it mechanically without apparently taking it in, what would have happened to him? He does suddenly understand why the rose back on his planet is meaningful, for he says, "Oh, I have wasted a lot of time. So that is why she is unique to me! And that is why I have to be responsible for her and not take her as one of the many." That realization looks as though he had understood the fox, but what is lacking?

Answer: He wants to go back to the planet.

It helps him to go back to the rose later, perhaps even to choose death. But what he does not notice is that he has one friend on the planet, the rose, and one friend down here, the fox! If he had really understood, he would not only have made up his mind to go back to the rose, but he should have fallen into a conflict about what he was going to do. The fox is here on earth and that friendship must last, for otherwise it is meaningless; but now the fox makes him realize at the same time that he has an obligation to the rose. There is again a fatal constellation! He should not have fallen into the realization that he has to return to his rose; he should have fallen into a conflict, because now he has a friend on each of the two planets. But it does not even occur to him that through the fox he has gotten into a conflict! His only conclusion is that he must return to his rose. So the fox's teaching, which really would be something to tie him to the earth, operates just the opposite way in him; namely, it liberates him from earth and makes him long to go back to the asteroid. That shows how deep and fatal the death pull is in

Saint Exupéry. It would have meant a conflict if he had realized that he had to say yes to the fox here, and yes to the rose over there. Then he would have fallen into an adult psychological stage where one is constantly in that conflict, with obligations to the figures of the Beyond—to the unconscious; and obligations to human reality on this side. For instance, if a man has an obligation to his anima and also to the woman whom he made a friend or married, then he gets into the typical duality situation of life. There, one always has a real conflict and a double pull; he is always torn between obligations to this side of life and to the inner, or other side. That would be the realization, or the crucifixion—the basic truth of life: that life is a double obligation, and that life itself is a conflict because it always means the collision of two tendencies. That is what makes up life, but that realization escapes the little prince completely, or he escapes the realization. It is one more of those little, but fatal, turns in the story which point toward the tragic end.

CHAPTER FIVE

Last time, we ended with the problem of the fox; namely, that when the fox taught the little prince that the feeling function establishes ties and changes statistical thinking (for feeling thereby makes one's own situation and one's own relationships unique and breaks the harmful spell of statistical thinking), then the little prince at once made up his mind to go back to the rose without it occurring to him that he also has some tie to the fox. Later, he says to Saint Exupéry:

"You must return to your engine. I will be waiting for you here. Come back tomorrow evening . . ."
But I was not reassured. I remembered the fox. One runs the risk of weeping a little, if one lets himself be tamed . . .

You see, he only feels some slight sorrow at leaving the fox. It does not occur to him, as I pointed out last time, that he *could* get into a conflict and take that conflict seriously, asking himself to whom he was now bound. The decision is one-sidedly in favor of a return to the rose and to the Beyond.

Then follows one of the most poetic episodes of the book. Saint Exupéry begins to suffer from thirst and runs away into the desert. The little prince goes with him and causes him to find an imaginary well whose water refreshes him and fills him with joy—a *fata morgana*. They walk and walk, and the little prince always says that there is a well somewhere. Finally, they see one. Saint Exupéry begins to doubt if this can be true, knowing that where there is a well in the desert, there is also a village. With this well however, there is no village. But the little prince runs towards it and tries to work the pulley, and the two drink from this imaginary well. In *Terre des Hommes*, Saint Exupéry says of the water:

Oh water, thou has no colour and no taste. Thou canst not be defined. One tasteth thee without knowing thee. Thou dost penetrate us with a joy which cannot be explained by the senses. Through thy blessing all the dried-up sources of our heart begin to flow afresh. Thou art the greatest treasure on earth. Thou dost not suffer any mixture or brook any alternation. Thou art a dark divinity but thou dost impart an infinitely simple joy.

This episode in the book goes back to the time when he was lost with his mechanic, Prevost. They had walked and walked, and he had the experience of a *fata morgana*. At the last minute, they met a Bedouin who gave them a drink of water from his bottle, thereby rescuing them. In this moment, he probably had the experience which he related in *Terre des Hommes*, and here he describes it again. It was one of his deepest experiences and therefore repeats itself in his books.

Since the divine child, which the little prince represents, is a symbol of the Self, he is also the source of life. Like many mythological saviors, or child-gods, he *has* the source. How can you explain that? Why is the motif of the source of life, the water of life, so often combined with the motif of the divine child? What are the practical links?

Answer: He has the force of renewal and is the symbol of the Self.

Yes, but how does that work out in life, practically? Why does the child side represent the flow of life and the possibility of renewal?

Answer: Because the child has a naive view.

Yes, because the child has a naive view of life, and if you recall your own childhood, you remember you were intensely alive. The child, if it is not already neurotic, is constantly interested in something. Whatever else from which the child may suffer, it does not suffer from remoteness from life, normally—only if it is thoroughly poisoned by the neuroses of its parents. Otherwise, it is fully alive, and that is why people, thinking back to their own childhood, long to have that naive vitality which they have lost in becoming a grown-up. The child is an inner possibility, the possibility of renewal, but how does that get into the actual life of an adult?

What does it mean, for instance, if an adult dreams about a girl or a boy? What does that mean practically?

Answer: A new venture, or a new relationship.

A new relationship, perhaps. I would simply say a new adventure on the level of those functions which have remained naive. It has to do with the inferior function—through which the renewal comes—which has remained childlike and completely naive. Therefore, it conveys a new sight and a new experience of life when the worn-out superior function comes to its end, and it imparts all those naive pleasures which one has lost in childhood. That is why we have to learn to play again, but on the line of the fourth, or the inferior, function. It does not help if, for instance, an intellectual person starts some kind of intellectual play. If a thinking type were to quote the Bible, saying that unless you become like little children you will never enter the kingdom of heaven, and then would go to a club to play chess—that would not help at all, for it would again be on the main function. There is a great temptation to do that; namely, to accept the idea of play and of turning to something else, something noncommittal, but to do it within the field of the main function. I have often seen feeling types whose feeling functions have run out. I tell them that they must do something which has no purpose, something playful. Then they propose working in a kindergarden, or something like that. But that is nonsense, for that would again be on the feeling side; that would be a half-way acceptance and an escape at the same time. The really difficult thing is to turn directly to the inferior function and play there. For this, the ego must give up its directing line, because if you touch your inferior function, *it* decides on the kind of play; *you* cannot decide. The inferior function, just like an obstinate child, will insist that it wants to play at something or other, though you may say that is not suitable and would not work well. For example, in an intuitive, the inferior function may want to play with clay, but the person lives in a hotel room and would much prefer something clean because clay makes a lot of dirt in a hotel room! But you cannot dictate to the inferior function! If you are an intuitive and your inferior function wants to play with stones or clay, then you have to make the effort to find an ambiance where that would be possible. That is exactly the difficulty. That is why the ego always has thousands of objections to turn to the inferior side. It is always something very difficult to arrange in practical life.

The inferior function is a real nuisance, just as children are, whom you cannot put in a box and take out when it suits you. It is a living entity with its own demands, and it is a nuisance to the ego which wants to have its own way. The half-concession of giving the enemy something so as to be left alone, which most people try when they see they have to turn to the inferior function, always reminds me of the Greeks who went about with their pockets full of honey-cake, for if one threw something to the dark powers they would leave you alone—a kind of buying oneself off by throwing a sacrifice. In the descent to the underworld, the Greek heroes always had honey-cakes to throw to Cerberus so that he would fall asleep and they could slip by. That can work sometimes, but it does not work for the main conflict. You cannot appease these demands by throwing them a little sacrifice. But if you accept the humiliating experience which makes the ego submit itself to the demands of the inferior or childish part of the personality, then the divine child becomes a source of life; then life has a new face, you discover new experiences, and everything changes.

Naturally, the child is also a uniting symbol, bringing together the separated or dissociated parts of the personality, which has to do with the quality of being naive. If I trust my naive reaction, then I am whole; I am wholly in the situation and wholly in life. But most people do not dare do this because one exposes oneself too much; however, one just needs the courage, being somewhat shrewd at the same time, so that one does not expose oneself to those people who do not understand. One should be clever and not just childish.

When you begin to play with the inferior function, you touch uniqueness, which is at the bottom of all the tests! In the tree test, or the Rorschach test, you tell people to do whatever comes into their minds, and they give themselves away at once, because play is genuine and therefore also unique. That is why children play. In two minutes they reveal their whole problem, for in that way they are themselves. Very often, I try to help a feeling type by suggesting that they take some striking motif in a dream, a numinous dream motif, and try to do some real thinking on that— not to look up the indexes in Jung's books, but to find out what they think about the symbol themselves. And then, very often, they suddenly get quite passionate and have the most amazing thoughts —sometimes what seem to be very naive thoughts to a thinking type.

I often notice that when the feeling type begins to think, he does so exactly like the early Greek pre-Socratic philosophers. He has thoughts like those of Heraclitus or Democritus, and such people, and is as fired by these as were the early Greek philosophers. If you read Empedocles or Heraclitus, you will find an eternal youth in the way they think. That is why I love those philosophers so much. Nowadays, it seems very like mythological thinking—not very scientific. For instance, the atomic theories of Democritus are awfully naive, if looked at according to modern theories, but there is a kind of wholeness and enthusiasm about them, together with the idea that now they see the whole picture. Naturally, the material is full of projections of the symbol of the Self, so one gets quite carried away when reading it. There is a kind of springtime of the spirit; the early Greek philosophy is like the blossoming spring of philosophy. Very often, if a feeling type gets down to his own thinking, he comes to this kind of experience; when that happens, the thinking type must retire to his own estate and not say that one knew that twenty-thousand years ago! The same thing applies to the thinking type if you get him or her to bring up naive real feeling, rather than something organized. Usually, the thinking type is so much a thinker that he even organizes his feelings appropriately, and because he does not get on with his real feelings, because they are unadapted, he generally has a pseudo-adaptation to feeling. I would say that the main method for getting to the playfulness of the inferior function is to scratch away the pseudo-adaptation with which we all cover the inferior function. The feeling type, for instance, is usually full of school and university theories and imagines that those are his thoughts. But they are not: they are pseudo-thinking adaptations to cover up the fact this his real thinking is awfully embryonic and naive. The same holds true for the thinking type who has very naive feelings; for instance, "I love you, I hate you." If he went round the world saying that, or saying, "I can't stand you," you can imagine what a stumbling block it would be! It would not work for two minutes! Even in school, you cannot tell your teacher that you cannot stand him! I am a thinking type myself and I loved certain teachers and hated others. But I could never dissimulate my feelings sufficiently; I always showed how I felt. I knew it would have been much more diplomatic not to show too clearly how much I despised a certain teacher, but it was always quite obvious. When you become adult, you hide these reactions and acquire a pseudo-feeling adaptation. Thinking types are often very amiable and seem to have very balanced, amiable feeling reactions, but never trust that! That is just a pseudo-adaptation, because the other is so painful and helpless and childish that one cannot show it. But if you have to go to it, then you must again dig up the naiveté of your thinking or the naiveté of your real feeling and get the crust off the pseudo-adaptation.

Intuitives very often have no relationship to the body and are likely to dress badly or be dirty, but since that does not work, they learn to wash and put on nice clothes, and so on; although they may be quite correctly dressed, there is no personal style. If they would dig up their real sensation, their taste would be artistic, but weird and very much out of the ordinary. Intuitives who get down to their sensation cannot buy ready-made clothes; everything has to be made for them. Neither can they eat hotel food; they must either have a cook or they must cook for themselves, and it must be very special. It gives them a lot of trouble to discover this, and, what is worse, it is a nuisance and expensive both in money and time. You can have the tailor and the cook, but that is not quite genuine, or you can go down to the inferior function, but that is the greatest time-thief in existence, because it is primitively slow.

You know that in primitive countries it is impossible to hurry people. If you travel in Egypt, it is no good ordering the cars for 9 A.M. and expecting to be beyond the Nile or in the Kings' Tomb at 10 A.M. Everyone who travels in the Orient knows that he must put up with being two or three hours late; he cannot arrive on time as Europeans do. But once you have made the adaptation, life is much nicer, because you have all kinds of experiences: the car breaks down and causes a lot of fun, and instead of arriving at the Kings' Tomb, you get into the desert and do a lot of swearing, and so forth. But that's life too! You cannot organize the inferior function. It is awfully expensive and needs a lot of time, and that is one reason why it is such a cross in our lives: it makes us so inefficient if we try to act through it. It has to be given whole Sundays and whole afternoons of our lifetimes and nothing may come out—except that the inferior function will come to life. But that is the whole point. A feeling type will only bring up his thinking if he begins to think about something he cannot use in this world, neither for examination nor study; but if he will think about something which interests himself—that is how to get going, because it is not possible to yoke the inferior playfulness to utilitarian motives. The essence of play is that it has no visible meaning and is not useful. I would tell a feeling type to learn what he needs by heart for his exams, and not try to think, because he won't be able to do so. He should make pseudo-adaptations, and if the thinking type gets into a situation where he has to behave—say he has to attend a funeral—then he must on no account pull out his personal feelings. He must just behave and do the conventional thing with flowers and condolences; that is the right pseudo-adaptation for him. To get at his real feeling, the thinking type must find a situation where he can play with it, and then it will be quite different. So the first thing to do is to take it out of the adaptation field and keep the pseudo-adaptation for those cases where it is necessary. I think nobody can really develop the inferior function before having first created a *temenos;* namely, a sacred grove, a hidden place where he can play. The first thing is to find a Robinson Crusoe playground, and then when you have gotten rid of all onlookers, you can begin! As a child, one needs a place and time and no interfering adult audience.

To return to our book—after this climax of happiness where they have found a well, the tragic end follows relatively quickly. The little prince asks Saint Exupéry to draw him a muzzle for the sheep so that it may not eat the rose on his asteroid, and by that, Saint Exupéry guesses that the little prince intends to leave the earth. Saint Exupéry continues working on the repair of his engine and has accomplished it just on the evening when he hears the little prince arranging a noctural rendezvous with somebody. He rushes to see with whom the little prince is talking.

Beside the well there was a ruin of an old stone wall. When I came back from my work, the next evening, I saw from some distance away my little prince sitting on top of this wall, with his feet dangling. And I heard him say:

"Then you don't remember. This is not the exact spot."

Another voice must have answered him, for he replied to it:

"Yes, yes! It is the right day, but this is not the place."

I continued my walk toward the wall. At no time did I see or hear anyone. The little prince, however, replied once again:

"—Exactly. You will see where my track begins, in the sand. You have nothing to do but wait for me there. I shall be there tonight."

I was only twenty meters from the wall, and I still saw nothing.

After a silence the little prince spoke again:

"You have good poison? You are sure that it will not make me suffer too long?"

I stopped in my tracks, my heart torn asunder; but still I did not understand.

"Now go away," said the little prince. "I want to get down from the wall."

I dropped my eyes, then, to the foot of the wall—and I leaped into the air. There before me, facing the little prince, was one of those yellow snakes that take thirty seconds to bring your life to an end. Even as I was digging into my pocket to get out my revolver I made a running step back. But, at the noise I made, the snake let himself flow easily across the sand like the dying spray of a fountain, and, in no apparent hurry, disappeared, with a light metallic sound, among the stones.

I reached the wall just in time to catch my little man in my arms; his face was white as snow.

"What does this mean?" I demanded. "Why are you talking with snakes?"

I had loosened the golden muffler that he always wore. I had moistened his temples, and had given him some water to drink. And now I did not dare ask him any more questions. He looked at me very gravely, and put his arms round my neck. I felt his heart beating like the heart of a dying bird, shot with someone's rifle . . .

"I am glad that you have found what was the matter with your engine," he said. "Now you can go back home—"

"How do you know about that?"

I was just coming to tell him that my work had been successful, beyond anything that I had dared to hope.

He made no answer to my question, but he added:

"I, too, am going back home today . . ."

Then, sadly—

"It is much farther . . . It is much more difficult . . ."

I realized clearly that something extraordinary was happening. I was holding him close in my arms as if he were a little child; and yet it seemed to me that he was rushing headlong towards an abyss from which I could do nothing to restrain him . . .

His look was very serious, like some one lost far away.

"I have your sheep. And I have the sheep's box. And I have a muzzle. . ."

And he gave me a sad smile.

I waited a long time. I could see that he was reviving little by little.
"Dear little man," I said to him, "you are afraid . . ."
He was afraid, there was no doubt about that. But he laughed lightly.
"I shall be much more afraid this evening . . ."
Once again I felt myself frozen by the sense of something irreparable.

The little prince trembles when Saint Exupéry rushes towards him and takes him in his arms and scolds him, but Saint Exupéry feels that he cannot hold him back; that it is too late and that nothing will help him. The experience of helplessness and of being unable to save anyone from death has been impressed on him through the death of his brother. If he describes somebody's death in his novels, he always describes this terrific feeling of helplessness. One stands there with the feeling that the person is slowly slipping away, floating away from you, and that you are utterly helpless. You cannot hold them back anymore. Here is the same experience, for he realizes that the little prince has arranged a meeting with the snake in order to be killed by the sand viper, but Saint Exupéry feels that he cannot do anything to stop it.

The little prince then tries to comfort him instead of being comforted or helped by Saint Exupéry. He says:

All men have the stars, but they are not the same thing for different people. For some, who are travelers, the stars are guides. For others they are not more than little lights in the sky. For others, who are scholars, they are problems. For my businessman they are wealth. But all these stars are silent. You—you alone—will have the stars as no one else has them—"
"What are you trying to say?"
"In one of the stars I shall be living. In one of them I shall be laughing. And so it will be as if all the stars were laughing, when you look at the sky at night . . . You—only you—will have the stars that can laugh!"
And he laughed again.
"And when your sorrow is comforted (time soothes all sorrows) you will be content that you have known me. You will always be my friend. You will want to laugh with me. And you will sometimes open your window, so, for that pleasure . . . And your friends will be properly astonished to see you laughing as you look up at the sky! Then you will say to them, 'Yes, the stars always make me laugh!' And they will think you are crazy. It will be a very shabby trick that I shall have played on you . . ."

And he laughed again.

"It will be as if, in place of the stars, I had given you a great number of little bells that knew how to laugh . . ."

And he laughed again. Then he quickly became serious:

"Tonight—you know . . . Do not come."

"I shall not leave you," I said.

"I shall look as if I were suffering. I shall look a little as if I were dying. It is like that. Do not come to see that. It is not worth the trouble. . ."

"I shall not leave you."

But he was worried.

"I tell you—it is also because of the snake. He must not bite you. Snakes—they are malicious creatures. This one might bite you just for fun. . ."

"I shall not leave you."

But a thought came to reassure him:

"It is true that they have no more poison for a second bite."

Though Saint Exupéry promises not to leave the little prince, he misses going with him. The text runs:

That night I did not see him set out on his way. He got away from me without making a sound. When I succeeded in catching up with him he was walking along with a quick and resolute step. He said to me merely:

"Ah! You are there . . ."

And he took me by the hand. But he was still worrying.

"It was wrong of you to come. You will suffer. I shall look as if I were dead; and that will not be true . . ."

I said nothing.

"You understand . . . It is too far. I cannot carry this body with me. It is too heavy."

I said nothing.

"But it will be like an old abandoned shell. There is nothing sad about old shells . . ."

I said nothing.

He was a little discouraged. But he made one more effort:

"You know, it will be very nice. I, too, shall look at the stars. All the stars will be wells with a rusty pulley. All the stars will pour out fresh water for me to drink . . ."

I said nothing.

"That will be so amusing! You will have five hundred million little bells, and I shall have five hundred million springs of fresh water . . ."

And he too said nothing more, because he was crying . . .

"Here it is. Let me go on by myself."
And he sat down, because he was afraid. Then he said again:
"You know—my flower . . . I am responsible for her. And she is so weak! She is so naïve! She has four thorns, of no use at all, to protect herself against all the world . . ."
I too sat down, because I was not able to stand up any longer.
"There now—that is all . . ."
He still hesitated a little; then he got up. He took one step. I could not move.

Saint Exupéry sat down, and then suddenly the little prince got up and took one step—and now comes the decisive sentence: "I could not move." Saint Exupéry cannot do a thing. He remains sitting.

There was nothing but a flash of yellow close to his ankle. He remained motionless for an instant. He did not cry out. He fell as gently as a tree falls. There was not even any sound, because of the sand.

After a while, Saint Exupéry remembers with horror that he had forgotten to draw the strap for the sheep's muzzle, so that the little prince will never be able to fasten it on. From now on, he is tormented as to whether the sheep has eaten the rose or not, every time he looks up at the stars. Then follows the last picture. He says:

This is, to me, the loveliest and saddest landscape in the world. It is here that the little prince appeared on Earth, and disappeared.
Look at it carefully so that you will be sure to recognize it in case you travel some day to the African desert. And, if you should come upon this spot, please do not hurry on. Wait for a time, exactly under the star. Then, if a little man appears who laughs, who has golden hair and who refuses to answer questions, you will know who he is. If this should happen, please comfort me. Send me word that he has come back.

✍

We must discuss this part at some length, because it is full of symbolism. First, it must be said that the little prince has to be killed like a mortal human being in order to return to his star. He says that his body would be too heavy for that. This is a very strange motif, because if you think of the little prince as a psychological inner figure—a symbol of the Self within Saint Exupéry—then he certainly would not need to be deprived of his body. He would already be in the psychological realm and could return whenever he wanted—could come to earth and go back to the star again. He came down holding onto a flock of birds, and at that time he had already a certain amount of body. He could not fly through the air or fall down through it to the earth, but needed the help of the birds. It is strange that this idea does not occur to him again, but the only point I want to press is that he consists of psyche *and* body. What does that show?

Answer: He has gotten into the human realm.

Yes, he has incarnated to a certain extent. He is not a content of the unconscious which has remained in the Beyond, in the unconscious. It has already incarnated in the human realm; it has become physically real, so to speak, and shows that this symbol is a mixture of a childish shadow and a symbol of the Self. In a way, the little prince is an impure symbol; that is, it is partly the childish shadow, which is already incarnated, and it is a symbol of the Self, which is not incarnated. As a symbol of the Self, it is in the Beyond and is eternal, and there is no such thing as death; there is only an appearing and a disappearing into, and out of, this realm—just as an experience of the Self comes to us, and then we lose it again. If we look at it from the Self, it means that it sometimes touches the realm of our human consciousness and then disappears. But insofar as it has a body, it has incarnated in us—in our realm. It has become audible and visible through our own actions; it has become a part of ourselves, and then the problem is difficult. The snake kills the shadow, for the snake can only poison this body and thereby free the symbol of the Self from the body it has inhabited. The other possibility would have been that the incarnation would have gone on, and the symbol of the little prince would have evolved on a more adult and different level. But in this inbetween situation, the development is suddenly interrupted by the snake's poisoning of the little prince.

Saint Exupéry describes the coincidence very artistically: at the exact moment when he can repair his engine and return to the human world and his fellow beings, the little prince makes up his mind to leave. Saint Exupéry departs towards a human world and the other departs to the Beyond. Because this story is such a mixture of right and wrong symbolism from the very beginning, one does not know at this moment if this departure of the two is really a positive development; you could say that now, after this experience of the Self and the Beyond, Saint Exupéry can return to his normal adaptation in this world, and the symbol of the Self, which was only meant to meet him at this crucial moment, can return to the place from which it came. That would be a positive aspect of this tragic moment. But at the same time, somehow one feels that this is negative, insofar as Saint Exupéry himself did not return to his adaptation to this world but soon after followed the little prince to the Beyond. So we can say the departure has not really happened or was not quite carried through; they were not cut apart. The human part, namely Saint Exupéry, followed the other, and thus the departure of the little prince becomes an anticipation of Saint Exupéry's death. With this goes the fact that Saint Exupéry had not accepted the departure, as you see from the last few words:

Then, if a little man appears who laughs, who has golden hair and who refuses to answer questions, you will know who he is. If this should happen, please comfort me. Send me word that he has come back.

Saint Exupéry had not given up. He cannot accept the departure as such, though it is quite unlikely that the little prince will ever return. He has not sacrificed the relationship. That is another fatal hint, because if one does not sacrifice such an experience after having had it, then there remains a constant pull towards death and unconsciousness in the hope of finding it again.

That is a very dangerous and typical experience. It belongs to the neurosis of the *puer aeternus* who generally, because he is so close to the unconscious, has overwhelming experiences of it which convey to him a positive feeling of life. But then he cannot let them go. He just sits there, waiting and hoping for the experience to come back. The more one sits and waits, the less it can approach consciousness again, because it is the essence of these experiences that they always come in a new form. The experience of the Self does not repeat itself, but generally turns up again at those desperate moments when one does not look for it any longer. It has turned completely in another direction and suddenly stands before you in a different form. Because it is life and the renewal of life itself and the flow of life, it *cannot* repeat itself. That would be a contradiction of its very essence. Therefore, if one has an experience of the Self, the only way not to get poisoned and on the wrong track afterwards is to leave it alone, to turn away—turn to the next duty and even try to forget about it. The more the ego clings to it and wants it back, the more one chases it away with one's own ego desire. It is the same, for instance, with positive love or feeling experiences. People who make childish demands on other people every time they have a positive love experience, or feeling experience, with another human being, always want to perpetuate it, to force it to happen in the same way again. They say, "Let's take the same boat trip because of the magical Sunday when it was so beautiful." You can be quite sure that it will be the most awful failure. You may try it, just to show that it does *not* work. It always shows that the ego has not been able to take the experience of the Self in an adult way, but that something like childish greed has been awakened. The positive experience has called up this childish attitude—that this is the treasure which should be kept! If you have that reaction, you chase it away forever and it will never come back. The more you long and the more you seek, the more you get into a cramped state of conscious desire, the more hopeless it is.

The same thing applies to an artist's work when, through an inspiration from the unconscious, he produces something outstandingly beautiful, and then wants to go on in the same style. It has been a success and the work has been admired, and he feels that now he has got it and that something of value has been produced. He wants to repeat it, to repaint or rewrite in the same manner, but it's gone! The second, third, and fourth draft are nothing—the divine essence has disappeared—the spirit is out of the bottle and he can't put it back again. It often happens that young people produce something which is a big hit and then become sterilized for a long time, for they cannot go back; ego greed has gotten into it. That is the downfall of the *Wunderkinder*, the outstandingly gifted children who are sterile afterwards because they cannot get out of this difficulty. The only solution is to turn away and not look back one minute. But Saint Exupéry looks back—*"Tell me, send me word that he has come back"*—as though he were constantly hoping to recapture the experience. And that is fatal.

The snake bites the little prince on the heel, which is obviously where a snake would bite. This is also a mythological motif. You know of the Achilles heel, the only place where Achilles could be wounded. Many other savior gods were often wounded in the feet. An example is Philoctetes, written about by Kerényi in his paper, "Heroes Iatros," which means "the healing hero." There, he has collected all the Greek material on the healing gods and demons: Asclepius, Chiron, and so on, all of whom are, according to certain versions, wounded, and therefore, healing. One must be wounded to become a healer. This is the local image of a universal mythological motif, which is described in Eliade's book about the initiation of medicine men and shamans. Nobody becomes either one or the other without first having been wounded: either cut open by the initiator and having certain magical stones inserted into his body, or a spear thrown at his neck, or some such thing. Generally, the experiences are ecstatic—stars, or ghostlike demons, hit them or cut them open. But always, they have to be pierced or cut apart before they become healers, for that is how they acquire the capacity for healing others. How would you interpret that psychologically?

Answer: He would know the whole process of suffering and of being wounded and healed.

Yes. But many people have the experience of suffering and do not become healers; practically everyone could become a healer if it depended only on the experience of suffering, for we have all suffered. At that rate, everybody would be a shaman.

Answer: By overcoming suffering and having been wounded.

Yes. The natives in the circumpolar regions, for instance, say that the difference between an ordinary person who suffers and the healer is that the healer finds a way to overcome and get out of his trouble without outer help. He can overcome his own suffering; he finds the creative way out, and that means that he finds his own cure, which is unique. Eliade tells a story about a very successful reindeer hunter, a provider of food, and therefore a big man in his tribe, who has no thought of becoming a shaman. However, he gets a nervous disease which keeps him from going hunting, and then he discovers that as soon as he learns to drum like a shaman, his disease disappears; as soon as he begins to "shamanize" by drumming, calling ghosts, and making cures, he cures himself. But once he is cured, he has had enough of being a shaman and goes back to hunting. Then the illness gets him again. In the end, he sullenly puts up with it and becomes a healer, since it is the only way by which he can keep himself fit. Against his wish and his will, reindeer hunting is finished forever. This is a striking illustration of a man's having to find his own cure after having been wounded by a neurotic disease and forced into a healing activity. Naturally, when he was initially confined by his illness, he got a shaman to try to cure him. But no shaman could cure him. He had to cure himself; he had to shamanize, and then he was cured. The healing hero, therefore, is the one who finds some creative way out, a way which is not already known and does not follow a pattern. Ordinary sick people follow ordinary patterns, but the shaman cannot be cured by the usual methods of healing; he has to find the unique way—the only way that applies to him. The creative personality who can do that then becomes a healer and is recognized as such by his colleagues.

That, I think, is the most convincing explanation of this motif and the most simple one. But you can also see it differently, and that comes into our story.

When the Self and the ego come together and get in touch with each other, who is wounded? As soon as they come together, both are wounded because to get in touch with the ego is a partial damage to the symbol of the Self, just as it is a partial damage of the ego to get in touch with the Self. These two entities cannot meet without damaging each other. One way in which the Self is damaged is that instead of being a potential *wholeness*, it becomes a *partial* reality; in part, it becomes real within the individuated person—in the realizing actions and words of the person. That is a restriction for the Self and its possibilities. The ego, however, is wounded because something greater breaks into its life. Which is why Dr. Jung says that it means tremendous suffering to get in touch with the process of individuation. It causes a tremendous wound because, put simply, we are robbed of the capacity for arranging our own lives according to our own wishes.

If we take the unconscious and the process of individuation seriously, we cannot arrange our own lives any longer. For instance, we think we would like to go somewhere and the dream says no, so we have to give up the idea. Sometimes it is all right, but sometimes such decisions are very annoying. To be deprived of an evening out, or a trip, is not so bad, but there are more serious matters where we greatly want something which is suddenly vetoed by the unconscious. We feel broken and crucified, caught in a trap or imprisoned, nailed against the cross. With your whole heart and mind you want to do something, and the unconscious vetoes it.

In such moments there is naturally an experience of intense suffering, which is due to the meeting of the Self. But the Self suffers just as much, because it is suddenly caught in the actuality of an ordinary human life. That is why, in this connection, Jung refers to the saying of Christ in the Acts of John, in the Apocrypha. Christ stands in the middle of the dancing apostles and says, "It is your human suffering that I want to suffer." That is the most simple way to put it. If it is not in touch with a human being, the divine figure has no suffering. The divine figure longs to experience human suffering—not only longs for human suffering, but causes it. Man would not suffer if he were not connected with something greater, or he would suffer as an animal does: he would just accept fate and die from it. If you submit to everything that happens like an animal, you do not suffer intensely, but in a kind of dumb way. Animals accept things as they happen: a leg is lost in an accident, and they hobble along on three legs; they are blinded and try to carry on without eyes and will probably starve. That is what happens all the time in nature, but man *feels* what happens to him. He has a greater capacity for suffering because he is more conscious. If his legs are cut off or he is blinded, the feeling is deeper and more intense because there is more ego, and therefore, the ability to rebel against fate. If you have ever worked with people who have met a horrible fate, you will have seen what a terrific revolt it can mean. Such people say, "I cannot accept it! I cannot! Why has this happened to me? It is irreversible, but I cannot accept it!"

The animal does not show such intensity of suffering. It tries to carry on until it dies; even if its hind legs are paralyzed, it tries to move, and usually dies by being eaten—a quick and merciful end. It is worse for us, because with modern medicine a human being is not killed quickly. We are preserved in hospitals, and then comes the problem: What does this mean? Why do I have to go on living? In such cases, the suffering becomes intense and terrible and a real religious problem. One can say, therefore, that man is more open to real and intense suffering, and this has to do with the fact that there is something within us which thinks that this should not be; but if it is a part of my life and inescapable, then I must know what it means. If I know its meaning, I can accept the suffering, but if I do not, then I cannot. I have seen people who could take what had happened to them with a certain acceptance and composure when they saw a meaning in it. Although the suffering continued, they had a kind of quiet island within because they had the relief of feeling that they knew why they suffered. But we have to follow the way of our individuation process to discover the reason for such suffering, because the reason is something unique and different in each individual; therefore, one must find that unique meaning. That is why in seeking for the meaning of your suffering you seek for the meaning of your life. You are searching for the greater pattern of your own life, which indicates why the wounded healer is the archetype of the Self—one of its most widespread features—and is at the bottom of all genuine healing procedures.

Question: Would you say that suffering, if accepted, could become a medium of communication with the Self?

That depends on whether it is accepted in the right way. It if is accepted with resignation, it does not work. Many people accept their suffering, but with a tinge of resignation. They put up with it, and then it does not help. It must be a *positive* acceptance, and I would say that you can only get the meaning if you accept. So it generally works out as an endless struggle and then a moment of grace, where suddenly one can accept it and the meaning dawns upon one. One could not even say which comes first. Sometimes it is the meaning and then the acceptance, or one makes up one's mind to accept it and then at that moment the meaning becomes clear. But it is strangely interwoven.

Remark: Christians have an idea that suffering is of value, but as a rule there is too much resignation, is there not?

That is what I have been trying to describe. If they have a living faith, then they accept suffering without resignation because they already have understanding, and then it is all right. But if you have a kind of cramped faith, such as people have who *try* to believe, saying, "I must believe because Christ suffered on the cross. I must accept this suffering," which is what is preached to them, that does not help at all. The person is merely preaching to his own consciousness, and since it is not an experience, it does not help.

How do you interpret the fact that this last picture, which is the most tragic of them all, has no color? Could you analyze the picture? There is nothing but the star and the two lines.

Answer: It is lifeless. Life is receding.

The feeling experience, yes; emotional participation is receding. Now what would that mean? In what way do you mean that life is receding?

Answer: When the little prince and Saint Exupéry came together, there was a possibility of something real happening.

Yes. I only want to know from what life is receding. At the beginning, there were very highly colored pictures; there was the one which Saint Exupéry himself called the "urgent picture." That was the one of the baobab trees, which he says he has drawn much better and which has much more color. And now there is this— quite without color.

Answer: It is a picture of his microcosm at the moment, isn't it? It is a kind of mandala.

No. I would say that it is a picture of the loneliness left after the departure. The picture shows the crossing point of two sand dunes and the star, the idea being that the prince returned to that star. It is a picture of the loneliness which is left, but what is bad about it? It would be normal to feel lonely and lifeless after the little prince had departed. It is not a bad symptom; that is natural.

Answer: It is a desert and there is no life in it; there is nothing growing at all.

Yes, but that is how it would feel. If the divinity left, that is exactly how one would feel. I would say that it is the drawing which expresses his disappointment, and therefore its sadness and emptiness are right. But what is objectionable about it is that the disappointment is not more intense. It is a poor and inadequate drawing of a disappointment and of loneliness. You have to think about it; you cannot get the feeling of it. Try, all of you, to make a picture of how you feel when you are deserted by the gods; try to draw that, and you will see, or I hope so for your sakes, that your imagination will run in a more vivid way than this. It would take some artistic effort—but after all, Saint Exupéry was an artist—to depict the loneliness of the desert. But draw a wide, wide plain, and get the feeling of the atmosphere into it, its nothingness, and try to express the sad coldness of a sky which has only one star looking down on the earth, with its cold light. You have all seen paintings of being lost, and of despair, which wring your heart; in which you feel all the "lostness" and the despair and the emptiness, but here you don't. You have to imagine what he is trying to express. You think that it must be the loneliness, but it doesn't hit you or wring your heart, because there is no color. Why didn't he make it all gray? If it had been a sad gray, you might have gotten the feeling of it. Why didn't he make the sky so that it appears as a vast, color orb overhead, so that it chills you to look at the picture? Here, you feel neither sad nor chilled. You have to replace that reaction by your own thinking. There is something lacking.

Remark: It is just dead.

Yes, it's dead—it's not even a disappointment! It does not even express sadness.

Remark: But the description in the book is full of nostalgia!

Yes, the description is, but not the drawing, and though the description is nostalgic, it is very childish. There is just the hope to get it back again: "Please send me a word." It suggests a postcard, the cheapest means, just public help—like a radio announcement for some missing person—a request that the next police station be informed. But, except for the greedy child who wants to have his toy back and the poor expression of it, it is a very weak goodbye.

Remark: Perhaps he did not realize that it was a god. Otherwise he would never have asked to be sent word like that!

Quite right! Fancy appealing to the world to send you word—"if you find my god!"

Remark: You can see the incongruity between his thoughts and his emotions.

Yes. You are confronted with the extinct volcano again. The emotional intensity is not great enough, and that is the dangerous thing; that is typical of the person who simply reacts by saying, "Oh yes, yes!" in such tragic situations. Sometimes it is pretense and understatement. They pretend to have no emotion, but then you can tell by the cold hands and other symptoms that emotion is there; then it does not matter, for it is just pretense. But if they really have no emotion—when the volcano is burnt out—then it is dangerous.

Remark: I think that Saint Exupéry himself was quite intuitive and he thought that it was an episode which had to come to an end, just as when he crashed in the desert. Throughout the book, you have the feeling that the experience is only meant to last for a short time and then will be over. The flatness in his picture, together with the experience itself, makes me feel that there is no disappointment, because he knew that it would have to come to an end and he could do nothing about it.

That would place too much weight on the intellect. I think you are quite right, but that is a morbid reaction on his part. Suppose there is someone you love and that person dies from an incurable disease. Your intellect knows too! It knows that the experience has to come to an end. The relationship must end, the doctor has warned you, saying that the patient will last another three weeks, but that does not mean that you have no reaction. Even if you know that the relationship has inexorably to come to an end, that doesn't stop your feeling. That is exactly it! It is clear that such an experience as Saint Exupéry had in the desert with the little prince had to come to an end; it belongs to the experience that it must do so. But that is exactly the weakness of a personality such as Saint Exupéry's. People who cut themselves off from their feelings and the emotional layer in order to avoid suffering, or because they are incapable of feeling and suffering, replace all that by reflection; they simply say, "All right, that had to come to an end." That is an intellectual argument.

Remark: Saint Exupéry has really been preparing himself for this all along. There has always been a borderline, but by constantly preparing himself for it, it is almost humorous at the end because "it is just another experience to be gone through and which will come to an end." Basically, that expresses his whole life.

Yes, that is exactly the lack of intensity of feeling. If you are constantly penetrated by the feeling of transitoriness of life and therefore are always preparing for an end before you get there—that is typical for the *puer aeternus*. For instance, when he makes friends with a girl, the *puer* knows that the end will be a disappointment and a parting, so he does not give himself wholeheartedly to the experience; instead, he is always getting ready to say goodbye. As far as reason is concerned, he is right, but then he does not live; reason has too much say in his life. He does not allow for the unreasonable human side which does not always prepare for the retreat because there will be a disappointment. Why can one not say, "Of course there will be disappointment, because all experiences in life are transient and may end in disappointment, but let's not anticipate it. Let us give ourselves with full love to the situation as long as it is there." The one does not exclude the other. One need not be the fool who believes in nothing but happiness and then falls from the clouds, but it is a typical and morbid reaction if one always retreats at the beginning in anticipation of the suffering. Still, it is something which many neurotic people do. They try to train themselves not to suffer by always anticipating suffering. One person said, "I always think ahead of the suffering to come and, like that, I am trained against it. I try to anticipate it in fantasy all the time." But that completely prevents you from living. A double attitude is required: that of knowing how things are likely to turn out and that of giving oneself completely to the experience all the same. Otherwise, there is no life. Reason organizes it ahead of time so that one may be protected against suffering—in order that one shall not get the full experience—naively—just when one does not expect it. In that case, reason and consciousness have taken too much away from life: exactly what the *puer aeternus* tries to do all the time. He does not want to give himself to life and tries to block it off by organizing it with his reason.

Remark: When you think of the pictures of van Gogh, even the most melancholy are full of energy and force and emotion.

Yes, even desolation is fully experienced and even what is lost is fully expressed, in contrast to this. Sometimes, one thinks how much more alive such people would be if they suffered! If they can't be happy, let them at least be unhappy, really unhappy for once, and then they would become human. But many *pueri aeterni* cannot even be quite unhappy! They have not even the generosity and the courage to expose themselves to a situation which could make them unhappy. Already, like cowards, they build bridges by which they can escape—they anticipate the disappointment in order not to suffer the blow, and that is a refusal to live.

Question: Isn't it possible to say how the locked-up feeling tends to express itself? I suppose it must express itself somehow; the feeling that is refused must be there.

I do not see it here, except in the temperamental spontaneity of the rose.

Question: Is it because the volcano is burnt out that there is none?

I think there is none in him, but you have it in the very temperamental outbursts of the rose, where there is a certain amount of feeling. She is fully involved in what she is doing. When she boasts, she boasts thoroughly; when she is angry, she is thoroughly angry; and when she is haughty, she is thoroughly haughty. She has a certain totality of expression. She is right *in* her momentary mood, one could say, and that, at least, is something. Apparently, that was the case with Saint Exupéry's wife. She was amazingly spontaneous, even to a shocking extent—she threw herself into instantaneous reactions.

Remark: I think it runs through the whole book in a more negative way as the slight sentimentality.

Yes, that always indicates a lack of feeling, for sentimentality replaces real feeling. That is another aspect of the picture.

How would you interpret the fact that the little prince wants a muzzle for the sheep so that it should not eat the rose? You see how the thing has to work: he wants a sheep to eat the baobab shoots, and, naturally, if he just lets the sheep loose on the asteroid, it will not be able to distinguish between rose and shoots and will eat anything. So the little prince probably plans to put the glass shade over his rose and then let the sheep eat up all the baobab shoots; then put a muzzle on the sheep and take the shade off the rose. In that way he could keep sheep and rose naively apart! Since drawing is a form of creation in his world, he wants Saint Exupéry to draw the muzzle, which he can put in the box with the drawing of the sheep and thereby prevent the rose from being eaten. But the strap for the muzzle gets forgotten in the upset of the departure, and when Saint Exupéry suddenly thinks of it afterwards, he says, "Now what will happen?" And then he thinks that he will be tortured to the end of his life by wondering whether or not the sheep has eaten the rose. To that question he gets no answer, but it is a thought which will torture him from now on. How would you interpret this?

Remark: His animal side is not assimilated and there is a danger that it may become destructive.

Yes, but the important thing is to remember that you are dealing with this earth and the Beyond. You will remember that when we talked of the sheep, I spoke of it as being possibly the little mistake which causes a deadly accident, as, for instance, when there are sheep on the airfield and the plane lands on one of them and crashes. We have already spoken of it as representing the mass man, the crowd soul. The sheep's negative aspect is the collectivity of its instinctual makeup. Formerly, there were always a few goats among the sheep, because if wolves attacked, the goats did not lose their heads and the sheep might get away; whereas if a ram were the leader, it would panic and the whole flock would follow after him. To compensate for the stupidity of the sheep, goats were kept, but wolves learned to kill the goats first and then make the sheep panic. If the sheep is the collective element that destroys the process of individuation by its collectiveness, it would not be surprising if it ate the rose. As a mandala, the rose is also the nucleus of the process of individuation, and in the book the terrible thing is that it is destroyed on the other side—in the Beyond. On this earth, the sheep is not wholly negative; the *puer aeternus* does not need collective adaptation. He is usually a wrong kind of individualist and does not adapt sufficiently to collectivity; for instance, most *pueri* flunk their military service because of not wanting to be sheep. In such cases, it sometimes does them a lot of good to be sheep and to have to adapt to the collective. But in this case, collectivity extends to the star, where there should not be any sheep. This is a mechanism which is tragic: if one is too extreme in one's refusal to adapt to collectivity, then one gets collectivized from behind and from within; if you pretend to be more individual than you are and flunk adaptation by thinking you are something special—with all the neurotic vanity of being someone special and misunderstood by everybody, and so lonely because so misunderstood, because all the others are such tough, insensitive, stupid sheep, while you are such a delicate soul—if you have these false pretentions and because of them do not adapt to humanity, then you will be just the person who is actually not at all individual.

I have already spoken of the fact that if I talk of the *puer aeternus*, people always have the reaction that they know many such persons; they have in their minds a whole crowd of examples of such men, which goes to show that the *puer aeternus* is not at all original! He is really a very collective type—the collective type of the *puer aeternus*, and nothing else; that is, the more he plays the part of the prince, with the idea that he is something special, the more he is really an ordinary type of neurotic person—a type you could describe clinically and cover almost the entire personality with such a description. Precisely because the *puer* entertains false pretensions, he becomes collectivized from within, with the result that none of his reactions are really very personal or very special. He becomes a type, the type of the *puer aeternus*. He becomes an archetype, and if you become that, you are not at all original, not at all yourself and something special, but just an archetype. This is why sometimes, when you are confronted with a *puer aeternus*, you are able to say to him, "Isn't that, and that, and that, your philosophy? And haven't you trouble there, and there, and there? And isn't this the case with girls? Isn't such and such your experience with girls?" And then he replies, "But heavens! How do you know? How can you know me?" If you are identical with an archetype, I can describe all your reactions, because an archetype is a definite set of reactions. One can partly foretell what a *puer aeternus* will look like and how he will feel. He is merely the archetype of the eternal-youth god, and therefore he has all the features of the god: he has a nostalgic longing for death; he thinks of himself as being something special; he is the one sensitive being among all the other tough sheep. He will have a problem with an aggressive, destructive shadow which he will not want to live and generally projects, and so on. There is nothing special whatsoever. The worse the identification with the youthful god, the less individual the person, although he himself feels so special. If people are really schizophrenic and mad and think they are Jesus Christ, then they all say the same thing. Dr. Jung once had two Jesus Christs in the asylum, and he put them together and introduced them, saying, "Here is Mr. Miller. He thinks he is Jesus Christ. And this is Mr. Meyer, and he thinks he is Jesus Christ." And then he went out of the room and left them alone. After a while, he found one sitting in a corner, drumming with his finger on the table, and the other was standing, drumming on the window. So he asked them if they had made out who was the real Jesus Christ, and both turned to him and said, "He is completely megalomaniac!" In the other, each saw it quite clearly! The diagnosis was correct as far as the other was concerned.

CHAPTER SIX

In order to illustrate what we saw in *The Little Prince*, I would like to go into some material. I cannot call it case material because, as you will see, my contact with this *puer aeternus* was a very strange one; one could not call it a treatment.

It is the case of a young man who, when I met him first, was thirty-one years old. He came from a central European country, and his father had owned a small florist's shop and had been a decorator, but he had committed suicide by shooting himself when the boy was six years old. I could not find out why the father had killed himself, and the boy did not know. The marriage apparently was very unsatisfactory, and the boy remembered that there had been constant quarrels. The mother had brought him up and continued to run the florist's shop after the father's death, and the boy himself wanted to become a painter. Actually, I think he was quite gifted in this way. From the age of about eighteen, he had suffered from a prison phobia to such an extent that he could hardly go to any town, for as soon as he saw a policeman he became so frightened that he ran away, thinking that he would be arrested and put into prison. This made life very difficult for him, for he was always running away and sneaking round the corner as if he were a persecuted criminal. He was also very afraid of the night, and every dusk was an agony to him. He was frightened at the approach of evening; at night he couldn't sleep, and lying awake through the night terrified him. He also masturbated, one might say, naturally. Another phobia, which came out much later was that he could not cross a frontier or a border of any kind, and it is pretty disagreeable to live in Europe if you cannot cross a frontier! It was in connection with this difficulty that I first heard of him.

I had gone abroad somewhere and had lectured on some Jungian theme. Afterwards, I received a postcard saying that there were a few things about my lecture which he would like to discuss with me, and he also had a personal problem, and that he would arrive at such and such a time and date. I set aside some time for him, but nobody came! Later, I received another postcard, with no apology, simply saying, "This is me again, and I am coming at such and such a time." Again, nobody appeared! As I found out later, he always went to the Swiss border and then couldn't cross it, and so returned home. Since he didn't want to explain this in writing, he simply didn't turn up. Then I got a third postcard, again without apology, and again saying he would be coming, but this time I decided not to keep any time for him. Then suddenly, a young man stood at my door and explained, quite politely, that he had written twice and had not come because he had been afraid. The only explanation he could give of his phobia was that once he had been painting very near the frontier somewhere without knowing that he was practically on the border. He had been arrested by the frontier guard who had asked him for a passport, which he did not have, and had then locked him up for two or three hours while the guards telephoned to his home town to make inquiries, after which he was released with many apologies. He said that the experience had not really frightened or upset him, and later he confessed that he had had this fear of crossing the frontier before, so that we cannot take this very seriously; the incident just reinforced the existing phobia. He also told me very vaguely that he had once had some shock treatments and that he had been in an asylum, but I was never able to find out any details, for he did not want to talk about that experience. In a way, you could probably call it a post-psychotic case. He had practically no money, and he wanted to live nearby in a tent and consult me. He was very tall and had golden locks and blue eyes. He looked just like a beautiful young sun-god, and he had a Jean Cocteau coat and hood in a heavenly blue, which suited him very well. I talked to him for a few hours that afternoon and found out what I have told you above. Then he took his tent to sleep in a field nearby, but in the night—it was summertime—a thunderstorm came up, and he became so frightened of the night and the storm that he had to rush into a hotel and spent the little money he had.

So he had to leave the next day, and I never saw him in person again. In that one short discussion, I told him a few things about the problem of the *puer aeternus* and outlined a few of his problems, which he did not like at all. I did not expect to hear of him again; I thought he would be just like a meteor in my life, coming and disappearing again forever. But after a fortnight, I received a letter in which he said that he had very much disliked what I had told him and had been very angry with me and very disappointed that the heroic expenditure to meet me had ended so badly. Then, afterwards, he had thought it over and had come to the conclusion that I was not quite so wrong about the things I had told him after all, and, moreover, something had happened which proved that I was putting my finger on the right spot. Then he told me the story which I will relate later. He asked if he might write from time to time and if I would answer his letters. That went on for about a year, during which time we exchanged only about three letters, after which the correspondence lapsed. That was about ten years ago[18] and I knew no more until about five years ago, when I met someone who had known him and who said that he was all right and working at his painting. Since then, I heard that he married and that later he died from cancer at the age of 45.

At the end of his first letter, he wrote, in a very challenging kind of way, that he had had a dream shortly after he had left me. He said he could not make anything out of it and he wondered what I would say to it. The dream was as follows:

"I was on the crest of a mountain and was walking with a girl along the ridge. I did not know the girl. Two men jumped from below and attacked me. During a wild wrestling match with them, they took me and threw me down into the gorge below. I had the feeling that I was lost, but there was a lonely fir tree in which I got caught and so did not fall to the bottom of the gorge."

This shows the problem of the *puer aeternus* in a nutshell. He is too high up, and that was his attitude. He always wanted the cream of every experience. He was the Don Juan type and had been with any number of girls with whom he usually lived for about a fortnight or three weeks before walking out on them. As soon as things became a bit too personal and too binding or too committing, he just walked away. He did not know, or had not realized, that this was an

---

[18]This lecture was given December 2, 1959.--ED.

unsatisfactory way of behaving; he thought everybody behaved like that, and that was the way for a man to live. He was, in a way, completely innocent about this. The valleys in which people live, jammed together, but also rooted, held problems about which he knew nothing. For example, he had never dealt with the money problem. He got some money from his mother and lived on that somehow, I must say very modestly, saving money by living in a tent and so on, but he never thought of earning any himself, in spite of the fact that he was thirty-one. When I suggested that a sexual relationship with a woman might also be a human relationship with some feeling and some commitment in it, he stared at me in amazement, for such a thing had honestly never occurred to him. He did not like the idea, but at least was quite innocent about it. This aloofness of his attitude would be the crest of the mountain, but if you walk along the ridge, then, whichever way you go, you have to go down—you cannot go higher up, for all four sides lead down. This shows his psychological situation very clearly, for he could only either get stuck or in some way come down from his height, which is what I wrote him. It is however, very dangerous to have a dream analysis by correspondence with someone whom you do not know at all, so I kept to vague generalities such as, "You are too high up. To go on like that will simply mean that somewhere, or somehow, you will have to go down,", and I left it to him to make the practical application, for I did not know what possibilities he had.

We know that he was afraid of the night because, when he was lying awake in the dark, he very often had the hallucination of a big, very strong, primitive type of man who stood near his bed and stared at him. He said he was like a boxer, and he would stare steadily at him. This terrified him. It is obvious that the man represented a split-off part of his masculinity. He did not look very feminine, but he was very nervous and anxious and did not go in for any kind of sport. It was clear that this other man represented a part of the instinctive masculinity which was lacking. This type of shadow is very common among *pueri aeterni*. On account of the mother complex, they are usually split off from the physical spontaneity of masculinity. In the present case, the shadow is relatively harmless, and I thought that the prospect was not too bad because such a type is not very dangerous, whereas a really cruel gangster type is a highly dangerous shadow.

It is the physical spontaneity that the animus of the mother tends to split off; masculine spontaneity is what the mother who intends to keep, or destroy, her son, instinctively fights. I had an amazing illustration of this once. A woman in my neighborhood had a little boy of four to whom the parents gave a watering-can as a Christmas present. Because it was winter, he naturally could not use it, and when he was given the can he was told not to use it in the sitting room. The boy probably would not have thought of this, but of course, as soon as the mother was out, he took the can and sprinkled the carpet. The mother blew up, ranted and raved, beat the child terribly, making a fuss out of all proportion. I heard the noise and decided to interfere. The boy was screaming at the top of his voice, and when I asked the mother what was the matter and she told me the story, I could not help laughing. I told her that she had put the idea in his head and that of course he could not wait until spring. She said, "Perhaps not, but this behavior must be stopped, because otherwise, when he is sixteen he will go out and kiss girls." That was literally her answer! The child had shown a little bit of spontaneity, independence and disobedience—the wish to enjoy life and do something on his own—and the mother realized that this was the little *man* in the boy, which must be crushed at once. Naturally, there is also the symbolism of the watering-can— the obvious one—which would later lead him into kissing girls in the dark at the age of sixteen. The mother's fantasy had already anticipated that; she felt the little man standing up and being spontaneous—and she could not tolerate it.

You see how the mother's animus pounces on these manifestations, such as coming in with dirty shoes, spitting, using bad language, or the phase that young boys go through of speaking of women in a belittling way, as though women were God-knows-what—despised because one is attracted. Such things are primitive—one could even say ape-like—manifestations of masculinity. A certain wildness is natural in a boy, a certain lack of adaptation, and while one has to oppose such behavior to a certain extent, a certain amount of it should be allowed to live. Every mother who has a healthy instinct just shrugs her shoulders and says, "Oh well, boys are impossible," or something like that. But she leaves them alone and tries to ignore what they do although she swears a little because it is a nuisance. This mother, however, revealed exactly what the fantasy was about; she felt the germ of future independence in her little boy's action.

That is why, when the mother has "eaten" the son, she has largely destroyed with her animus such physical manifestations of masculinity as being dirty, wild, aggressive, and slamming doors. But such things strengthen the boy's feeling of being alive.

In your youth, probably all of you have been in Bacchanalian, Dionysian festivals of wildness where you felt on top of the world and completely alive, when you felt you could smash up the whole world. This feeling of vitality is typical in a healthy young person. It makes one feel alive and enterprising, and that is what the devouring mother hates most. She hates it in the son because that is the impulse of life which will lead him away from her, unconsciously, as it were. It will make him forget her, which is why usually, in such a son, one finds this split-off shadow of a gorilla, or a big strong boxer, or a criminal, who represents the shut-off masculinity. It also compensates for the weakness of the ego.

In the dream, the shadow figure is double. Two men spring at the dreamer and wrestle with him. In general, as I have pointed out before, when a figure appears in a dream in a double form, it means that it is approaching the threshold of consciousness. In this case, it also means something else; i.e., that the shadow has a double aspect, a dangerous and a positive aspect; a regressive and a progressive aspect, which in this case is only too obvious. For example, the shadow figure could come into the life of the dreamer in the form of homosexual seduction; he could easily have been seduced by a homosexual man of that strong type. Actually, as we shall find out later, he had a friend of that type, although nothing homosexual ever happened between them, but the fascination was rather tinged in this way. One could say, therefore, that this boxer shadow is now in a double constellation in the unconscious: it is either something which can blend with him and, in that case, will add to his consciousness and strengthen the lacking masculinity; or it can remain outside and become projected, and in that case, he will probably become homosexual and run after this shadow in an outer projected form. So this split-off content can either damage him, or can get him into a wrong way of realizing it, or can help him. From its behavior, one can see also how ambiguous this double shadow figure is: the two men throw him down the side of the mountain. If there had been no fir tree, he would have fallen to his death, which means that the shadow suddenly attacking ego consciousness is responsible for the sudden death, and the crashes, of the *puer aeternus* type. This shadow can save him or possibly destroy him. I have seen cases where the latter has happened.

I remember the case of a young man who was completely devoured by his mother and was half a girl. He was also a kind of artist, and terribly unreal. When both his parents died and he was left in a difficult financial situation, a very cynical, realistic type of cousin turned up and gave him the opportunity of joining in a scheme to cheat the insurance company. The young man had never worked before, had never faced reality, and was suddenly stranded. Then this criminal appeared and said everybody behaved in a crooked way and that he should just sign the paper and he would get the insurance. He did so, without quite realizing the moral implications of what he was doing, and very soon landed in prison. The cynical, realistic friend had carefully arranged that *he* should not appear in it, but the *puer aeternus* boy sat in prison for having tried to cheat the insurance company.

Another case where the shadow produced a sudden crash was also of a mother-bound boy who hitherto, having been kept completely away from life under a plastic cover, got away from his home for the first time in his life, and into a big town. Having never had any kind of freedom, either sexual or other, always having had to be so over-civilized at home, he ran completely wild for a time. He went to the Friends-of-Nature huts (*Natur Freunde*)—a communistically inclined group of young people who live a very free life—and there he drank too much and had a different girl every night. He switched right over to the shadow side. There would have been nothing wrong in it, except that he overdid it in a kind of nervous, hectic way. I only met him once in my life and then saw that he was absolutely worn-out, and his health was completely run-down. I warned him, saying that I did not mind what he did, but that he should not overdo it to such an extent that he would ruin his health, and that he was running a great risk. He looked at me mockingly as if I were a kind of clucking aunt, and that was all the return I got. Three weeks later he rang me up. He had caught polio and was lame for the rest of his life. I am sure that the fact that he was in such a poor state of health had added to the bad outcome of his illness. That is how the shadow, in practical life, hits the *puer aeternus*: he either crashes to his death from an airplane or dies in an accident on the mountains, or in a car crash, or he lands in prison—half-innocently, in many cases. Those are all examples of what falling down the mountain means or what it means to be thrown down from the mountain into the abyss. So you see, this shadow had a double aspect: it contains the necessary vitality and masculinity but, in addition to that, a possible destruction—something which might really destroy the conscious part.

The two shadow figures (he had no associations with them) fling him down. He must go deeper, and that might be the right or the wrong thing for him. If he goes too far, it is wrong, and if, as here, some saving force comes in, it turns out well. In this dream, you can see for the second time what I have already pointed out to you in *The Little Prince* material. In the case of the *puer aeternus*, the material is very often double in a strange way: the healing and the destructive factors are close together, and you can interpret everything almost on a double line. An optimist might say that the *puer aeternus* was too high up and, thank God, the shadow seizes him and brings him lower; there is the tree, a symbol of growth, and that is how it must go. But the tree can mean death just as much as life. It could be said that the *puer aeternus* was too high up and that an ambiguous shadow overwhelms him and throws him down, involuntarily, instead of his going of his own free will. It *looks* like an accident. Actually, this man, in the state I saw him and when he had this dream, was in very great danger of death. He could have died any moment, and therefore, to myself, I gave the dream a fifty-fifty interpretation, which can also be seen in the double figure of the shadow. We cannot say how it may come out, but we do know that there is a lysis, a solution; namely, that he does not fall down the whole slope of the mountain, which would probably have killed him, but that something stops him half way—an isolated fir tree which stands just where he falls and in which he is caught.

As you know, there were several mother cults in Asia Minor and Syria whose center was the mother-goddess Kybele. Later, Kybele was also identified with the goddess Aphrodite. Her son, Attis, or in some versions, her lover, her priest-lover, was the beautiful youth Attis. When Attis got interested in a nymph and was no longer interested in the mother-goddess, she jealously drove him into madness so that he castrated himself. He did this under a fir tree. According to other versions, he was also persecuted by the lover of the mother-goddess Kybele, the war-god Ares. We could say that it was the aggressive animus of the mother-goddess which killed or castrated the young god. In Rome, and in several towns in Asia

Minor, there was a spring festival in which fir trees were carried around in the streets with an image of Attis, generally only his upper part, hanging in the top of the tree. There are also mythological versions according to which he was, after his death, changed into a fir tree himself. All this naturally belongs to the mythological cycle of the young dying sun-god, the mourning which accompanied his death, and the spring ceremonies connected with the cult of this god. Here, the great problem is the tree. Attis is suspended in the maternal tree; Christ suspended in the tree of life, or of death, portrays the same idea. One could say that Attis regressed into a pre-human form; he became a tree numen, the vegetable spirit in a tree. He has grown out of the tree; that is, his life comes only from his mother complex, or from his connectedness with the collective unconscious, and he is no living system in himself. He is like a parasite living on the tree. That is a very serious thing to consider. There are cases of mother-bound young men where it is not advisable to try to detach them too much from their mother complex because they would die. You could say that they can only survive in that parasitic connection with the maternal tree. If you put them on earth as an independent living system, a fruit of the tree, they cannot survive, for they lack the vitality to become an independent individual—which shows that one should approach such problems without prejudice. If such a man goes about with an elderly woman, many people say that he is just going about with his mother and should be thrown into life, and so on, but one should never go on such common-sense general opinions, which are absolutely destructive. Instead, one should follow the dreams and the unconscious material, for only that can show if the detachment from the maternal tree is possible. If it is not, one is just working for the death of that individual.

The suspended youth in the tree is an ambiguous figure. You can interpret the dream positively and say that the tree is a symbol of life; that it is something rooted, which grows, and has a place on the earth. Taking it in this way, we can say that through the clash with the shadow, the young man is forced into being rooted, into having a place in life, and into beginning to grow or mature. But if you interpret it negatively, with the tree—the mother—as a coffin and death, you can say that through the clash with the shadow, the young man is thrown back into the symbol of the death-mother and returns to the source of life; namely, into the mother—in this case, into death. The *puer aeternus* is, in a way, the opposite of a tree, because he is a creature who flies and roams about. He always refuses to be in the present and to fight in the here-and-now for his life, which is why he avoids attempting to relate to a woman. Woman represents the tie to the earth for a man, particularly if she wants to have children; a family would tie him forever to the earth. For the bird that flies about, the *puer*, the woman is the tree principle. In accepting this side of life, he accepts the just-so situation of life, which he constantly tries to avoid. The tree shows clearly that being tied inevitably means losing one's freedom and the possibility of roaming about. The *puer aeternus* and the tree symbol belong together. The tree fixates him, fastens him to earth, either in a coffin, or in life.

On the afternoon when I met the dreamer, he told me principally of his outer life in a superficial way, without relationship to the unconscious. In the middle of the conversation, he pointed out that when he was in a certain town in his home country, he once suddenly lost all his symptoms. He complained that he was afraid of the night, that he had borderline and police phobias and how intolerable his life was for that reason, but when he stayed in this place he had no symptoms: he did not masturbate, his prison fear vanished, and he had no fear of the police. Then he looked at me very sadly and said that three weeks later it started again—and even worse. I said that we should look at those three weeks more closely, that it was always very interesting when someone temporarily lost their symptoms because it meant that for a short time the person must have been in a situation where things were right, which was very important. So I asked him what he had done during that time. He seemed to ascribe the beneficial influence to the town and its atmosphere, but then it came out that he had lived with a girl there, then left her after three weeks and went somewhere else. I asked him if that was not strange and if he never made any connection between the fact that, while he was with the girl for three weeks, all his symptoms had disappeared. Such a thought had never occurred to him. I asked him why he had left, but he said he had just gone. After some further questioning, I got from him the following story to which I previously referred.

He had known the girl since his boyhood. She was the daughter of a rich neighbor, and he had always admired her from afar. She was introverted, very unapproachable and respectable, and he had always looked upon her as the beautiful girl whom one admires and can never get. From his early twenties, he had been friends with a very strong masculine type of man, a sculptor, who, in a way, resembled the man of his nightmare. The two were always in contact, and one evening in the sculptor's atelier they began talking about this girl and whether it would be possible to seduce her. The sculptor, who was a Don Juan type, was quite sure that he could do it—one could get any woman if one only knew how to set about it. But the dreamer said in this case it would be impossible, and while they were a bit drunk they had a bet on it. The dreamer then arranged a meeting, introduced her to the sculptor, and helped on the situation. Somehow, the poor girl got caught in the plot and the sculptor succeeded in getting her for one night. Somehow, the girl must have unconsciously felt that she had stepped into an intrigue and had realized that the sculptor did not love her and that the thing was a cold, devilish plot. After that night, she ran away terrified and completely avoided both men.

The young man got a terrific shock from the fact that the sculptor succeeded with the girl, but not simply because he had lost his bet. He did not know why he had such a shock and did not bother to think much about it. He never tried to contact the girl until later, when he met her again in the town and was with her for three weeks. And that was the time when he lost his symptoms, which returned after leaving her.

In the conversation, it became apparent that actually it was he who wanted the girl, but he had not the courage nor the virility to approach her himself and so had made his shadow friend do what he should have done. It was so much a projection that he had not realized that if the shadow friend succeeded in getting the girl, he himself got nothing! He was so identified with his sculptor friend that, at the time of the bet and under the influence of drink, it had seemed as though he were to get the girl himself. Then, when the sculptor triumphantly showed the scalp, it dawned on him that he was out of the picture; that the other fellow had won out and he had made the sculptor live his split-off shadow. To me, that was the simple explanation of the shock. Then—again swimming along in his unconscious—he started once more with the girl and lost his symptoms, but still, he did not ponder what that meant. To me, the girl seemed to be a very important factor in his life, for with her he had once been happy in the normal way of life. But when I suggested this, he saw me as a matchmaker and a witch. Therefore, I had to retire and say that I did not want to push a relationship with her, but that I did think it would not be bad if he thought about her again and perhaps carried on the contact, or tried to think about the possibility of a relationship. But even that very careful kind of advice made him so angry that he left. He wrote to tell me that it was the one part of our afternoon's conversation which finished me for him—apart from the fact that he had no money. He then returned sadly to his studio and thought that it had not been worthwhile to come to see me and waste all that money. But after a fortnight, he thought that perhaps there might be something in it after all, and he might write to the girl to suggest a meeting, nothing more. At that time she lived in another town. He wrote in the evening, but did not mail the letter, for he wanted to think it over a little longer. When he opened his own letters the next morning, there was a letter from the girl! She had never taken the initiative in any way, so it struck him tremendously that he, the evening before, had made up his mind to write to her but had not mailed the letter, and had received a letter from her that very morning. Both had made the same proposition in their letters—that they should meet once more and, since there was a national festival day during the next week, why shouldn't they spend it together. The girl put it practically in the same words as those he had written. That was a typical synchronistic event. Of course, he knew nothing about synchronicity, but still, it had a very convincing effect. Then he thought that perhaps I had not been quite so wrong. He forgave me after that and wrote me about the whole thing. He would never have resumed contact with me if this synchronistic event had not taken place, because he was disgusted with what I had told him.

The two met on this summer day and went out on a bicycle trip. They stopped at the edge of a wood and lay down in the grass. He put his head in her lap and, strangely enough, while lying in her arms, he had a little nap during which he had the following big archetypal dream:

He was standing at the edge of a cliff. (He made a drawing in the letter, showing himself standing at the edge of the cliff looking down into the valley below—it is much the same as in the Grand Canyon with the plain on either side.) He looked down: there were steep cliffs on both sides of the valley; at the bottom of the valley were the heavens with the sky and the stars. He crawled down very slowly towards the valley, making movements with his legs as though he were bicycling, in order to slow up the slow descent still more and (he had bicycled quite a while before, so in part it is the continuation of a physical stimulus when he still bicycles in his dream, but there is a deeper meaning) to keep his balance. There is a certain amount of anguish, and he is a little afraid of what is happening, but he is still in control of the situation. He has the feeling that there is something near him, but it is very blurred; it might be a dog. Suddenly below, there is a sort of explosion, the welling up of an enormous outburst of light. The light spot is quite flat and he has the feeling that he is absorbed in it, but he continues to fall down through the air. Then there comes a change in the dream when the whole thing disappears and he no longer sees the sky below him, but rather a quadrangular pattern, as you see a landscape from an airplane, with the fields in rectangular patterns. There are no trees. Then there comes another shift when he is again in the same landscape. There is stagnant water at the bottom of the valley. It is gray, and dirty, and does not reflect. He wakes up and says to himself, "I am not afraid, but this water is a symbol of the mother and I don't want to fall into that. (He had had some Freudian analysis so he knew that he had a mother complex, and so on, but only in a narrow Freudian sense of the word.) It is like ice at the bottom of the valley and it does not mirror." (He repeats that twice.) He is a bit afraid. Suddenly this spark of light appears again at the bottom of the valley. It is quite round, but the borders are a bit blurred. It explodes like a soap bubble, and in the spot he sees a skull and thinks to himself, "How funny!" What does death mean in all this? What does death mean here?" He is not terribly afraid, but he is still falling slowly at the same spot (that means that he is falling and not falling; it is a dream paradox). Then the whole thing disappears and is replaced by a floor covered with linoleum at the bottom of the valley. It is yellow with brown spots. (At first it was the sky with light stars, and now there is a yellow linoleum with brown spots on it.) The landscape has completely lost its gigantic proportions, and he asks himself, what is a piece of linoleum doing at the bottom of the valley? (This is really surrealistic.) He can see it all very clearly. He laughs a little about the idea of the linoleum.

He then added, in his letter, that he does not like linoleum; he thinks it cold and not aesthetic. It was very difficult to get the associations. Those he did not write voluntarily I could not get, so I had to make do with what he wrote in his rather superficial letters. That was all he said about linoleum.

This dream contains in a nutshell the drama of the *puer aeternus* who has to come down into life. Usually, a landscape in dreams, especially if it is worked out with so much detail and love as in this case, can be said to be a soul-landscape. It mirrors an aspect of the Romantic period in which the landscape takes on the qualities of the painting's atmosphere—a storm coming up or the peace of evening or a dark, threatening forest. These typical landscapes are attractive and, in a way, are mirrors of certain moods or convey the atmosphere of being psychologically tuned in a certain way. Therefore, where there is a worked-out description of a landscape in a dream, it can always be taken as a description of the psychological situation. Here again, as with the dream of the crest of the mountain, he has come to the edge, to the end. He cannot go farther in the way he is now going, which is why he alighted so briefly in my neighborhood— really like a bird lighting on a tree and flying off again. He felt he had come to an end and could not go on in the same way. He has one split in his psyche, a very deep one. But from a clinical viewpoint, it is important to note that his is not a typical schizophrenic landscape. In the landscape made by schizophrenics there are several splits: there will be canyons here and there, indicating that the field of conscious reality is falling apart. In one way, the case of this young man is not psychotic because there is only one split—the earth is not falling apart. I have often seen this type of split in compulsion neuroses, which are frequently diagnosed as being on the borderline of psychosis—between neurosis and psychosis. There you often find the very deep split, but only one; naturally, that is more hopeful, because there is only one big problem. In this case, you can say that there is one big problem behind his border-frontier phobia, but that his whole structure is not dissolving.

Naturally, I have not commented on the symbolism of this man's phobia because I thought it obvious: the policeman putting him in prison, and the frontier. When he has to go over the border into another country, he projects the idea that now he is going to fall into the hole in his psyche. The prison phobia is very obvious, too. He is like a bird; he never gets pinned down to earth, he never stays anywhere, either with a girl or in his profession or anywhere else. He doesn't even stay in the same town all the time, but wanders around with his tent. So the prison is the negative symbol of the mother complex (in which he sits in fact all the time), or it would be prospectively just exactly what he needs, for he needs to be put into prison—into the prison of reality. But he runs away from the prison anyway, wherever he turns. He has only the choice of two prisons: either that of his neurosis or that of his reality; thus, he is caught between the devil and the deep blue sea. That is his fate, and that is the fate of the *puer aeternus* altogether. It is up to him which he prefers: that of his mother complex and his neurosis, or that of being caught in the just-so story of earthly reality.

He now comes into a situation where he is confronted with his inner split and he is slowly falling, and while doing so, he makes bicycling movements with his legs in order to stop the rate at which he is falling. There might be a sexual implication in this too, but there may be also a physical stimulus because he had been bicycling for several hours before the dream. Beyond that, there is also something positive in the sense that he keeps moving; he does not just passively sink into the situation—he maintains a certain amount of movement himself—and in that way, the fall is slowed down. That is very important, for when an individual falls into the inner split—a depression or an inner accident, so to speak—the danger is less if the ego complex can keep a certain amount of activity; if it can keep moving. This is very often done instinctively by people when they are going off into a psychotic episode. One of the last attempts to save themselves—I have seen it in several cases—is that they try feverishly to write all their fantasies. They write day and night and keep on and on until they snap. It seems rather crazy, but it is really a last attempt to keep a certain amount of initiative, to keep going with the ego complex and to do something about the flood of unconscious material by separating it and putting it down on paper. The ego complex is drowning, but it still has an instinctive need to struggle and keep moving. If one can encourage that, it is sometimes possible to bridge the dangerous moment. As long as the ego keeps a certain amount of initiative, it does not just sink completely and inertly into the unconscious. If we link this with the actual situation, the very fact that this man went on a bicycle trip with the girl was such a movement. Instead of waiting till his bad fate caught up with him, he met the relationship half-way for once, and showed some enterprise by making a contact with the girl on a more feeling level, which was exactly the movement that kept him from falling completely into his split. You will notice that during the whole dream he keeps on repeating that he is not afraid, or that he is only a bit afraid. Such insistence always means that people *are* afraid, and the very fact that he must keep asserting that he is not afraid shows his tremendous fear of falling into the split, but, with a kind of autosuggestion, he tries to keep his head.

This is a great improvement on the other dream in which he is thrown down by the shadow into the gorge and was saved by sheer chance. This time he retains a certain amount of movement himself, and that slows up the fall. You see how important it is not to push a man who is caught in this kind of constellation into reality too abruptly, because that might constellate being thrown down by the shadow. It is as if an airplane, too high up, were running out of fuel, and it has to land slowly to avoid a crash. That is the great difficulty in dealing with such cases—in one way it helps them to approach reality, and in another way, they cannot be pushed too much, because there is the danger of crashing. The dream shows very delicately how one can fall slowly, like a parachutist, but it also shows that this man has such a severe split that he needs very careful handling.

The crash landing means what I explained before, when I spoke of the young man who had polio, or the young man who landed in prison, or similar possibilities—or else it can happen completely inwardly, rather than outwardly. Then, instead of being a brilliant *puer*, such a person suddenly becomes a cynical, disappointed old man. The brilliance has turned into cynical disappointment, and the man is too old for his age and has neither belief nor interest in anything any longer. He is absolutely and thoroughly disillusioned, and thereby loses all creativeness, all *élan vital*, and all contact with the spirit. Then money, ambition, and the struggle with colleagues become paramount, and everything else disappears with the romanticism of youth. There is very often an embittered expression on the face of such a man. Here is a dream which illustrates that situation very clearly.

A very romantic young man of the Don Juan type with a positive mother complex, married and built up a profession. Unfortunately, he decided to go back with his wife and children to the town where his parents lived. Naturally, there were the usual quarrels between wife and parents-in-law. The man had a good sexual relationship with his wife, but not much human contact with her; he did not know her, really. He had also tremendous illusions about his own mother, whom, because of his positive mother complex, he had idealized as he idealized his wife. When he got into the situation where the two women started fighting, he couldn't help but be very disappointed by the way in which quarreling women behave: lies and slander and outbursts of affect, both of them pulling him apart and telling him poisonous things about the other—the usual weapons which women use in such situations. He felt literally out of the clouds and wrote everything off; he drowned himself in work and just tried to ignore the fighting cats who made his life a hell. Instead of shouting from time to time at one or the other, he took very little stand himself. When I met him again, I was absolutely shocked at the change in him. He was a disappointed, pale-faced man, with a bitter expression. I asked him how his work was, and he said it was going well and that he had a lot to do, and then the whole story came out. Consciously he was not disappointed. He thought that was just life and that he had dealt with the situation quite all right in a practical way, but he had not realized the shock to his feeling. Then he told me the following absolutely archetypal dream:

He came into a strange town where there was a prince who had loved a beautiful woman, but she had become a film star and had left him, and now he was engaged to a second woman. It was doubtful, however, whether he loved her as much; it looked as if he still loved the film star, to whom he had given, as a kind of farewell present, a jewel he had made for her—a huge diamond in the form of a tear. Then suddenly, the dreamer was standing in the street of this strange town, and he saw the prince walking away with the second woman. He had his arm around her. A lot of cars were racing by, and the dreamer thought that now the couple would be run over, but they succeeded in crossing the street, and then, in a rather slummy part of the town, they went into a dark backyard. Then he saw dark men jump out of a nearby building, intending to attack the prince. But there came a switch in the story, and the dreamer himself was lying sprawled on the pavement, knocked out but not dead, and wondering if the attackers were still around or whether help would come.

In this dream, you see that the prince is the archetype of the *puer aeternus* with whom the dreamer is no longer identical. This man has fallen out of the identification with the prince and is no longer a *puer aeternus*, and the prince is now an autonomous figure within him.

Let us say that ten years before he had been a prince himself, a typical *puer aeternus*, but now he has come into reality. He has disidentified with that archetype, which, however, is still alive in his psyche but independent from the ego. When the ego has disidentified, the figure that was previously a kind of mixture of the infantile shadow and the Self becomes a pure symbol of the Self. The association he gave me was that the prince had loved a beautiful woman who had now become an American film star and gone completely into cheap extraversion. This is a kind of normal development where one part of the anima seduces the man into life—that was the part which had seduced him into marriage, into a career and into getting involved with life, founding a family, finding a big flat, and so on. He had, with a part of his will-to-live, gotten fascinated into life, so to speak. That was all right, but it left out the romantic prince within him, who could not follow into this part of life. So the prince chose another woman as his fiancée, which would mean that now another part of the anima—probably not the exogamous, but the endogamous aspect—is linking itself with the Self.

In the development of the anima, youths, perhaps when at school, often have a girlfriend whom they admire but cannot marry because they are not yet of an age to marry, and sometime later they marry another type. Then later in life—probably between forty and fifty— this admired anima-imago frequently turns up again and generally plays the symbolic inner role of being the one who leads to the Self. This aspect of the anima takes on the role of Dante's Beatrice; namely, that of the leader into the inner man whilst another aspect of the anima seduces him into marriage and into life. So you can say that there is an exogamous marriage, and with that, generally, involvement with outer life, and an endogamous aspect of the same image which remains within and which in later life, becomes the guide towards the realization of the inner life. The new fiancée of this disappointed man would be this endogamous aspect of the anima, but she is nondescript, not yet clear, and he has not yet grasped what she means.

The prince gives a diamond in the form of a tear to the film star, who is leaving, which clearly expresses his sorrow at her departure and also alludes to the fact that he still accords her high value and is tragically hit by her departure. He probably would still cling to her if she had not left him. Although this man had an expression of deep sadness and of bitter disappointment, he had not realized how profoundly he was hit by the disappointment of his past life, how much he felt betrayed by the fact that he was now involved in the human, all-too-human, ordinary life of this planet. In a way, the prince in him was still longing for the lost *élan vital* which had seduced him into life and which had now faded. When he connects with this new form of the anima which turns towards inner development, he is nearly run over by a lot of cars when he crosses the street.

In our civilization, we still have a *Weltanschauung* that approves of the young man who leaves his parents and goes off to start a family. In the present case, the mother resists that, but the collective attitude approves of this kind of development. When a man turns to the inner life, however, the pace of outer life works against him. It demands that once a man has established a family, he should go on building a career, getting more money and a better position, striving to become the boss and super-boss. Here, however, the middle-aged dreamer ought to give that up and turn to another sphere of life. But, he is not supported in this need—he is threatened by the speed and the demands of outer life. In actuality, the dreamer was in a situation where he was completely overworked. He was very successful, and therefore it was all the harder for him to see that although he had great success in outer life, he nevertheless had the face of an embittered old man.

The prince is not destroyed by the mechanical speed (i.e., the dreamer's overwork—indicated by the traffic in the dream), but has the courage to go into the darkness of a city backyard, which means into his inferiority and human misery—the inferior function: to misery, poverty, and the atmosphere of backyards, where dogs eat out of dustbins, where cats mate, where woman gossip, and so on. The backyard represents the place of the big city's hidden misery— a beautiful image of the neglected unconscious and the neglected inferior part of life. As if in a fairy tale, the prince must enter the darkness of this aspect of life, and in this moment, the dark gangster-shadow attacks the archetypal prince. This shows that the danger within the dreamer's psyche is that he will cynically throw away his secret longing for a meaningful life. Actually, he had already begun to do that. His cynicism is now attacking his inner prince and he is in danger of giving up any search for an inner ideal or truth, or for what he once had felt was the aim and meaning of his life. And then, suddenly, he is in the situation of the prince himself and lies helplessly on the ground. I told him that he was just awfully "down," that he felt "down"—depressed. He could not answer for about five minutes, he was so surprised by the idea that he should be depressed. But I said, "Well, you are lying on the ground, just knocked down by the situation and you don't know what to do anymore. You feel helpless and had better realize it, because if you realize that you are knocked down, you might do something about it. You might call for help or find people who would pick you up, or something like that." That clicked with him at once, and he saw it. The dream really wanted him first to realize that nothing could happen until he saw how deeply disappointed and depressed he was by the situation as it had developed.

That is a typical middle-life situation and crisis of a *puer aeternus* who has successfully moved out of his *puer* neurosis, but is now confronted by a second difficulty. It is always like that, for once you have solved a problem and feel that you have done so, then wait! The other comes round the corner at once. So this man had not pulled out for more than about two years when the steering wheel was turned around by the unconscious; he had to reevaluate the whole thing again and do just the opposite. He was very angry when he heard this interpretation, but it clicked. There you see the danger of crashing, the danger of falling down: if you have succeeded in falling down, you are not at the end of the story; you just have to climb up again. Falling down is only one rhythm in life. The glorious spark is like a star plunging from heaven that must fall into the mud. But then it has to rise out of the mud again.

Now we come to the abnormal theme of the other dream, the theme of the stars below; however, this is such a complicated subject that I would rather discuss it next time. You can take it as simply the old image of the earth being flat instead of a sphere. At one time, it was supposed that the earth was like a pancake, or something shaped like that, and when there was a split in it, you could see the stars below. You can draw one conclusion from the dream: namely, that the dreamer had a flat world—that his reality was not round but flat, which was true. There were no dimensions and no polarities in his psyche, as you can see by the way in which he walked into, and out of, situations and into, and away from, relationships with girls, never wanting to waste a thought on them. Naturally, his life lacked any kind of conflict or polarity. it was just flat.

CHAPTER SEVEN

We stopped last time at the motif of the stars below. The dreamer looked down into the valley and saw that much was being transformed there, but what he noticed first were the stars. I mentioned that his world of consciousness was not round, but flat. His personality is not rounded and his field of consciousness is like thin ice over the abyss of the collective unconscious. He has not yet built up any solid reality of his own. You could also call it the picture of his ego weakness. In the middle of this flat world is a huge split, and he sees the stars below, as if you could see through the firmament below.

There is a famous alchemical dictum which says:

> Heaven above,
> Heaven below,
> Stars above,
> Stars below.
> All that is above
> All that is below.
> Grasp this
> And rejoice.[19]

At once, I was reminded of this old alchemical saying, whose origin we do not know—we only know that it comes from an ancient Hermetic writing. In general, the stars can be interpreted as the archetypes of the collective unconscious—as nuclei in the dark

---

[19]Carl Gustav Jung, *The Practice of Psychotherapy*, vol. 16, *Collected Works* (Princeton: Princeton University Press, 2d ed., 1966), par. 384.

sky of the psyche. We see them as luminosities, as single lights, and usually they are interpreted as gods or archetypal contents. For instance, the Lord of Sabaoth is the Lord of Hosts (i.e., of the heavenly army) because it was thought that the stars were his army, the soldiers of God, and that God led this heavenly army. Then there is the theory of the stars as the individual gods; the order in which they are constellated would represent the secret order of the contents of the collective unconscious. In mythology, there are also the motifs of the many eyes or the many stars. The dragon Argos, for example, is covered with eyes, and sometimes that is also projected onto the sky.

The zodiac was thought of as a huge snake, a kind of uroboros biting its own tail, and was represented as being covered with stars. In a Gnostic treatise, one of the oldest representations of the uroboros is that of a snake eating its own tail, the head speckled with stars and the rest black, thus illustrating the double nature of the unconscious totality with a dark, nefarious aspect and a light aspect that is characterized by the stars. Exactly the same representation is to be found in the alchemical treatise of the so-called *Codex Marcianus*, in which there are drawings that characterize the "whole in one.' The tail of the uroboros is the material and dangerous end, and is very often the seat of the poison (quite in contrast to a real snake). The head is the light, spiritual aspect. That was projected onto the sky because the uroboros always appeared at the borders of human knowledge. In antiquity, for instance, it was believed that the ball of the sky was this huge uroboros snake, upon which the signs of the zodiac were constellated. In the flat form of the world, the ocean circled the earth as a round snake biting its own tail. In old maps, the uroboros stood for the outermost circle; when man reached the end of his field of consciousness, he projected that type of snake. When he came to the point where he could say that he did not know what was beyond, the picture of the snake with the stars on it would appear. You see how much the star motif has to do with unconsciousness, especially with the collective unconscious.

If we look naively at the dictum previously quoted, we see that it must have to do with a double aspect of the collective unconscious which is above and below us, as though it surrounds us in two forms. Again and again, in the analysis of mythological material and in dream interpretation, people make the mistake of identifying what is above with consciousness and what is below with the unconscious; they call the unconscious *Unterbewusstsein* (subconscious) —that which is below consciousness—implying that consciousness is what is above. If one goes downstairs in a dream, that is taken as going into the unconscious, and going upstairs is interpreted as going into consciousness. That is superficial nonsense. If you look at the mythological maps of the world, you see that above is a realm consisting of the mysterious, the unattainable for human beings, home of the gods. Mount Olympus has gods above and below. In Sumer and in Babylon, there is a myth about a man who tries to fly up to heaven with the eagles, but he is incapable of transcending a certain barrier above; he is hit by the gods and falls down. He encounters the same difficulties and obstacles in going to the gods below. If we are objective, we have to admit that there is a field of the unconscious both above and below us. This same duality applies to the symbolism of the house: the cellar often represents the unconscious in some form, the area where the drives exist. There are innumerable dreams in which coal and a fire are in the cellar; awful animals are in the cellar, or burglars have broken in. But exactly the same things happen in the attic. For instance, a crazy person, overwhelmed by the unconscious, has "bats in the belfry" or mice in the attic. Ghosts usually rattle their chains in the attic and walk about over our heads. So up in the attic, where it is dark and full of cobwebs and we are a bit crazy, there is just as much a realm of unconsciousness as in the cellar. People frequently dream of thieves breaking in from off the roof, or of demons sitting up there and taking off the tiles, and so on.

Therefore, we must look at the above and the below from a different standpoint to see if there is any kind of qualitative difference between the unconscious when it is represented as being the powers above, or when it is represented as the powers below. There are exceptions, but in general, the above is associated with what is masculine—ordered, light, and sometimes spiritual—and the below, with the feminine—fertile, dark (not evil; there are no moral designations in the original mythological counterpositions), chaotic, and the realm of the animals. The sphere above is connected with birds and angels—with winged beings of the spiritual world. For instance, if something comes from below in a dream, you might expect it to surface in the form of an emotion or a physical symptom such as sleeplessness, or in the form of some emotional disturbance of the sympathetic nervous system; or it often comes in the form of synchronistic occurrences which have materialized in the outer world. If an invasion from the unconscious comes from above, it can take the form of an enthusiasm for some idea: communism or Nazism. Such an "above" unconsciousness erupts into the system in the form of an archetypal idea. If it is characterized as positive, then it can be said to be the Holy Ghost; if it is negative, then there are the winged demons, bats in the belfry, and other negative winged creatures; that is, destructive ideas. Whether constructive or destructive, such ideas have a strong collective dynamism of their own. Dynamic representations belong to the "above" aspect of the unconscious, and the emotional, instinctive impulses to its "below" aspect.

Egyptian mythology is an exception to this formulation, because certain aspects are inverted; thus, as far as sexual symbolism is concerned, the heavens above are feminine and the earth below is masculine. This probably has to do with the Egyptian's inverted concept of life: the main value was placed on life after death and little value on life in this world. For instance, the amazing pyramids were built in connection with life after death, but until the very end of the Syncretistic Period, except for the king's palace, no decent houses existed for the living. To the Egyptians, ideas were concrete and real, while actual life forms were abstract and, therefore, masculine. Studying Egyptian religion, one is struck by what could be called the concretism of ideas; for example, the idea of immortality had to be realized by the chemical treatment of the corpse to preserve it for the longest possible time. We consider immortality as being symbolic, but to the Egyptians, it was not (as in very primitive magic), and the preparation of the mummy was meant to establish immortality. This shows the concreteness of the idea. To the ancient Egyptian, the earth was masculine, whereas the spirit and the ideas were concrete. While these conceptions were specific to Egypt, there are traces of this reversed constellation in some other civilizations. Therefore, whenever above and below appear, we have to think in a qualitative way and study the context carefully, rather than simply identify what is above with consciousness and what is below with the unconscious.

In his paper, "On the Nature of the Psyche,"[20] Dr. Jung compares the psyche to a color spectrum, with the infrared at one end and the ultraviolet at the other.

[20]Carl Gustav Jung, *The Structure and Dynamics of the Psyche*, vol. 8, *Collected Works* (Princeton: Princeton University Press, 1960; 2d ed., 1969), pars. 343ff.

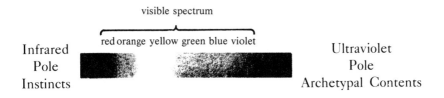

Infrared
Pole
Instincts

visible spectrum
red orange yellow green blue violet

Ultraviolet
Pole
Archetypal Contents

Beam of Light =
Ego consciousness and
mores between these poles

He has taken this as a simile to explain the connection of the psyche and the body—the archetypes and the instincts. Compared in this way, our ego consciousness is like a ray of light, with a nucleus in it to represent the ego, which is a kind of field of light that can shift along the spectrum. The infrared end would be where things become psychosomatic and finally end in physical reactions. At that end, the psyche is somehow connected (we do not yet know exactly how) with the physical processes, so that its activity loses itself, or slowly enters, physical processes of some kind: psychosomatic and then somatic. This would be the end that represents the body. At the other end, the ultraviolet end, would be the archetypes. From within, we do not know what the body in itself is—or from without either—except to a certain extent. Here there is a big question—the mystery of the living organism. At the ultraviolet end that same mystery is expressed in the form of representations, realized as ideas, emotions, fantasies, and so on, of which it is the source. As you know, the origin of dynamic fantasies and ideas that come up in our psyche is unknown, but we ascribe such fantasies to the activity of the archetypes. Probably these two poles are in some way connected; although we do not know how, they may be two aspects of the same reality. At the one end is the body, and at the other are the ideas and representations that suddenly seize upon the human mind. Generally, our consciousness shifts between the two poles. We know that somatic processes and physical behavior are directed by the instincts, such as: the sexual instinct, with its play of hormones in the body and its physical aspects; the instinct of self-defense automatic-fighting gestures; the instinct of running away, a part of the instinct of self-preservation, which takes over automatically in certain life situations without reflection on the part of the subject, either when we run away from danger or when we withdraw upon contacting a burning object—an automatism or reflex of the body that we could call instinct. The difference between instinct and archetype is the following: instinct is represented by physical behavior, similar in all human beings, while archetypes are represented by a mental form of realization, similar in all human beings; that is, *homo sapiens* mate in the same way all over the world, die more or less in the same way, run away, and go erect, all over the world, but certain patterns of behavior characterize us as different from other animals. *Homo sapiens* also tend to have emotions of the same kind, ideas of the same kind, religious reactions of the same kind, seen best in the mythological motifs which are similar all over the world. So at the one end are the instincts, and at the other, the corresponding inner experiences.

Jung does not assert it with certainty, but he says he has not yet met an archetypal constellation which does not have a corresponding instinct. Therefore, one could say that every archetype has a corresponding instinct-connected counterpart. Let us take the archetype of the *conjunctio*, which appears in all the myths of the origin of the world—the mating of a male god and a female god and the creation of the world, or union in an eternal embrace, as Shiva and Shakti. It appears, in the whole mystical experience of the soul's union with God, as a *conjunctio* in a feminine or masculine form; it exists in some form in most religious symbolism. Sexual instinct is the corresponding physical instinct. Self-preservation in the form of fighting is connected with the archetypal idea of the shadow or the enemy, the dangerous counterpart, the figure which appears in dreams as the attacker or the person from whom one runs. On the physical side, it is represented by the instinct to hit, or to run away, which is physically inborn in us.

It seems, therefore—for so far, we have not met with any exceptions—that every archetypal content has a counterpart in some form of an instinct. This is a way of looking at things; that is, instincts are what we see from the outside, while representations— ideas and dream fantasies and images—are what we observe from within. If we observe the human being from the outside (we can photograph it in all its actions), then we get the infrared aspect. Nowadays, that is often done in anthropology and in anthropological writings, where concentration is directed onto what the human being does in contrast to other animals: how it mates, how it builds its abode, how it fights and survives, and so on. Such writers try to describe a human objectively, as though he were just one species of animal, as compared with elephants, tigers, and other creatures. In this way, we can obtain a scientific photograph of physical, instinctual human behavior which is absolutely correct. But if we follow up the same thing from within, which is what we do, we observe what wells up in the human being: its ideas and representations. We have an anatomy of the human being that is photographed from within, an introspective picture of the human being, by which we discover the realm of the archetypes. In an unknown way, the two are probably one—the same reality observed from outside and from within. If we adopt the idea presented in mythology of the human reality of consciousness and the unconscious as being between two poles—the heavenly pole above and the underworld pole below— we might compare this to the scientific model of the psyche and call the infrared end of the spectrum the "heavens below" and the upper end, the "heavens above."

Our dreamer is in the middle field of general human consciousness; through the break, he can see the heavens below, and the movement of the dream is to make him sink down into that. One should also remember how the little prince had to descend to the earth, investigating, or rather rejecting, certain qualities on his way down. Usually, the *puer aeternus* is too caught up in the realm of archetypal representations. Generally, through his mother complex, he is actually possessed by it. This means that he underestimates living experiences; that is, the infrared realm. It is quite a different thing if I think about a beefsteak or if I eat it: the thought of the beefsteak and the sauce *béarnaise* can be very delightful, but if I eat it, I will have still other experiences. The same thing is true for the archetype of the *conjunctio*. It is certainly one thing to fantasize about a love affair and to try to get your fantasy into every detail of the inner experience, but the actual living experience is different.

The *puer* generally tends to avoid the immediate friction of realization. He does not go into the heavens below, which he underestimates, nor into the instinctual realization of life. That is why the little prince meets the fox on earth and needs the sheep, but, as you know, the realization of the heavens below did not work out. This is a generalization, however; the *puer* sometimes lives a certain amount of instinctual life, but he blocks off the psychological realization, so to speak. He makes a cut and lives his experience automatically, as a split-off shadow affair. In that form, his archetypal fascination with the idea of the great love and the *conjunctio* has remained a wishful fantasy—one day he will meet the woman who will bring perfect love, perfect warmth, perfect harmony, eternity of relationship, and so on—clearly a mother-image illusion. In the meantime, he does not abstain from sexual contacts, for that would frustrate him too much, so he has twenty or thirty affairs with women, as in this case, but he does not let himself be affected by them. He does not actually live the experience through. You could say of such a person that he was as innocent, in the wrong kind of way, as though he had not lived at all, because he lives it without being in it. He makes a mental reservation, saying to himself that this isn't it, but that, meantime, he needs a woman. Then he has the physical union with a woman, but it does not count mentally or in the inner aspect of fantasy—in the feeling of the man himself. And if it is not taken seriously, if he does not let the impact of the experience touch the psyche, then it is as though it had not been lived.

I once analyzed a professional prostitute who had the makeup of an old maid. Her dreams always showed untouched little girls or old maids who had never had any experience, and this was completely true! She had shut herself off from what she lived. She just wanted the money; she was not involved in it for she neither admitted to herself the pleasure of certain contacts, nor her disgust over others. She had made a rational decision that she needed the dollars and had said to hell with the rest of it. Thus she was, in a way, untouched by life. Though she had rather severe psychic symptoms, she was not miserable. One of the results of the analysis was that she suddenly realized her own miserable condition, which she had not previously done. It was all carried on by intellectual decision; she never admitted that certain men disgusted her and others attracted her, for that would have disturbed business. Therefore, though she was really a very emotional woman, she did not allow herself to have the emotional experience of what was happening. If she had done so, she would have earned less money by refusing certain men.

The same thing sometimes happens with the *puer aeternus* who, although he lives the instinctual side, does so in a cutoff way: he makes an artificial emotional barrier, separating what he is living from his real self. In such a case, the stars below are not seen, so the dream says to take them and enjoy them. Life is incomplete if you live it in its fantasy aspect; it has to be lived through on the instinctual level. But that means really accepting it—letting yourself be hit by the experience and not limiting it by living it in a conditioned way. To have a mental reservation about it means that it is not lived at all, and that is why the *puer aeternus* is sometimes cut off from the stars below. It is also why the solution for the dreamer is that he should sink into the world of the stars below.

Remark: Dr. Baynes[21] *once told me that a friend of his made a psychological investigation of Parisian prostitutes and discovered that, without exception, they all had major father complexes and that they made a reservation; they "cut" in some way—perhaps that the man should not kiss them on the lips, or something like that.*

Yes, they would do that to cut off feeling and the emotional experience of what was happening. Like that, you can have the most adventurous life, but you don't really live, for it doesn't count.

I think, therefore, that the stars below mean the living experience of the instinctual or archetypal pattern. One has to live life through before one is able either to know oneself or to realize what the thing is.

Remark: So often, it happens that people who are regarded as pueri aeterni *among their associates, such as this man you mention, are very much envied as being able to throw themselves into life with great vigor, so that they appear to be living successful lives. We could say that was the shadow and that we know that they are really cut off. But how do they achieve this appearance of so vigorous a life?*

They can act! Many people are actors, and to act something simply means to play a part. Those people, as far as I have come to know them, act to themselves to convince themselves that they are living, until they land in analysis and have to confess that this is not the case and that they are not happy. Other people consider them to be successful, but they themselves do not feel so. The criterion is simple: Do you feel that you are living? Those who do not feel alive themselves describe it as being as though they were acting, acting to themselves.

Remark: Or wearing costumes!

Yes, and people will fall for that, unless they know some psychology and look at the eyes to see the real expression. Then

---

[21]Dr. Peter Baynes was Jung's assistant at one time. See Barbara Hannah, *Jung, His Life and Work: A Biographical Memoir* (New York: G. P. Putnam's Son, 1976)).--ED.

one can tell that something is wrong, even though such people seem to be so successful.

Remark: If one were fixed at the ultraviolet end and had numbers and numbers of experiences at the other end, then I suppose the ultraviolet end would be too beautiful for the infrared end; even though there might be nineteen experiences, they would be sordid and miserable because one would always be looking for the ultraviolet.

Yes, exactly. That is a quite correct formulation. You can say that if you live one end in a split-off way, then one end cannot communicate with the other. Put quite simply, you have the experience but it is not meaningful, and an experience which one does not feel is meaningful is nothing. It only becomes real when it is connected with an emotional perception of meaning. Without that, one is just bored. I knew of one man who had a lot of affairs, but was so detached that in the middle of the sexual act he would look at his watch to see how much time he had! Obviously, it meant nothing to him, or else it was purely narcissistic, for all he experienced was his role as a male.

Question: And what would be wrong with the woman who would go into a relationship with such a man?

She generally makes the same cut with the animus. For example, in the case of that prostitute, her idea was that if she tried to earn her living by typing in an office, she would have to be at the office at 9 A.M. and work till 6 in the evening for weeks and weeks on end and would never be able to do anything else. Since she was a very undisciplined, childish woman, that was unacceptable to her. Her animus said that that would go on forever, which was animus-opinion number one. She could just as well have started an office job and found a boyfriend all the same, but her animus logic was that if she worked in an office, she would have to submit to discipline—which she hated—and that she would never have a love affair, though why one excluded the other, one does not know—but her animus thought so. Then at fifty, she would be an ugly old woman still typing in an office! Since she wanted to live and did not want an office life, but she needed the money for food and could not afford to live freely with a lot of men whom she could have chosen, the animus said that she should combine the two things and to hell with her moral prejudices. One could say that in her case, she just resigned herself to it because she had no faith in the irrational. She had landed in New York as an immigrant, but when

she saw that immense city, she felt she would be lost in it. She had
no faith in herself, in life, in her own personality, or in God. So she
mapped it all out and thought that being a prostitute was the thing
to do. In the case of a woman, it is the animus who engineers
things, and he is always a professional pessimist who excludes the
tertium quod non datur (the third which did not exist).[22] The animus
animus says to the woman that he knows that there are only so
many possibilities; he says that the thing can only go in such a way,
thereby blocking off any possibility of life producing something
itself.

*Question: Do you mean that a woman who had a good relation to her
instincts would not fall for such a man?*

Yes, I think that is correct, or she might start a relationship on
this unreal level, but then she would try to pull the man into a
definite or meaningful relationship. I will give you an illustration,
though it does not quite fit, because in this case the man took the
initiative. It is the case of a woman who had rather too many affairs
which she ran in accordance with her animus decisions. But she met
a man who really loved her and whose instincts were more sound
than had been the case with the others. He was very sensitive and
felt that often she went to bed with him without being there herself
or in feeling-tune with him. He felt the autonomy of her sexuality
and revolted against it. He got nasty with her about it because it
hurt him. He said that that was how she was with all her other
lovers, of whom he was jealous, feeling himself to be just one of
them. He knew nothing about psychology and was rather clumsy.
He just gave a nasty reaction and called her a "cheap" woman, and
such things, which was not just, for she was not that at all—her
feeling had been cut off. But through his strong, emotional,
instinctual reactions, combined with the fact that he was a mature
man who had had much experience and had great physical self-
control, he was able to help her regain her feeling—naturally a very
difficult task. Usually the man is so sexually impulsive that he
cannot hold himself back, but this man said that he would not go on
unless they were both on a feeling level. She had a dream that there
was a dirty, poisonous, muddy hole in the ground into which he
dived and brought up a golden key to her. I think we can say that

---

[22]Jung, *Archetypes and the Collective Unconscious*, vol. 9, part i, "The Psychology of
the Child Archetype," especially pars. 285ff.

he really rescued her feeling because he loved her as an individual and did not just make use of her. He wanted her as a whole person with her feeling, and resented it when that did not function. Through his resentment and after a lot of quarrelling and trouble, he brought up her feeling personality.

Naturally, one can go on discussing and expanding this problem endlessly because it is really the key to the whole dream. In a former series of lectures, I presented a motif from a Russian fairy tale which can illustrate this: At a dinner party, the czar says that none of his sons had yet picked his flowers, so the three sons ask for his blessings and set out on the search. Each takes a horse from the stable and sets forth. All three come to a signpost which says: "He who goes to the right will have enough to eat, but his horse will be hungry; he who goes to the left will have enough for his horse, but will himself remain hungry; and the one who goes straight ahead will die." The first brother would be robbed of the instinctual experience and therefore his horse would be hungry. The brother who goes that way finds a copper snake on a mountain. When he brings it home, his father is furious and says he has brought home something dangerous and demonic and puts him in prison; that is, he only finds a kind of petrified life and falls back into the prison of the traditional spirit; i.e., the father. The next brother goes to the left and finds a whore who has a mechanical bed to which she invites him. Having jumped out of it herself, she presses a button, the bed turns over, and he falls into the cellar, where there are a lot of other men—all waiting in the dark. That's the fate of the one who goes to the left! Then comes the Great Ivan, the hero of Russian fairy tales. When he gets to the signpost, he begins to cry and says that a poor fellow who has to go to death will find neither honor nor glory, but he gives his horse the whip and goes ahead. His horse dies and comes to life again, and he finds the witch and conquers her. Then he finds the princess, returns home, and becomes the czar. He has a normal, successful fairy tale career. He chooses to remain in the conflict, which seems like death to the ego, for ego consciousness wants to know what is ahead. If this woman who arrived in New York had had the strength and psychological courage to accept the fact that she faced nothing but misery no matter what she did, and that she could not see a glimmer of light or life ahead; if she could have faced that mental death and still have remained herself—then the fairy tale, the path of individuation, would have begun. But she couldn't, and in her case she chose the path to the left. Others chose the path to the right.

It can therefore be said that human consciousness must always be crucified between the pull of the two poles: if you fall into the one, you die, just as much as if you fall into the other. Life, in its essence, means crucifixion; to the rational ego it seems to be death, and that is what this Russian motif expresses in a most beautiful and clear form. The third son chose what seemed to his ego to be the road to death, but in fact, as the story says, he had chosen the road of life. The others, who wanted to be clever and chose the relatively lesser evils—one, the way on the right and the other, that on the left—lacked the nervous strength and the guts to face the unknown, so they rationalized the situation. Apparently, for the human being to face the unknown—not to know in advance what is coming and yet be able to keep steady in the dark—is the most difficult task. Man's most ancient fear and cause of panic always seems to have been the unknown. The first time a primitive sees an airplane or a car, he runs away, for everything unknown is inevitably terrible! That is the old pattern; in analysis, it is the same. When people are confronted with a situation where they cannot, by their own inner reason, see what is coming, they panic. That is painful, but it would not matter so much if they did not rashly come to some decision—to turn to the left or the right—and thereby fall into the unconscious because they have not been able to stand the tension of not knowing what is ahead.

However, it would not be so bad if the *puer* went too much to the right or left, because sometimes one must find the copper snake first, then land in the whore's cellar, and only afterwards make up one's mind that it would be better to go on the road that leads to death. But in reality, the *puer* does something much worse: he risks neither way completely, but ventures a little both ways to be on the safe side. He bets on the one horse but puts a little on the other too, which is his self-destructive act. It is worse than going too far either way, for the excessive reaction gets punished, and one has to wake up and pull out. The natural interplay of psychological opposites corrects the one-sided business. Life forces one into the middle path. But in order to avoid suffering, the *puer* plays a dirty trick which boomerangs on him: he splits himself by throwing a sop to the dragon, but inwardly remains on the other side and has illusions about himself. So he arrests the process of life and gets stuck, for even the interplay of the opposites is thwarted. His weak personality tricks him into it so that he may escape suffering.

As the matchmaking witch that the young man considered me to be, I had tried to push him into taking up a relationship with a woman with whom he had already had his Don-Juan affair and whom he had already cast aside. But after he had planned and written his letter saying that he wanted to see her again, the synchronistic event took place—she wrote a letter similar to his own, which he had not mailed—then, for the first time, he got a whiff of meaningfulness with this woman. After this strange synchronistic event, he couldn't avoid naively thinking that this woman must stand for something beyond what had already passed between them, and that the relationship must have some meaning. Thus, for the first time, he accepted something unknown. The doubt which I had cast into his mind would not have helped, except for the synchronistic episode. But as it was, his attitude towards life was touched by an experience which seemed marvelous and mysterious: Therefore, he went on the bicycle ride with a different attitude, instead of knowing all about everything. For the first time, he was puzzled about a relationship; you see what the unconscious produced when he slept in her arms. It was as though the heavens below—the meaningfulness of such sexual experience—dawned on him, which explains why he fell slowly into the heavens below while making the motions of riding a bicycle.

The next theme in the dream is the explosion of light in the heavens below, which would mean a sudden realization and an illumination from below. It is a very interesting motif if you compare it with the experience of the medieval mystics who spoke of a light which they experienced from above. Here, it is the light experienced from below, which comes from accepting the unknown of life and the unknown unconscious. We might say with the alchemists, "Heaven above, Heaven below." It is the same light, but it comes from the midnight sun and not the sun above. When Apuleius was initiated into the Isis mysteries, he described how he was illumined not by the heavenly sun but by the midnight sun, which he met face-to-face when he descended into the underworld and to the gods below. That would mean an experience which cannot be reached by intellectual effort, or exercises in concentration, or yoga, or the *Exercitia Spiritualia*, but an experience of the Self, which one can only have by accepting the unconscious, the unknown in life, and the difficulty of living one's own conflict.

When the dreamer gets further down, suddenly the heavens below solidify and look like the earth as seen from an airplane, with a quadrangular pattern of fields. It is a very positive image, for now the split is beginning to close. A difference of levels still exists, however, for between the earth above and the earth below is a very sudden change of level, such as that which often appears in the psychological geography of a dream where there are the two levels and no connecting steps. Such a dreamer might switch between intellect and instinct in his way of living, without any bridge between. But that would not show a very dangerous situation, since it is one that occurs frequently in the case of young people who have not yet harmonized the relationship between the two. The wound in this dreamer's psyche is healing; the earth level is rising through the fact that by accepting, for once, an unknown situation and venturing into it, he is touching human reality for the first time—he is touching the earth upon which we live. How would you interpret this? He could have seen woods below, or just the ground, but he sees the fields.

Answer: Man in relation to the earth.

Yes. It is cultivated earth on which labor has been expended and which has been distributed among different individuals, but with the disadvantage of the many walls, fences and roads, and all the different regulations and controls concerning admittance and respect of property. It is the civilized earth and suggests work, so that one is reminded of Dr. Jung's words that work is part of the cure of the split and the difficulties of the *puer*—just ploughing some plot of earth, no matter which, is helpful. I remember him saying to a *puer-aeternus* type, "It does not matter what job you take. The point is that for once you do something thoroughly and conscientiously, whatever it is." This man insisted that if only he could find the right occupation, then he would work, but that he could not find it. Dr. Jung's answer was, "Never mind, just take the next bit of earth you can find. Plough it and plant something in it. No matter whether it is business, or teaching, or anything else, give yourself for once to that field which is ahead of you." Everybody has in front of him a field of reality where he can work if he wants to, and the childish trick of saying, "I would work if it were the right thing," is one of the many self-delusions of the *puer aeternus*, by which he keeps within the mother and his megalomanic identification with the god—because the gods, as you know, do not work. Except for

Hephaestus, who was very much despised by all the others, there are no working gods in Greek mythology. Fields would also imply limitation. That is the drawback of getting in touch with reality, because in that way one becomes limited: there are restrictions. One comes to the miserable human situation where one's hands are tied and it is not possible to do as one would like, something which is particularly disagreeable to the *puer aeternus*. What one produces is always miserable compared with the fantasies one had lying in bed dreaming about what one would do, if one could!

Next in the dreams comes an autonomous switch, for the valley is suddenly replaced by stagnant, icy water. The dreamer identifies it as the mother complex, into which he does not want to fall. It is treacherous, and what had previously looked like an explosion of light now resembles a soap bubble, and within it, a skull. The same world into which he is sinking down now shows its completely destructive and negative aspect, without anything happening in the dream to justify such a change. If the dreamer does or thinks something in a dream, after which the whole landscape turns negative, you can say that there was a wrong thought which made things go wrong. If, while sinking down, the dreamer had the thought that he did not like this narrow reality, and then the change had come about, then the dream would be easy to interpret. If one refuses the earth, then it becomes eternal stagnation and being haunted by the mother complex and, at the end, death. That would be a cheap and easy way of interpreting the dream, but here the thing is very mysterious, for he goes on—one would think rightly—towards the bottom of the valley and the earth. Quite of itself, what had looked so positive turns into something uncanny: stagnant ice water and a soap bubble with a skull in it. I do not pretend to have understood this in all its aspects; I intend just to tell you what I think about it.

Let us begin with the stagnant ice water. That suggests stagnation in reality, where the water of life does not flow. Ice suggests being frozen in the cold. Obviously this man was very cold. If he were not, he could not have behaved as he did with his girlfriend. His feeling was either nonexistent, or had been destroyed by the family situation, or he was so deeply tied to the mother that he had no feeling for other people. As you remember, I had met him only once, so I could not say where his feeling was—whether it was tied up with the mother or whether he was just an unfeeling, cold fish, but certainly he was a cold fish in his behavior. He associated the world below with the mother complex, into which he does not want to fall. There, I think, we get on the track of the trouble. In general, a soap bubble is a simile for an illusion, which can be pricked. It has a great volume and a marvelous and beautiful surface if the sun shines on it, but it is an empty sphere which, when it comes into contact with some real body, dissolves into nothingness. It is possible that that is accompanied by joyful fantasy with little children who love to blow bubbles with their spittle. Building castles in the air, or fantasizing, is like the inner cinema where you are the wonderful stag or the beautiful woman. All those wonderful daydreams are bubbles which can be pricked. Here, something appears below which means stagnation, coldness, illusion and death, without apparently any fault on the part of the dreamer, except that when he sees the stagnant, icy water, he identifies it as the mother complex, into which he is not going to fall. I think that gives us the key. We must not forget that this man had had a Freudian analysis, and what effect does that have on a human being? It produces an intellectual attitude towards life, which is robbed of its mystery: one knows all about it, and if one does not, then the doctor in the white coat, who sits behind the couch, does. Freudian analysis explains everything to you as the Oedipus complex, and so on, and dreams are no mystery; they are quite clear! All long objects are phallic, the others are feminine, and the rest have some sexual connotation. If you know just a little anatomy, you know all about it, and you just have to make the connection. So dream interpretation becomes very monotonous and easy. Once, Freud even complained to Jung that he no longer worked much on dreams because that was too monotonous! Of course! He knew what would come out, so he played the magician's trick and first dropped a rabbit into the hat and then pulled it out! That is Freudian dream interpretation: one already knows what it is driving at; namely, the Oedipus situation, which you first put in the hat and then triumphantly pull out again. Your mind is no longer open to the fact that something might exist which you do not yet know, or that you might dream about something which is not yet known to you. The ego is therefore fed with the conscious illusion that it is just a question of knowing all about it, and with that comes the complete stagnation of life.

A certain type of man with a mother complex is quite attracted by Freudian psychology because its effect on the individual is similar to that of the mother complex itself; that is, it is another prison, and this time you are imprisoned in a situation which is known to your intellect. The Freudian system has its gaps, but these were not approved by its founder. Freud created the system as something entirely known, except for the physcial aspect, where there are openings left for biological chemistry. On the religious or philosophical side there are no openings, however; there, everything is precisely defined. For this reason, Freudian analysis seems attractive to the victim of a severe mother complex, with his anxious and ungenerous attitude, because it offers him another cage of protection. One learns the language easily, and anyone who has had a Freudian analysis for six months or so knows all about it. If you have a patient who has had it, he will bring his dream to you with a ready-made interpretation. You feel puzzled by the dream and wonder what it means, but he will interrupt you and ask if it is not again the Oedipus situation. Such people have it all down pat; therefore, life cannot flow.

Freudian analysis is often completely unfeeling; this is also expressed factually, inasmuch as the doctor is not allowed to have any personal feeling for his patients and avoids them by putting on his white coat and sitting in the rear; any personal feeling or feeling reaction is suspect. (Here, I am speaking of the strictly Freudian school—there are now modified schools, but I am referring to the original attitude.) If the patient's feeling function is already damaged, the situation can be catastrophic; the split will be worsened. Our dreamer, like a clever monkey, had assimilated the Freudian standpoint as a justification for his Don Juanism. I am not accusing his Freudian analyst of that; I think that at least was his own trick. I do not know. But every time he got too close to a girl, he thought that was the mother complex again, so he moved out; in this way, the Freudian way of thinking helped him to carry on his Don Juanism. What is so damnable about it is there is even truth in it! Naturally, in Don Juanism, the partner who is sought in different women (Goethe formulated it aptly as "seeing Helena in every woman") is the mother complex, so that to have an affair and then walk out of it because it is the mother complex again is quite justifiable. It is a wonderful excuse for escape! And it is quite true that these first fascinations are due to the mother complex—that is, to the play of the anima—and they do prove to be an illusion. I have not seen a man who has gotten into touch with a woman, with feeling, for a long time; who has not suffered from certain disillusion-ments and disappointments; and who in the end, has not realized the transience and corruptibility of all earthly life.

I would therefore propose to take this dream more philosophically: If you venture into life—into reality—instead of keeping outside to avoid suffering, you will find that the earth and women are like a fertile field on which you can work, and that life is also death. You will find that if you give yourself to reality, you will be disillusioned, and the end of it will be that you will meet death.[23] If you accept your life, you really accept death in the deepest sense of the word, and that is what the *puer* does not want. He does not want to accept his mortality, which is why he does not want to go into reality: the end of it is the realization of his weakness and of his mortality. He identifies with the immortal and does not accept the mortal twin, but he would assimilate the mortal brother by going into life. Therefore, you could say that this dream contains a philosophy of life which would not surprise an Easterner. An Indian would say, "Certainly, if you go into life, if you love a woman, then you embrace an illusion, and every illusion will show itself as Maya—the great illusion of the world—the end of which is death." All those who have read some Eastern mythology and philosophy will not be surprised by this, but it is surprising that such deep philosophy is brought up in a modern European young man's dream. The thought is put plainly before him: life and meeting a woman mean coming together with reality; to work means to meet the earth—disillusion, stagnation, and death. That is an honest answer to one who has doubts about whether he should live or not. We should not forget that as a child, this young man had met death in a very shocking way. The father had shot himself when the boy was six; living in a small town, the child undoubtedly heard gossip. It seems probable that he peeked into the coffin and saw the remains of his father; if he did not hear outside talk, very likely the maid in the kitchen made comments. He had met death in a terribly shocking form as a small, sensitive boy of six, so death already belonged to his experience. We should remember this, for probably it partly accounts for hesitation about going into life. The unconscious does not pour any balm over the facts at this moment or comfort him about them, but presents him with the plain truth: life is death, and if you

[23] I have heard that the dreamer died at 45! So this part could also be seen as a premonition.

accept life and move into it, as you are now trying to do with this girl, you are moving toward your own death. Death is the goal of life.

This fascinated me from a therapeutic standpoint, because the tendency of the analyst is to look at one part of the analysand's life and endeavor to infect the other with a certain optimism; namely, that one ought to go into life, one should believe in its meaningfulness, and so on. But see what the unconscious does here! It shocks the dreamer with the absolutely dual aspect of reality. If he wants to say yes, he should have no illusions about that, for this is how it is. Now he can say yes or no on an honest basis. And if he prefers to kill himself, that can be his honest solution too.

Later on, the dreamer left the girl again, in spite of all that had happened. In a big town, he fell into the hands of a Russian prostitute whose chief customers were Negroes. These Negroes hated the young man because he was the only white lover, and they made several attempts to kill him. The Russian prostitute was the Mother-Earth aspect of his mother complex—which the girl in whose arms he had dreamed was not, for she was a sensitive, introverted girl and not a very earthy person. With the Russian, he fell into the stagnant water of his mother complex and he nearly met death. His mother complex made him desert his relationship with the girl, which would have been difficult, but human, and then made him fall into the complex itself.

CHAPTER EIGHT

The last lecture ended in the middle of the dream which the man had when lying on the girl's lap. In the dream, he was slowly falling into the big split within the earth. First, you will remember, he saw the stars in the heavens below, then an explosion of light; afterwards, he saw fields, as one sees them from an airplane, and then a gray and dirty stagnant pool of water which was like ice, but did not reflect. He half wakes and says to himself that he is not afraid, but that water is a symbol of the mother, into which he does not want to fall. At the bottom of the valley, a round spot of light appears, the borders of which are a bit blurred. This bursts like a soap bubble. In this spot of light, he sees a skull and thinks that this is strange, for what has death to do with all this? He repeats that he is not terribly afraid, but continues to fall slowly in the same place. Then, the dreamer says, the whole thing disappears and is replaced by a yellow linoleum floor with brown spots. The landscape has completely lost its gigantic proportions, and the dreamer, wondering why there is linoleum at the bottom of the valley, says that it is really surrealistic. It is all very clear and he can see it quite plainly. He laughs a little about the linoleum, and in the letter he sent accompanying the dream, he added, "I don't like linoleum. It is always cold and not aesthetic. I don't like it." He obviously has a strong feeling against it.

We have discussed the problem of the skull and said that, in a way, the dreamer is right in saying that falling into this water would be falling into the valley with the skull; that he would be falling into his own mortality and the stagnating aspect of matter. I mentioned last time that he did actually leave the girl in whose company he had had this dream. Afterwards, he had an affair with a Russian prostitute, who had a number of Negro lovers who tried to kill him several times. One could say that he really did fall into a dirty pool, risking death and complete stagnation. The Russian prostitute was a fat, earthy woman—obviously a mother figure. In spite of his not wanting to fall into this condition—according to the dream—he did go through this phase and, so to speak, completely lost his wings. He already had the fear that a woman would lead him there when he made his contact with the girl, which was why he was afraid to continue the relationship. It was for this reason that he always left women so quickly, feeling that behind every woman was a whirlpool of matter which sucked men down. Falling into death does not always take such a concrete form, and many *pueri* die between thirty and forty-five years of age for this very reason. But there is another way of falling into something like this.

After the *puer* loses the ecstatic, romantic *élan* of youth, there is danger of an enantiodromia into a completely cynical attitude toward women, life, work in general, and money. Many men suddenly fall into an attitude of disappointed cynicism. They lose their ideals and romantic impulses and naturally, all of their creativeness, writing it all off as the fantasies of youth. They become petty, earthbound, small-minded people who just want to have a family, money and a career. Everything else is regarded as romantic nonense—what one wanted and did when one was young, which now must be written off. It is as though Icarus had fallen into the mud, and life had stopped. This is due to a weak consciousness, which cannot conceive of the possibility of enduring the difficulties of reality and not sacrificing one's ideals, but testing them on the touchstone of reality instead. Such men take the easy way and say that ideas merely complicate life and must therefore be written off. This is a giant danger.

This dreamer, as you know, was very weak on the feeling side, and the cold ice at the bottom of the valley mirrors his own coldness—his basically cold attitude and lack of feeling. It is the feeling function that gives life its color and values. In this case, there had surely been a great shock to the boy's feeling when his father committed suicide, and life then became icy, stagnant, and dull. If you talk to such people, they say that there is always the same human dirt, and that from now on they will just get up in the morning and have breakfast . . . and continue to exist.

I told you last time of a man who had fallen into this state and then dreamed of a prince whom he had to follow again. There, the *puer aeternus* reappeared and wanted to be followed, but as a figure separate from the ego. Having been identical with the prince, the man fell into the mud of the road, after which they became two; when the prince reappeared, he was still in love with his bride, to whom he gave a jewel shaped like a tear. The man had to follow him and the bride, but was knocked down by shadow figures. One could say that in order to avoid this stagnation, it is necessary to face the shadow again and again. When you are identical with the *puer aeternus* archetype, the shadow must be faced in order to come down to earth. But when you are identified with the shadow, the archetype of the *puer* must be faced again in order to connect with it, for facing the other side is what leads to the next step. I have seen several cases where this disappointment was not so much concerned with the mind and the spiritual side, but has affected the man's attitude towards marriage.

When this kind of Icarus loses his wings and falls into the stagnating aspect of the mother and matter, some very independent men cannot make up their minds to marry. They feel that marriage would be a prison—a thought which is typical for the mother complex and the *puer aeternus* mentality. After having married, as Dr. Jung once said of such a man, "He curled up in his little basket like a nice little dog and never moved again." They never move again; they don't dare look at other women, and they generally marry (even though she may be beautifully disguised in youth) a devouring-mother type of woman. If she is not already that, they force her into the role by being submissive and boy-like and son-like. Then the marriage situation is changed into a kind of warm, lazy prison of habits with which they put up, with a sigh. Such men continue on the professional side quite efficiently and generally become very ambitious, for everything is boring at home: there is the basket for the dog, the sexual problem is parked, as is the food problem—so all ambition and power goes over into the career, where they are quite efficient. Meanwhile, they stagnate completely on the Eros side. Nothing goes on there anymore, for marriage is the final trap in which they got caught. That is another way in which the *puer aeternus* can fall into stagnating water—either on the mental side, when he gives up his creativeness, or on the Eros side, when he gives up any kind of differentiated feeling relationship and curls up in the habitual conventional situation.

We also said that naturally the skull could represent the problem of death. One of the problems is that if the *puer* enters life, then he must face the fact that he is entering upon his own mortality and the corruptible world; he must realize his own death. That is a variation of the old mythological motif where after leaving Paradise, which is a kind of archetypal maternal womb, man falls into the realization of his incompleteness, his corruptibility, and his mortality. From this skull, this realization of death, the dream then says that light explodes again, showing that in such a realization there is still more light to come; that is, the dreamer would be illumined if he could think about and accept these facts of life. Afterwards, the landscape changes completely and loses its gigantic proportions; now there is the linoleum at the bottom of the valley. First, the dreamer looked down into the split and saw the stars below; then came the dark sky with the light stars; and afterwards, the yellow linoleum, when what were light stars became brown spots. He is looking at the same picture again, but there is an enantiodromia in the color: what was light is now dark, and vice versa. This, he says, is really surrealistic. I have no further amplifications for the linoleum other than his dislike of its coldness and its unaesthetic effect; we must add our own material, though it may be arbitrary to do so. One could say that linoleum is the typical floor covering in little bourgeois dwellings and poor people's homes. It is cheap stuff, and brings to mind the rather disgusting atmosphere of cheap little flats that smell of cabbage. Now, for the first time, nature no longer covers the ground. Instead, there is an artificial, man-made substance in all its smallness, which complements the fact that the landscape loses its gigantic proportions and that everything is flattened. The stars have become dark spots, and what was the brown earth has become a yellowish linoleum. Here again is the danger of falling into banality, connected with the fact that the floor is now artificial and man-made. I discussed this part of the dream with Jung. In response, he wrote the following: "Linoleum is the essence of unaesthetic, banal, bourgeois-poor reality: marriage, taxes, address, milkman, cleaning woman, rent . . . it is the squareness of the Earth with its hard angles, in which one sees no symbol. (It is) that which crushes, suffocates, imprisons the just-so-ness. This is the very demonic power of a real symbol, from which the *puer aeternus* would like to escape, which binds him like a magnet, but to which he should surrender—he who goes to the place of fears has overcome fear. The mystery of being is hidden in the banal; he who runs away falls into imaginary fear. The just-so-ness is 'sartori'; close to the Self. One has to become small and ugly to get rid of the eggshells of Bardo. Only in utmost smallness can one see and achieve greatness. He should sit on the linoleum and meditate: *Tat twam asi.* The son of the mother can find himself only in matter,"[24] ad lineam.

Now, in the dream, the gigantic proportions disappear and there is some leveling up, which means that even if he does fall into banality, the great polarities and—for his weak personality—the too-great tension in his psyche have been flattened out, and the opposites are nearer each other. The stars, however, which are the illuminating aspect of archetypal complexes in the collective psyche, have now turned into dark spots."

How do the archetypes of the complexes appear to normal people? They would say that life was quite clear except for a few disagreeable spots, the dark spots—the complexes! Actually, when Jung discovered the complexes of the unconscious, he did discover them as dark spots; namely, as holes in our field of consciousness. By making the association experiment, he found that the field of consciousness was nicely and tightly put together; that we can associate clearly and correctly except when a complex is touched, and then there is a hole. If a complex is touched in the association experiment, there are no associations, or they are delayed. That, therefore, is the normal view of the unconscious: everything is clear except for those disagreeable dark spots of the complexes, behind which are the archtypes. That is, for instance, what one always realizes if a strong enantiodromia is present. If, after a psychotic episode, people go through what is called the regressive restoration of the persona,[25] they then call that which had meant illumination to them (the source of the too-bright insight which one experiences when one has fallen into the collective unconscious), the dark spots which have to be avoided. This is a very unhealthy state of affairs. If you get people out of their psychotic episodes by pharmacological means, they frequently tend to push away the whole experience of the collective unconscious, with its excitement and illumination, and

[24]Translated by the author from an unpublished letter dated August 28, 1952. Quoted with the kind permission of the Jung family.

[25]Jung, *Two Essays,* pars. 461ff.

call that a dark spot about which they do not want to hear any more. This is the typical compensation in a case where the ego is too weak to stand the opposites and see both sides of the issue: namely, that the archetypes are the source of illumination on the one side, but that one must also keep one's feet firmly on this world at the same time. From this dream, it looks as if the dreamer were in danger of falling into the opposite—complete banality—but when I wrote him about the dream, I said that this was a phase he had to go through; that after he had fallen into it, he must trust the unconscious to take him the next step further; that for the time being, this is where he must land, which is a process which cannot be stopped; that he will fall into utter banality and write off all his former ideals—and become an angel who has lost his wings.

Remark: One could say that at least he could walk on such a floor, whereas on the sky he could not.

Yes, that is sò, and he could also walk on the fields, which appeared first, after which came the skull, where again he could not walk, and then the linoleum, where he could. There are, therefore, really two changes: the fruitful earth, then death, and then something he can stand upon. I think it is a pity that the dream did not stop when the fields appeared, for that would have been a complete solution of the problem. But he was not capable of looking at reality as something which one could form and work upon; his nature was too passive. He looked for something on which to stand, but he could not turn to the masculine attitude toward reality; he could not say that if things were not as he liked, he would change and form them, and impress his own mind upon them. The creative masculine gesture of taking the clay and molding it according to his own ideas was what he could not do. He remains passive and accepts reality, but then it has to support him and be something upon which he can stand; however, that is better than before, when he would have fallen into a bottomless abyss. He has not yet found his masculinity, but is still dependent upon the mother base. How much it is still a problem of not having found his masculinity is shown in the next dream.

Question: Could the yellow floor mean intuition?

To an intuitive person, reality is always what creates difficulties and what one knocks up against in life. The yellow color would have to do with the intuition, but I cannot quite fit in this floor as intuition—except that he was clearly a very intuitive kind of person, and it might mean that at least he had now found the basis of his main function. He was so completely unborn that he had not even developed superior and inferior functions. The ego complex was weak, and there was no developed consciousness, so at least his function of intuition could become something he could rely upon. Its opposite would be reality (which is related to through the sensation function), and intuition is always at odds with reality. To the intuitive type, earthly reality is the great cross.

Question: Could you say that the one aspect must be lived in order to get to the other? It seems to me that if he has his linoleum to stand upon, he might find the stars too, since one replaces the other, and the colors replace each other.

I would say that the first step of his birth of consciousness is that he begins to develop a superior function; later, after many, many years, he might touch the other. Practically, it would mean that, with a human being in such an unborn state, one would have to concentrate initially not on getting him close to his inferior function, but on developing his main function, something which normally takes place between the ages of ten and twenty. He still has to get to that; that is, to develop one main function, after which he could go on to the inferior function to discover the problem behind the irritating factors of reality.

In the next dream about which he wrote me, he tells that he is in a sort of *razzia* (i.e, a raid in which people are caught by the police). He does not try to run away because he thinks that his innocence will be revealed. He is put in a room, and after awhile he opens the door and sees that his guard is a woman. He asks her if she will let him go, since he is innocent, and she answers, "Yes, certainly I shall let you go because you are innocent, but first there are some questions to be put to you." Then he hears moaning coming from behind the wall, and realizes that questioning is accompanied by torture. Actually, people are being beaten on the sinus. He is very much afraid of the physical pain and wakes up.

He did not give me any other associations, but this refers clearly to this prison- and police-phobia complex. As you remember, he could not cross the Swiss border because he thought he would be put in prison, and he always ran when he saw a policeman. In connection with the woman guard, you will remember that he was a painter. He wrote that he had once painted the portrait of an unknown woman, an imaginary woman. For four years he worked on this painting, which became so vivid and significant for him that he had to keep it covered with a cloth—especially at night—because he was always afraid it might come alive and threaten him. He could not sleep in the same room with it for that reason, so he painted and then quickly covered it over; sometimes, he did not look at it for weeks, because it was a living thing to him. That is a really amazing example of the anima itself. The painting did not remind him of any concrete woman. It was the representation of the anima, of the imago of the woman within, and it had become so alive to him that he was terrified of it. The old Pygmalion motif!

Now we should go into this strange police-prison complex, which he had as a kind of phobia in reality. The dream is very important because it begins to link up with what I wish to arrive at at the end of my lecture: namely, that we are dealing with a problem that is not only personal, but also belongs to our time—the police state, the absolutist system which tortures thousands of people, is becoming more and more the great problem of our day. The strange thing is that it is mainly the *pueri aeterni* who are the torturers and who establish tyrannical and murderous police systems. So the *puer* and the police state have a secret connection with each other, and the one constellates the other. Nazism and communism have been created by men of this type. The real tyrant and the real organizer of torture and suppression of the individual are therefore revealed as originating in the unresolved mother complex of such men. That is what possesses them, and it is out of the state of possession into which such a complex plunges people that they act in this outrageous manner.

Since the dreamer is in the street, it can be said that he is in the collective. At present, in reality, he has no relationship to the collective since he is an isolated, lonely human being with an entirely asocial attitude. Nowhere is he linked up with his feelings; he has no real friends—only the man to whom he gave away his girl, but that had not been a strong feeling connection—therefore, he is lost in the collective. He is the anonymous man in the street, and that is where he is caught by the police system. Anyone who has a weak personality and who has not worked on his individuality is threatened from both sides; not only is he threatened with being swept away by the collective unconscious, but also by outer collectivity. The person with a weak ego complex swims between Scylla and Charybdis—between the devil and the deep blue sea.

Either the collective unconscious or conventionality in some form (collective movements, very likely)—one or the other—catches him. Identifying with the persona or identifying with a collective movement is therefore as much a symptom of a weak personality as to go mad and fall into the collective unconscious. It is merely a variation of the same thing, which is why the carriers of these collective, absolutistic movements are generally very weak as far as the ego is concerned.

I remember a medical doctor telling me that at the beginning of World War II, when he was a well-known stomach specialist, he had a high Nazi official under his treatment, who had stomach ulcers. He succeeded in curing this man, and as a result, he was spoken of in Nazi circles as being a good stomach doctor. Throughout the war, therefore, a great number of high-ranking Nazi officials came to him for private treatment. Under the *religio medici* (the medical code), he, of course, could not refuse to accept them as patients. He said it was amazing to see those concentration-camp torturers, those so-called heroes, take off the beautiful uniform and shirt and disclose a body tanned by sun and sport—and then to find nervous, hysterical stomach trouble underneath. These pseudo-heroes were merely weaklings—spoiled mamma's boys. He had to dismiss a large percentage, telling them the trouble was purely psychological—sheer hysteria. To the doctor, it was an eye-opener. It was not what he expected, although to us it makes sense. If he told them of a cure or a regime which was the least bit disagreeable, they would not try it. Moreover, if he poked into their troubles, many of them would begin to cry. He said that, when the beautiful hero persona had fallen off, he felt as if he were confronted with a hysterical woman.

Our dreamer thinks he can get away because he is innocent, so he still has the old-fashioned idea of a regular juridical State, such as we have in Switzerland, where one can only be arrested if one has committed some crime against the law. One need not fear the police, for if one has done nothing wrong, one can get away. It is quite clear from the end of the dream that the question of right or wrong plays no role here. He will get away, but he will be tortured by the police all the same.. His endeavor to plead innocent is not going to help him. How would you interpret his idea of being innocent? If you remember what I told you about him, about this beautiful, delicate, blond young being, with the heavenly blue coat, and if you ask what wrong he has done in his life, you could say that he has done practically none, except that he has *not* done anything! He has sinned by not sinning. *He has not lived.* If you live, you are forced to sin: if you eat, then others cannot have that food. We shut our eyes to the fact that thousands of animals are butchered so that we may live. Life is connected with guilt, and he, by not living, has not accumulated much active guilt, but he has accumulated a tremendous amount of passive guilt. Think of all the girls he has walked out on. True, he has not shouted at them nor given them illegitimate babies. He has not done all those things a more virile man might have done; he let women down by disappearing, which is as cruel and immoral as doing something which is called wrong. He has committed the sin of not living, but he is typical of the kind of man who, on account of his mother complex, has a too aesthetic and superior attitude towards life, and who thinks that by keeping aloft and out of things, he can keep up an illusion of purity and innocence. He does not realize that he is secretly accumulating dirt; this dream tells him quite clearly that he will not get away with that illusion. Life will catch up with him. He cannot continue as mamma's innocent little boy who has never done anything wrong, even if he would like to do so, for it wants to catch him all the same. Therefore, he is caught by collective forces in a negative form. You could say that his masculinity reappears in the police. Because he does not live it himself, it is lived against him. Whatever one has within oneself but does not live, grows against one, and so the dreamer is now pursued by the torturers and the police, and discovers that the real devil is the anima figure whom he had painted for so long. She is the real torturer behind the scenes. This anima figure is obviously a variation of the mother imago in him. It is the anima yet, *sensu strictiori*; it is the anima, but the anima is identical with the image of the mother, which is the devil behind the scenes. Do you know any mythological variations of the mother imago and her torturing questions?

Answer: The Sphinx.

Yes, naturally. The Sphinx is the Great-Mother image who asks torturing questions of those who want to remain innocent. Oedipus, too, wanted to be innocent; he ran away from home in order to avoid fulfilling the prophecy that he would kill his father and marry his mother, and by running away from it, by trying to avoid the guilt, he ran into it. In the dream, we have a modern version of the Oedipus motif: this man also thinks he can run away from fate, and he too falls into the grip of the Sphinx, who asks him an unanswerable question.

The motif of the Sphinx who propounds the riddle—or here, the sphinx-like woman who asks him questions while he is being beaten on the sinus—leads to an essential problem, widespread and archetypal, which I think has not yet been sufficiently commented upon. It has to do with what I call pseudo-philosophy—the wrong kind of intellectualism induced by the mother complex. The best example of this is to be found in the Russian fairy tale called "The Virgin Czar," which I spoke about in my last lecture. The story is about the Czar's three sons, who go out at his behest. As you remember, the two older brothers take the left and the right ways, the one who goes to the left being caught by a prostitute, and the other being caught, finally, by his own father (one falls into the imprisonment of the sexual drive, whereas the other regresses into tradition). Despite having been warned that he would be going to his death, the hero, as you recall, goes straight ahead. His horse goes through a death and resurrection process, but the hero stays alive. Then he comes to the great witch, the Baba Yaga, who is combining silk and who watches the geese in the field with her eyes, scratches the ashes in the stove with her nose, and lives in a little rotating hut built on chickens' feet with a cockscomb on top. First, he says a magic verse to stop the hut from rotating. He then enters it and finds the old witch scratching the ashes in the stove. She turns round and say, "My child, are you going voluntarily, or involuntarily?" What she really means is, "Are you going on this quest voluntarily or involuntarily?" In a way, they did start involuntarily, since the boys had been challenged by their father at the dinner party, when the father had said that none of his boys had yet done as much as he had: the impulse came from the traditional past and was handed on to the future. On the other hand, the quest is voluntary, particularly in the case of the youngest, who has been laughed at as someone who must not go because he will never get anywhere and should stay at home by the stove. So, although one can say that he really did go voluntarily, there is something wrong with the question. First, however, I should give you the answer because that shows how the problem should be resolved. Ivan answers, "You should not ask a hero such questions, old witch. I am hungry and want my dinner, so you hurry up!" And he ends with some threats—very vulgar and very delightful! He knows quite well, you see, that the witch does not want an answer and that the question is a trick designed to lame him. If he were to answer the question, it would mean slipping on a banana skin. It is just a trick—not something that should be discussed.

The question of free will is one of the philosophical problems which have never yet been solved by man. Free will is a subjective feeling. Intellectually and philosophically, there is a pro and a con, and you can never prove either side. If you ask yourself whether you are doing something because you have to or because you want to, you will never find out. You can always say that you feel as though you wanted it, but perhaps it is only an unconscious complex which makes you feel like that. How can you ever say which it is? It is a subjective feeling, but it is tremendously important for the ego to feel free to a certain extent. It is a feeling problem about the mood in which one finds oneself. If you cannot believe in a certain amount of free will and therefore free initiative of the ego, you are completely lamed, because then you have to delve into all your motives. You can go into the past and look into the unconscious more and more deeply, but you will never get out of it. And that is the spider's trick of the mother complex. That is how the witch tries to catch the hero; she wants him to sit and ask himself whether he really wanted it or not: whether or not it is a question of opposing his father. If he does this, is he falling for his father's suggestion, or is he showing off because he has been teased at home? After all, does he really want it? You can be sure that he will sit there forever and the witch will have him in her pocket. That is the great mother-complex trick.

Some *pueri aeterni* escape from the mother by means of actual airplanes; they fly away from Mother-Earth and from reality in planes, while many others do the same thing in "thought airplanes" —going off into the air with some kind of philosophical theory or intellectual system. I have not given much thought to it, but it has struck me that, especially among the Latins, the mother complex is combined with a strange kind of strong but sterile intellectualism—a tendency to discuss heaven and earth and God-knows-what in a kind of sharp, intellectual way, and with complete uncreativeness. It is probably a last attempt on the part of the men to save their masculinity. That simply means that certain young men who are overpowered by their mothers, escape into the realm of the intellect. There, the mother, especially if she is the earth type and a stupid animus kind of woman, is not up to it, so she cannot follow. Therefore, since it is an initial attempt to escape the mother's power and the animus pressure by getting into the realm of books and philosophical discussion, which they think mother does not understand, it is not altogether destructive. Such a man has a little world of his own—he discusses things with other men and can have the agreeable feeling that it is something which women do not understand. In this way, he gets away from the feminine, but he loses his earthly masculinity in the mother's grip. He saves his mental masculinity but sacrifices his phallus. He leaves behind his earthly masculinity which molds the clay, which seizes and molds reality, for that is too difficult, and so he escapes into the realm of philosophy. Such people prefer philosophy, pedagogy, metaphysics, and theology, and it is a completely unvital bloodless business. There is no real question behind such philosophy. Such people have no genuine questions. For them, it is a kind of play with words and concepts and is therefore entirely lacking in any convincing quality. One could not convince a butterfly with such "philosophical" stuff. Nobody would listen to it.

The pseudo-philosophical intellectualism is ambiguous because, as I said before, it is a way by which to make a partial escape from the dominant grip of the mother figure. but it is incomplete, being made only with the intellect, and only the intellect is saved. That is really what one sees in the tragedy of the Oedipus myth, where Oedipus commits the mistake of entering into the question instead of saying to the Sphinx that she has no right to ask such questions and that he will knock her down if she asks such a thing again. Instead, he gives a very good intellectual answer. The Sphinx carries on the play very cleverly by apparently committing suicide. He pats himself on the back and steps right into the middle of his mother complex—into destruction and tragedy—just because he complimented himself on having escaped that difficulty by answering the question!

To my mind, the way Freudian psychology has taken this myth and generalized it is quite wrong, for the Oedipus myth cannot be understood without the background of Greek civilization and what has happened to Greek civilization as a whole. If you think of Socratic and Platonic philosophy, you see that they discovered the realm of philosophy and pure mind in its masculine, mental operations. But when you know what happened to Plato when he tried to put his ideas into reality, you see that they had escaped reality and had not found a philosophy with which they could form it. It was a complete failure. They discovered pure philosophy, but not the philosophy which can be put to the test against reality. In the same way, they were the founders of basic physical and chemical concepts, but the Egyptians and the Romans had to change these concepts later into experimental science, for the Greeks could not put their ideas to the test in chemical experiments. Their science remained purely speculative, even in its most beautiful forms, and with it came the endless fight of the little Greek towns and the tragic decay of Greek civilization. As soon as they were up against nations with masculine and military physical self-discipline— the Romans—the Greeks had nothing to offer. Therefore, although they were the great philosophical fertilizers of the Mediterranean world, they could not follow up their own attempts in a creative way because they never solved the riddle of the Sphinx. They thought that the intellectual answer was the solution—an illusion for which the Greeks paid. The Oedipus myth is actually the myth of this stage of civilizational development; at the same time, it is the myth of all those young men who start with this same problem. That is why it is also a general myth.

The question of this Russian witch—her philosophical question at the wrong moment—shows that this is a trick of the devouring mother's animus; later, when the man is on his own, it is a trick of the mother complex to present a philosophical question at just the moment when *action* is needed. This trick is often practiced in actual life; for instance, a youth wants to go skiing or go off somewhere with his friends; he is filled with the *élan* of youth, which carries one out of the nest, eager to be with others of the same age, and he and his friends are enthusiastic about taking a boat down the Rhine to Holland. The boy tells his mother what he plans to do. That is just youthful exuberance, but the mother begins to worry about his being away from home. The boy is living and learning about life in a natural way, if only the mother does not hang onto him. But if she does, then she starts, "Ought you to do this? I don't think this is the right thing. I don't want to prevent you. I think it is quite right for you to go in for sport, for instance, but I don't think you should go just now!" It is never right "just now." Everything must be thought over first—that is the favorite trick of the devouring mother's animus. Everything must be discussed first. On principle, says she, there is nothing against it, but in this case it seems a bit dangerous. Do you *really* want to do it? If he is at all cowardly, he begins to wonder, and then the wind has gone out of his sails. He stays at home on Sunday while the others go off without him, and once more he has been defeated in his masculinity. He does not say that he doesn't care if it is right or not, he just wants to go! The moment for action is not the time for discussion.

I feel very negative in this regard for the generations who have to grow up under parents who have had analysis—irrespective of whether it's Freudian or Jungian or any kind of psychology—because I see that nowadays the mother's animus even uses psychology to lame the son: "I don't know if it is psychologically right for you to go skiing," or whatever it is. In the second generation, even psychology is dangerous; the children of unpsychological parents are often luckier. They can start something new, but not those whose parents' minds are spoiled by psychology. The same thing applies to analysts who want to keep the patient, for the moment he wants to go into action, they say one must look first at the dreams to see if it is psychologically right. The *puer aeternus* shadow often does the same thing to himself if no mother or analyst plays that role; every time he wants to go into action, he will argue that he will not act until he has thought it over carefully. One could call it neurotic philosophizing; philosophy at the wrong moment just when action is needed. That is the trick behind the myth of the riddle of the sphinx and the devilish question of the Baba Yoga in the Russian fairy tale. It is the mother's animus who says, "Oh, yes, you may go, but I must just ask a few questions!" And whether he answers the questions or not, he is tortured. But there is also a prospective aspect in it, for when the men are tortured in the dream, they are beaten on the sinus. In this young man's country, the language has Latin roots and he knows what sinus means in Latin: the curve, the bay at the seaside (or any kind of curve), but specifically, a female curve—the bosom. Therefore, when he is beaten on the sinus, he is hit on his hidden femininity. The sinus also is a cavity which can become infected, as doctors and others among you probably know. It is therefore a hollow, empty place, and "sinus" refers to something which, in a hidden way, is feminine and within the head; it refers to the fact that this kind of head activity, this pseudo-philosophy and pseudo-intellectualism, has hidden feminine qualities. Being this kind of philosopher implies having hidden femininity, and though it is the mother-devil who induces the man into this, that is where she hits him. One sees in real life how mothers do everything they can to castrate the sons: keeping them at home and making a woman of them, afterwards going about complaining that they are homosexual, or that at forty-three, the son is not yet married, and how happy she would be if he would only get married; that it is so irritating to have him sitting about at home so depressed, and how much she has to suffer because of him; how anything would be better than to have him at home in that awful state. But if a girl comes on the scene, then she goes off on another tack, for it is never the *right* girl; the girl in question will never make him happy, she can guarantee that; that must be stopped. So the mother plays it both ways. She castrates her son and then perpetually hits that weakness, criticizing and continually complaining about it. That is how it looks on the personal level; the same thing applies as far as the archetypal complex is concerned, for the cure can only be found at the place where the destructive complex lies.

In this case, you could look at such torture as a meaningless "neurosis-causing" activity of the unconscious psyche. He was terribly tortured by his symptoms at the time of the dream, for he could not go anywhere because of his prison phobia. The symptom by which the mother complex tortured him was at the same time a question, and if he could have understood it as such, he could have asked what it wanted of him: what was the trouble behind it? And then he would have found the answer. The torture has a completely double aspect: if he understands it as a question put to him by fate, then he can solve his problem; whereas if he only runs away from it, then it is eternal torture imposed on him by his mother complex. The decision is up to him. Unfortunately, the dreams ends: "I am very much afraid of the physical pain, and I wake up," which shows that this is one of the basic troubles. It is the quite simple, but widespread, trouble of a man who has fallen too far into the mother: he cannot endure physical pain. Generally, that is where the mother who intends to devour her son begins, when he is quite young, with her perpetual fussing care—putting cream on the sore place—telling him not to go with the other boys who are so brutal, and so on; and then when he comes home after having been beaten up, saying she will speak to the other boy's parents about the awful things their son does, instead of telling her own boy not to be such a coward but to hit back. So she already turns him into a physical coward, which forms a base for all the rest, for a physical coward has no foothold in life. I knew a man of fifty who would not go out with a woman because, he said, if he went with her to a bar and a drunken man challenged him, then he would be forced to fight, and that he would never be able to.

Remark: But think of Julius Caesar! He was afraid of physical pain, but you cannot say that he was a coward!

No, but he never gave in to his fear! To be sensitive is a different thing. There are people who feel pain more keenly, but the question is whether you give in to it. There is the story of a Frenchman and an Englishman who, during World War I, were in a trench together. The Frenchman nervously smoked one cigarette after the other and paced up and down. The Englishman sat quietly and then said mockingly to the Frenchman, "Are you afraid? Are you nervous?" And the Frenchman said, "If you were as afraid as I am, you would have run away long ago." It is not a question of being afraid: there are thick-skinned people who don't feel things, who have some lack of sensitivity and are really not so badly hurt, while others feel pain much more. But the question is whether one has sufficient stamina to stand it. Caesar certainly faced pain even though he hated and feared it. I would say that was really heroic. As the Frenchman intimated to the Englishman, it is not heroic not to be afraid. The Englishman was just unimaginative and therefore quiet. Many people are tremendously courageous, but simply because they are not sensitive and imaginative, they cannot imagine what might happen and are therefore not nervous. Highly strung, imaginative people naturally suffer much more, but the real problem of courage is whether one can stand it, or at least not lose one's fighting attitude, one's feeling of self-defense and honor. This is a very deep-rooted instinct, which exists not only in the human male but also in the animal realm, for the male of many species cannot lose self-esteem and honor without paying for it. It is essential to basic masculinity, and to lose it means castration in a deep way.

Among the *cichlidae*—a certain breed of fish—a male cannot mate with a bigger female. The reason is that these fish do not see very well, and there is no great difference between the two sexes. They swim towards each other, and the first thing the male notices is that the other is bigger, which alarms him slightly in case there may be a fight, and he goes pale; when he approaches and sees that it is a female, he cannot mate. A female meeting a bigger male may also be frightened, but she can still mate. The result, as the zoologists put it, is that in the male, sex with aggression can be combined, but not sex and fear. In the female, sex and fear can be combined, but not aggression and sex. There you have the animus-anima problem in a nutshell. In other areas of nature, it has been discovered that if certain male animals lose their self-esteem, they die. There is a beautiful story by Ernest Thompson Seton of a particularly good leader and cattle-thief wolf in an unusually good pack of wolves. This leading wolf was caught with much difficulty and, being such a famous animal, was not killed but tied up and brought home. At first, it got absolutely wild, with wild, manic eyes, but all of a sudden, to his astonishment, Seton, who had the wolf on his horse and was watching him, saw that the animal's eyes became quite quiet and had a faraway look, and the animal relaxed. He was left tied up in the courtyard, for no decision had been made as to what was to be done with him, and the Government had offered a tremendous price—but the next morning the wolf was dead for no apparent reason. It had died of humiliation, and that is something rather common, particularly in the case of male animals.

The same thing happens in primitive masculine societies. Statistics were compiled during World War II to discover whether primitive or more highly educated peoples stand imprisonment best. It was found that the more primitive the person, the greater the rate of suicide from despair. The Red Cross compiled the statistics, and I got the information from my sister who was working with the society. Apparently, among the most primitive people there were mass suicides; they just ran amok. In one American camp where there were well-treated Japanese prisoners, an enormous number committed suicide in an outburst of despair. It is also well known that primitive Africans cannot be imprisoned for more than three days. Bushmen, for instance, cannot be imprisoned, for no matter how well they are treated, they just fade away. They lose hope and die for psychological reasons. So it can be said that it is essential for the male human being to have a feeling of freedom and self-esteem and honor, and with that, a certain amount of aggressiveness and ability to defend himself. That belongs to the vitality of the male, and if that is destroyed by the mother, then he falls an easy prey to the mother's animus. She punishes the son in a humiliating way, thus robbing him of his self-esteem.

Another very wicked way by which it can be done is through mockery. I know of a mother who completely lamed her son by her witty tongue. Every time he wanted to assert his masculinity and be be enterprising, she would make a little mocking remark which killed all his *élan* and made him look ridiculous. A young man who goes off to perform his heroic deed does appear ridiculous to the adult, but he should be respected, for it means the growth of masculinity. Boys playing at being gangsters and Indians are funny, but one should recognize the necessity for the assertion of self-esteem and feeling of freedom and independence. That is esssential, and stress should not be laid on what is ridiculous about it. For that reason, in many primitive male societies where they endeavor to keep their independence and masculinity, the women may not look when the males go around wearing animal masks and tails attached to their behinds. The women are kept out of most male initiations in primitive tribes, for they could so easily make a little mocking remark about the heroes, or something like that, and immediately the thing would fall flat. The men know very well that they look completely ridiculous in those demonstrative displays of masculinity and for that reason, they exclude the women. Women also have their mysteries, with the girl's first attempt at makeup and hair styles, and the mockery by the brothers is terrible. They laugh at the way she has made her first shy effort at being a little feminine, so that usually girls prefer to get into groups at school and make their first attempts there. They are also ridiculous, so they hide from the boys.

Question: Hasn't the sinus also to do with the nose, and if so, would it not have to do with the breath of life? Isn't the nose stopped up when there is sinus trouble? Wouldn't beating on the sinus imply beating on the breath of life?

No, I don't think so. After the beating, one couldn't breathe anymore. In itself, the sinus is a cavity, but what the medical function is, I have never found out. It is a kind of remnant of the past, something like the appendix. Perhaps Dr. Mehmke can tell us about it. As far as I know, it doesn't have much functional meaning.

Answer: I think its function is that it can be infected!

So it must be like the appendix, a rather meaningless thing. It has no function in itself. I think that makes it more meaningful and makes the interpretation more prospective. The woman in the dream does not hit on the breath of life, but on something that is really unnecessary, and this is what gives the dream a meaning which is not only negative. In other words, if he did not have such a cavity, if he did not have this unnecessary feminine weakness in him, she could not torture him. One can say that if he were masculine and strong, and not already infected—and therefore weak—she would not be able to do anything. His lack of masculinity shows in the babyish cry that he is innocent. As if that matters! Instead of saying he is innocent, he should be furious and try to free himself. But he has this passive reaction, his hope that his innocence will save him—as if that would help in our world! According to Christian teaching, evil does not really exist, and if one is innocent, everything will be all right. But Christianity, by being misinterpreted in this way, has made us all infantile and has robbed us of our sound instinctual attitude towards life, because we all try to be innocent sheep, and then we are, of course, helpless. There, we link up with the sheep problem of Saint Exupéry, the idea of sheep mentality and infantilism. It is a certain kind of erroneous Christian attitude that since one is innocent, nothing can happen, for the protecting angels will apparently care for you. But reality contradicts this kind of teaching, because innocence does not help in this world and in nature. It invites the wolves.

CHAPTER NINE

Next, we will go into the *puer-aeternus* problem as mirrored in Germany, using a book by Bruno Goetz, *Das Reich ohne Raum (The Kingdom Without Space)*, the first edition of which was published in 1919; the second in 1925. It is interesting that it was written and published long before the Nazi movement came into being in 1933. Bruno Goetz certainly had a prophetic gift about what was coming, and, as you will see, his book anticipates the whole Nazi problem, throwing light upon it from the angle of the *puer aeternus*. Goetz predicted the whole movement in his book, including what is now happening in Germany. I believe that through the book we shall get nearer to the point at which I am aiming: the religious and the time aspect of the *puer aeternus* problem.

Goetz was born in Riga in 1885. His book is a novel, but it begins with two poems which I would like to quote:

When all we knew, destroyed, in ruins lay,
Encircled in death's mighty folds of darkness,
Our burning spirits strove along
After the dream which led us on.

Far from our home and our maternal land
On undetermined waves our ship drives on.
Laughing boldly, we had ventured forth
As Vikings, searching undiscovered shores.
And if by night and horror overtaken, THOU sing'st
Us songs of other homes,
Then phantoms vanish into gentle mist,

The world dissolves in dance and rhythm,
The stars disperse a fortune long delayed,
And radiant shines the kingdom without space.

Then comes a second poem dedicated to "Fo," who, as you will see, is the *puer-aeternus* figure in the novel:

When the dark cloud
Withdrew not from the sky
And from all the world
The sun was hid,

Out of the depths
A new light neared,
And in our sleep we knew
That Thou were there.

O the suns that come
From the depths of thine eyes,
And from thy lips
The flowing streams of love.

Across the waves of an ethereal sea
The splendor of thy limbs
Entices us
To flaming courage.

Eternal youth,
Encircled by the music of the stars,
Giver of comfort,
Sparkling, free, and beautiful.

Men and women
Dance in thy glory,
Driving into death
For sight of thee.

Forever into light
Thy white form calls
Wave after wave,
And never do we age.

As I said, the second edition of this book was published in 1925. I have not been able to find the first, but at the end of this edition it is said that this is the first unmutilated issue. The author was away when the first was brought out, and, either because he was so shocked or for some other stupid reason, the publisher cut out some of the chapters so that the first edition was incomplete. The book was then misunderstood as being a political pamphlet.[26] When the author returned, he insisted on its being completely reprinted, and, when speaking of the two editions at the end of the book, he says that he had never intended it as a political pamphlet.

It must be remembered that this was written just after World War I, the time of the great debacle in Germany, of mass unemployment and all the after-war miseries. It was at this time that a certain pathological dreamer, a soldier named Schickelgruber (later known as Hitler), went about trying to form a group of young people around him with his ecstatic and crazy political programs. Goetz's book was published fourteen years before the Nazis seized power in Germany, while they were already working underground. It was a time of the utmost collective, conscious despair and aimlessness, of collective disorientation, a time that, in certain ways, was similar to what we are now experiencing. Since the first edition of the book appeared in 1919 and since the author must have taken some time to write it, we can assume that it was being written just after the war and that the ruins alluded to in the first poem refer to the catastrophes of that time. The author mentions the dream, so passionately pursued, that takes them away across the sea to new lands and into some unknown horror, and then he tells about one who sings of a new country and of the emergence, before their eyes, of a "kingdom without space."

The second poem in the book begins with the same motif of a sky darkened by clouds; although the sun has disappeared, there is a new light which comes from the depths and which the still-sleeping people feel as an invisible presence. This invisible presence is described as "eternal youth encircled by the music of the stars" ("Ewiger Knabe umspielt von der Sterne Getön"). The author makes it clear that the eternal youth is the ruler of this kindgom without space and that one has to go into death in order to see him; that men and women dance ecstatically into death in order to see his completely transcendental realm. It is therefore apparent that he

[26]Frank Eaton, *Der Deihter Bruno Goetz*, Ria University Studies, vol. 57, no. 4, 1972.

entices people out of this world into another, and seduces them into death.

The first chapter, entitled "Schimmelberg" (white horse mountain), says that the inhabitants of a little university town—the University of Schimmelberg—well remembered the old sea captain, Wilhelm van Lindenhuis. (The name is north German, tinged with Dutch, and is made up of the words Linde-lime, and huis-house;—limehouse.) There had been a lot of talk about his sudden death. First, his gentle, rather woebegone and sickly wife had died, after which people noticed that he no longer took his evening walk. But when they saw a light in the house and his lean, furrowed face at the windows, they thought he must just have been indisposed for a while and was now recovered. One evening, however, two unknown youths appeared, wearing leather caps and what the author describes as "weather collars"; that is, turned-up collars for protection in bad weather. They rang the bell at the captain's house and he himself opened the door. Passers-by said that when he saw the boys, he recoiled at first, as if in surprise, but then let them in, and in a quarter of an hour they had left the house again.

Next morning, the postman could get no answer when he rang the bell, nor could he at midday, nor in the evening, so he informed the neighbors. When the door was broken open, they found the old man sitting in his armchair, dead. Apparently, he had died quite peacefully from a heart attack. Going through the house, a crown of thorns and an ivory cross were discovered on the son's—that is to say, on Melchior's—desk. Since there was no dust on these objects, they must have been placed there quite recently, for everything else was thick with dust. Every effort was made to advise Melchior of his father's death (Melchior is the hero of our story); telegrams and letters were sent to him in Rome, but all were returned, and he could not be found. People said he had always been a strange young man, and the following old story was dug up about him.

When he was about fifteen years old, he had had two friends: Otto von Lobe and Heinrich Wunderlich. Otto von Lobe was a very slender, gentle, blond, aristocratic boy, and Wunderlich was a strong, brown, bold young man. The three made friends and formed a mystical, secret club. They read a lot of alchemical and Rosicrucian literature and started alchemical experiments with the idea of finding an elixir which, when drunk, would enable them to change shape. After many attempts, they believed they had succeeded in producing such an elixir. Each of the three wanted to be the first to try it, and since they could not agree, they called the whole of their mystical club together. The others had been more fascinated by the romantic horror of the undertaking than by the details, which had been left to the three friends, and they knew nothing of the poisonous makeup of the drink. Lots were drawn and the lot fell to Otto von Lobe. It was decided to have an all-night carousel in which their fantasy ran off into future possibilities and what they could do when, like magicians, they could change their shapes, and how a new era would begin and mankind could be transformed. They became more and more ecstatic and in the early morning, they ran down to the sea and turned to the east. At the moment when the first rays of the sun appeared, Otto von Lube sprang up, tore off his clothes and, standing in the early light and laughing happily, slowly drank down the elixir. In a few minutes, he was dead. A strict investigation followed. Melchior was expelled from the school, having refused to make any statement, and the others were heavily punished.

Wunderlich, the strong, dark boy who had been the third in the group, changed noticeably after this event, dropping all unusual occupations and becoming very cynical and normal in a rather pointed and exaggerated manner. He studied medicine and retired, as a general practitioner, to a little village, where he lived as a very down-to-earth, practical man who wished to have nothing more to do with anything fantastical.

Here, we have the description of something we can recognize from former lectures: namely, the fallen Icarus who, after the elation of creative fantasy, now drops once and for all into banality. The third member of the trio, Melchior, having been expelled from his school, retired to his home and stayed shut up in his room for many months. His father, who was very interested in magic, Rosicrucian writings and alchemy, pardoned his son, neither reprimanding nor being angry with him. At first, Melchior would sit for hours and hours, brooding in his room, to which his food was brought up. Slowly, he began to regain confidence and started scientific discussions with his father who, although interested in magic and such things, had no faith in the possibility of the chemical transformation of the human being. He saw that, even if it could be done, it would have no meaning. But that was the son's fanatical idea: namely, that for its own sake and without any further purpose, it should be possible to burn the original shape of the individual to ashes and make the physical human being transparent—a mirror for the stars, as he called it. Melchior considered his father, who was more interested in astrology, to be muddle-headed, so they began to quarrel more and more. In spite of their similar interests they did not agree. They slowly drifted apart, and in time, ceased to talk to each other.

Melchior then began to visit Henriette Karlsen, the fifteen-year-old daughter of the director of the local museum. She was very beautiful, fair, and slenderly built, with pale, amber-colored eyes and limp, long-fingered aristocratic hands. Sitting locked up in his darkened room, Melchior once saw her crossing the street. The next day, he went out for the first time, and they met in the museum. She went up to him, took both his hands and looked at him for a long time without saying a word, her eyes full of tears. Then Melchior turned and hurried home. Thereafter, he met her every day in the museum, but during all this time, Henriette became paler and sadder. One day, by chance, the old director overheard Melchior telling her how a face had looked in through the window every night since his childhood. As a child, he would hear a knocking on the window and, looking up, would see a small, brown-faced little boy with eyes just like his own, staring at him through the window. When he ran towards it, the vision would disappear, and then he would sit and cry for hours. These visions faded, but while he and his friends were making the death potion which they imagined to be a transforming elixir, he saw the boy again, this time surrounded by other boys with mocking faces, looking through the window. Since the catastrophe of Otto's death, they had disappeared.

"Thank God," said Henriette.

At her response, Melchior went into a rage, asking how she could say such a thing, for since the boys had disappeared, he had been completely alone and nobody had helped him. Henriette replied that if he loved her, he must promise to forget all that, and if the boys called to him, he must not follow.

In despair, Melchior asked how he could promise that, and how she could ask such a thing of him. He wanted nothing more than to go with them and solve all their riddles, taking Henriette with him.

"Never!" cried Henriette, with deadly fear in her voice. "Do you want to kill me as you killed Otto?"

Melchior got very angry and, calling her a coward, he stormed out of the room, past the dismayed director, and back home.

On that same day, he asked his father to send him to another town to school, to which his father agreed; thereafter, Melchior only came home occasionally for a few days at a time and, after going to the university, remained away altogether. In the little town, all they heard was that he was studying chemistry, at which he was very good, and that he eventually got a Ph.D. for it at Oxford. Henriette died of tuberculosis the year he received his degree. So the one who did not want to die, who refused contact with Melchior because she saw that these boys represented a pull towards death, soon died herself. A year before his mother died, Melchior returned to Schimmelberg and stayed three days, after which he went abroad and traveled in India and China for a long time. Suddenly, it was stated in the newspapers that the famous Professor Cux of the University of Schimmelberg had taken Melchior as an assistant for his chemical investigations. He was coming back, and naturally everybody was very curious to meet the man about whose youth there had been such strange rumors.

When he returned, he seemed disappointingly normal. He had a very cold—and rather strange—personality, with still, gray eyes, and except for his rather strange look, he seemed to be an amiable and even impressive personality. People were pleased that he was married and were fascinated by his somewhat exotic-looking wife.

On the first day, Professor Cux told Melchior of the death of his father and of the strange apparition of the two boys who had deposited the crown of thorns and the ivory cross. When the boys were mentioned, Melchior seemed for a moment to have had a shock, but then quickly pulled himself together and pretended to know nothing about them. He just remarked that his father sometimes had strange ideas; for that reason he had contacts with other people, and that he himself did not know anything about the matter.

Melchior then took over and renovated his father's house, where he, but particularly his wife, started a very social life. The whole town met there, partly out of curiosity but also for other reasons, as we shall soon see. Large parties were given every evening, but Melchior himself always withdrew early, excusing himself, and went to his study, where he remained until far into the night.

Slowly, a scandal developed, Melchior began to be careless about his scientific activities and took more and more part in his wife's social life, which, through him, now acquired quite a different character. People were indignant over the mocking way in which he spoke of state and church institutions, but above all, they were upset by his ever-increasing influence over the students, whom he tried to incite against science and the scientific mind and to imbue with radical skepticism against the foundation and outcome of scientific knowledge and the institution of the church. He spoke of science as a modern form of intellectual illusion, saying that there was as little certainty in it as there was in faith, for science was also a pseudo-faith. At first, it was thought that Professor Cux might put a stop to this, but slowly it was discovered that he was completely under the charm of his young assistant; in the end, both were obliged to stop lecturing. The professor always supported Melchior in his views about science, saying that he was quite right and what was science? Nothing! People thought this was meant as a joke, but when it was discovered that in all secrecy, the old man had married a young dancing girl, everybody shook their heads and remarked that that was the fatal influence of a certain circle. Consequently, people drew away from Melchior; only a few remained true to him.

The circle continued to meet once a week at Melchior van Lindenhuis's house. There were very eccentric and orgiastic parties, and although reports were greatly exaggerated, there was said to be a terribly immoral atmosphere. People were very much astonished when the liberal-minded Lutheran priest of St. Mary's Church, Mr. Silverharnisk (silver harness), also joined the circle, but he justified his visits by saying that he was studying the disorientation and uprootedness of the modern soul! The real reasons, as you can guess, were quite different.

Melchior himself grew more and more peculiar, withdrawing entirely from the orgiastic parties given in his house. When the strange boys who wore the remarkable clothes were seen around the house in November, the townspeople remembered the curious conditions surrounding Melchior's father's death and the stories told by the old director of the museum about Melchior's conversation with Henriette when she was sixteen years old. People came to believe that there was some insoluble secret, and irritation and tension increased.

The second chapter is entitled "The Meeting." Melchior, in a very bad temper, sat on a bench, watching the heavy rain falling. He could not make up his mind to go home, for he was sure that his wife would have purposely forgotten to have his study heated in order to force him to join the party. He therefore preferred to freeze out-of-doors.

Steps on the gravel startled him out of his apathy, and with a shock, he saw a boy wearing a high collar and a leather cap loitering along the leafless alley of the city park. When the boy came nearer, Melchior saw a small brown face out of which the determined, yet shy, rather staring, gray eyes looked straight ahead. He walked past Melchior, and as he passed, looked at him briefly, smiled, and then disappeared. Melchior gave a little cry and suddenly began to tremble without knowing why. Then a tall man appeared at the other end of the alley. He looked around uncertainly, took a few steps, and then stopping again, looked around once more.

Before the man could have seen him, the boy suddenly rushed towards Melchior. He whispered to him to take his left hand and then quickly to put on his glove and not be surprised at anything and not tell anybody anything. The boy's voice expressed such panic, his eyes had such a feverish look, and his beautifully formed lips quivered in such fear as he spoke, that Melchior involuntarily seized the hand held out to him. At the same instant, the boy disappeared as though he had melted into thin air, and on Melchior's first finger there appeared a broad silver ring. Still under the influence of the boy's frightened request, Melchior drew out his glove and put it on. Then—he didn't know why—he suddenly had a feeling of tremendous happiness—that something he had long hoped for had now happened. His depression disappeared completely, and full of self-confidence, he looked at the tall man from whom the boy had fled.

When the strange man saw Melchior, he stopped and seemed undecided. He was clean-shaven, with clear-cut but rather faded features and a pointed, energetic chin. His mouth was thin and large, his nose small and bent, his cheeks sunken, and his eyes like bright, transparent stones. When he raised his hat, Melchior noticed that he had a very large forehead and beautiful, fair hair.

"Excuse me," said the stranger, "did you perhaps see a boy go by?"

"I haven't seen anybody," answered Melchior, absentmindedly.

"Is that so?" said the stranger. "Excuse me." And he sat down on the bench beside Melchior. "I am a little tired. I have been running about the whole day looking for my pupil."

"What does he look like?" asked Melchior; in spite of himself, he had to smile.

The stranger looked very suspicious and said, "But you did see him then? Did he speak to you? Did he . . .?"

"I haven't seen anybody," interrupted Melchior. "I have already told you so."

"I thought from your question that you remembered something," said the stranger. "So you didn't see him! What a pity! Excuse me for persisting, but I am very worried."

Melchior continued to look mistrustfully at the tall man sitting beside him. The outwardly immovable face of the man seemed to change in expression from one second to another. Sometimes it seemed like the face of an old man; sometimes there was a childish smile; and sometimes his features appeared severe and threatening and the eyes sparkled, cold and penetrating.

He got up and said, "Excuse me once more. I have a request to make of you. I don't know why, but I have the feeling that it will be just you with whom the boy will meet. I know that he will speak to you. Don't listen to what he says; it's not true. Don't take his hand if he asks you to. It might bring you trouble. I warn you! And if you see him, please be so kind as to tell me. Do not refuse to do so."

Melchior did not answer.

"My name is Ulrich von Spät," said the stranger. (Spät means "late.") "I am staying at the Grand Hotel and am passing through. You must think me completely crazy, and I cannot explain the whole thing to you, but please have confidence in me and do what I ask you. If you see the boy, he has a thin brown face, steady gray eyes, long black hair, and wears a coat with a high collar and a leather cap. You will certainly recognize him. His appearance must strike you . . ."

At this moment, Melchior dropped his head thoughtfully, but did not say a word. Von Spät waited a moment, then looked at Melchior and sighed, and then stretching out his hand to him, said, "Well, let us hope! Auf Wiedersehen!"

At this moment, Melchior suddenly felt a tremendously warm sympathy for the man and a deep inner relationship. He forgot the warning of the boy, took off his glove and shook Herr von Spät warmly by the hand, and the latter saw the ring. His eyes flashed for a minute, but he hid his excitement and walked quietly away.

Melchior, suddenly remembering the ring on his finger, felt as though he had betrayed the boy. Only when it occurred to him that the stranger might not have seen it, did he calm down a little, but without forgiving himself for his carelessness.

"What can that mean?" he thought. "I am losing control over myself. Things happen to me as though in a dream. Who was that stranger? What power had he over me that I suddenly loved him so that I forgot who he was? He is my enemy!"

The third chapter is entitled "Fo"—the name of the mysterious boy.

On the way home, Melchior felt as though he were dematerialized. Streets, walls, houses, surrounded him, tall and strange. They seemed to be made of air. It was as though he walked through them. They divided like curtains in front of him and closed behind him like clouds of mist. Everything was changed; buildings which he knew had existed in former times but no longer did, were suddenly there again. It was no longer the same town through which he walked.

The people also seemed changed. He caught fleeting glances and felt as though he looked into his own eyes as into a mirror. A smile, a wave of the hand seemed to him an indication, a greeting, a sign of secret understanding.

Near the station sat a fat old woman selling apples under a gigantic umbrella. He bought a couple of apples, put them in his pocket and, to her astonishment, stroked the wrinkled cheeks of the woman. "Yes, yes," he said, beaming. "We know each other. We are old friends. Do you see this ring on my finger? You never saw it before, did you? Nobody else may see it. That means I am going away now, far away. You know how it is when someone wants to go far away and suddenly it is time, and one goes."

The woman didn't seem to understand and looked uneasy.

"I know," he went on, "that I don't need to tell you all this. We know each other so well. We have known each other for long, ever since childhood . . ."

The woman, who had become more and more nervous, looked all around and at last, pulling herself together, interrupted Melchior. "Aren't you ashamed of talking like that to an old woman?" she asked.

"You don't know me?" asked Melchior. "Why, suddenly, don't you want to know me? . . . You always sat at some corner when I was on the road. I always saw you when I left a place or arrived somewhere. Don't you remember how you sat at the station at Genoa with a bright parrot on your shoulder, and on my arrival I bought oranges from you? And in Vienna? In St. Petersburg? In Stockholm? In a hundred other cities! You were always there and greeted me with your fruit when I arrived and watched me when I left."

Melchior looked her straight in the eyes and shook his head. Finally, he said in a low voice, "I understand. You are careful. You don't want to be overheard. The stranger is here—our enemy. It was careless of me to talk to you. We may have been watched. I was only so glad to see you. Now I know that I am going away."

At this moment, he saw a boy going past the apple woman's stall, who looked at him sharply and put his finger to his mouth in warning and then quickly went round the corner. It couldn't have been the same as the one who had disappeared, for this one's face was smaller, browner, bolder. Only the still, gray eyes were alike.

Melchior nodded a goodbye to the woman and quickly went away. "Who was it who warned me?" he thought. "He wore the same clothing as the one who disappeared. What circle have I run into? What is it that surrounds and captivates me? I have seen it all sometime in a dream. The many trusted faces on the street, the winks and nods and greetings, the two boys, the stranger . . . But I can't remember. And the apple woman . . . Why did I say all that to her? It was idiotic! How should she know me? Old women sit in all railway stations. And yet, it was the same face, the same hair, the same wrinkles, the same voice . . ."

When he got near his home at dusk, Melchior saw a number of boys who broke up at sight of him, hid behind the corner of the house, and peeped out curiously. "It is becoming more and more confusing," he thought. "Now there is a whole band of them!"

The windows of his dwelling, which was on the ground floor, were lit. There was the sound of laughter and confused talking and music. Among the murmur of many voices he thought he recognized the clear voice of von Spät. Then it occurred to him that he had never given von Spät his name nor told him where he lived, so how could he be here? Melchior decided he must be mistaken.

In order not to be seen, he went in at the backdoor and walked straight to his study. There it was cold and dark. He turned on the light and lay down in his damp coat on the couch, and the ring, which was loose on his finger, fell to the ground. In a fright, he looked up.

The boy who had disappeared stood by the couch and looked at him, smiling. "You're cold," he said. "I'll light a fire." He lit the fire in the stove and then threw off his coat and cap and stood by Melchior.

"I knew that I would find you, Melchior," he said. "I had seen in your eyes that you would help me. You belong to us even though you don't know it. I thank you. We all thank you."

"Who are you? Who are you all?" asked Melchior. "I don't understand what is happening. Who is the strange man? How do you know my name?"

"I have known about you for long. I am called Fo. I cannot tell you my real name. None of us may say that. We give ourselves nicknames so that we may speak to each other. Who are we? You will find out when you live with us. You have only to cry out that you want to go away and we will come and fetch you. But be careful of the stranger! He is our worst enemy! He saw the ring on your finger, and he will try to catch you. He has a secret which makes him very powerful. I was once in his power and could only get away by tricking him. I will tell you about it later, when you come to us. You are still living among the others, and I cannot yet tell you anything. And now—thank you, and let me go. The others are waiting for me."

Melchior heard a noise at the window and saw many faces pressed against the windowpanes.

"I won't let you go," cried Melchior, "until you have told me everything! How do I know that you will come when I call? How can I follow you when I don't know who you are? How can I resist the stranger when I don't know his secret?"

"Who we are you can only know by living, not by talking. You will follow us if your heart drives you. We are always there when called. We ourselves don't know the stranger's secret; if we did, he would not have any power over us. I have answered you. Now let me go."

"You want to run away from me," said Melchior, "but I know how to stop you with the ring."

"The ring won't help you, Melchior," said the boy, laughing. "It turns your life into mystery and confusion and change. But you won't get away. If you were to keep the ring, the town would always be to you as it was on your way home today. You would unravel nothing; you would take friends for enemies and enemies for friends, for you would not understand the signs which would explain them. Come with us and then you will be free. Call us when you want us. Until then, let me go. Open the window."

Still Melchior hesitated. Then he stood up silently, looked at Fo for a long time, and opened the window for him. The boy jumped out, and the crowd outside encircled him. They took one another's hands. A flame shot up in their midst, split up into sparks, and they had all disappeared.

You see that the story is very suggestive! It is something like Edgar Allan Poe's stories and might have been influenced by Kubin's *The Other Side*[27], and by E. T. A. Hoffmann's tales[28]. It is the kind of novel in which suddenly banal reality is dissolved in the mysterious events of the other side, where, in our language, the unconscious penetrates and dissolves the world of consciousness, and where from now on anything and everything can happen.

The name of the town, "White-Horse Mountain," is meaningful, for the white horse was a very well-known attribute, and sometimes a personification, of the old god Wotan, who either appeared riding on the eight-legged white horse Sleipnir, or was altogether replaced by this magic horse. Those who have read *The Other Side* know that a mad white horse who races through a destroyed world plays a similar role. Wotan retired to the mountain but will reappear at the end of time and reestablish his eternal and happy empire. Lindenhuis, the family name of the hero of the story, means "lime-tree house," and in olden times there was usually a lime tree in the center of most small German towns and villages. It is a feminine symbol that was dedicated to feminine nature goddessness like Perchta, Hulda, and Holle (plus all her other names). It was thought that the souls of unborn children lived under the leaves of the tree, and it was the mystical tree in the midst of the village around which the whole of life centered, very like the central pole which, for instance, you find in American Indian rituals. In the opening poem, there is an allusion to seafaring people, the still-living Viking spirit being a personification

[27]Alfred Kubin, *The Other Side*, trans. Denver Lindley (New York: Crown Publishers, Inc., 1967).

[28]Ernst Theodor Amadeus Hoffmann, *Tales of Hoffmann* (New York: Dodd, Mead & Co., Inc., 1932).

of the typical German restlessness and transcendental, eternal longing which is typical for German races. We cannot interpret the details in the book until later, for so far we have no key as to the meaning of the ivory cross and the crown of thorns. The explanation comes only in the later chapters.

The rumors which spread about the hero of the story contain a very typical feature. For instance, there are the three boys: Otto von Lobe, an aristocratic type, dedicated to death, and described as being very delicate; Heinrich Wunderlich, who is described as being very vital; and Melchior. The first two are obviously opposite shadow figures of Melchior's: von Lobe could be called a personification of the sensitive, artistic personality with a strong suicidal tendency; and Wunderlich, the vital side of Melchior's personality which pulls towards adaptation to life and who therefore cuts off all the juvenile, romantic longings. Otto von Lobe dies from drinking the elixir; through the shock, Wunderlich becomes quite cynical and realistic. You could say that one part of Melchior dies and another part of him reacts to that with a tendency to cynicism. The ego complex, which would be represented by Melchior himself, is between the two, and, as we hear, he retires into his room and into a deeply depressed introversion after the shock, while Otto von Lobe, the real *puer aeternus* in him, dies. It is well known that between the ages of fifteen and twenty, suicides occur frequently, for it is a period when the pull toward death is strong, and it generally is connected with *puer-aeternus* problems.

Melchior describes how he had always seen his double at the window. What does that mean? I will read you the exact passage: "Father was at sea or occupied in some way, and Mother leant over the Bible, and he himself felt lost and sad. And then he heard a knocking at the window and saw the pale brown face with eyes resembling his own, and that always made him cry bitterly. His mother never knew about it, but he told his father, who only smiled but gave no answer."

Naturally, you can say that that was Melchior's early experience, which foreshadowed all that was to come later, but I think we should amplify this with a very well-known fact: namely, that in early youth, lonely children tend to produce a double personality with whom they entertain themselves and play. This double is the coming-alive of the unconscious personality, due to loneliness. It is typical that it is described in this way: that he is a lonely child, and in moments when he sadly realizes his loneliness, this apparition appears. There are children who invent such a double, personifying it and playing with it for hours. Very often, this fantasy figure of early youth later reappears in dreams and really becomes a personification of the whole unconscious. It is the shadow, the anima, and the Self, still in one. It is the whole other side of the personality.

We are always inclined to think of the unconscious in terms of the different Jungian classifications, and therefore we might dispute about whether this first apparition is of the Self or of the shadow, but we should never forget that these concepts are only valid in certain psychological situations. When a human being first meets the unconscious, either in childhood in an autonomous form or, for instance, in the beginning of an analysis, there is no question of shadow, animus, or anima, and Self. The first experience we have when we enter the unconscious is with what we could best call the other side, which in those beginning stages is personified in different forms. It is advisable not to start introducing those classifying concepts in analysis, but to let the person simply experience that there is another side to the ego and its ordinary world. It is only after some time, when the fact that there is another side and a completely different part of the personality has been realized—that there is another inhabitant in our inner house—that we slowly discern figures in the half-darkness of the unconscious, such as that of the inferior man, whom we might classify under the name of shadow, and the figure of the heterosexual partner, which we might classify under the name of anima, just to bring some order into that other side. But in itself, as a reality, it is just the impact of the other part of the personality. You will find that the first meeting with the unconscious is very often with such a personification, or a double, in which shadow, Self, and anima (if it is a man) are completely one all over the world.

The same idea occurs in Persian teaching, which says that after death, the noble man meets either a youth who looks exactly like himself (because in death he turns again into his beautiful and noble stature) or a girl of fifteen (the anima), and if he asks the figure who it is, it will say, "I am thy own self." If the man has been virtuous, this figure is shining and beautiful. By living a virtuous, religious life, he develops a double in the Beyond, and the moment of death is the moment of reunion with the other half. This Persian myth has survived in certain Gnostic and Manichaean traditions in late antiquity. There, it is absolutely irrelevant whether the figure appears as a shining youth or as a girl, for its answer to the dying person is the same; namely, "I am thy own self, the other half." This is an archetypal idea. In many primitive societies, it is thought that on entering this world, every human being is only a half, the other half being the placenta; i.e., that part of the personality which has not entered this world. It is therefore ritually buried, or dried and worn in a capsule around the neck, and is the magic substance in which the double is supposedly located (the transcendental double, the other personality). After death, the two become one again. There is even a myth which says that the first man was complete in heaven, but when he was incarnated in this world he was only a half; therefore, the first man, who is mythologically exactly the same type as our figure of Adam, is called the "Half One." So you could say that any human apparition is only a half; the other remains in the land of death in the Beyond, and one joins it after death. What this means utlimately, we do not know, because it is an archetypal representation whose meaning we can never intellectually exhaust. But we can say that, among other things, it mirrors the basic realization that the growth of consciousness, which begins in early youth and increases, is a halving of the total personality; the more one becomes conscious, the more one loses one's other half, which is the unconscious. It mirrors, as it were, the split of the human being into a conscious and an unconscious personality, and there are those early-youth experiences in which this is already realized.

I once read in the *Neue Zürcher Zeitung* a story told by a Hungarian officer which illustrates this experience. He was the only child of an aristocratic Hungarian family before World War I and was so lonely, having nobody to play with, that he invented a brother whom he called Stepanek and whom he imagined as a very tough, red-haired little boy. In his imagination, this little boy would do all the mischief he had hoped, or would have liked, to do, but for which he hadn't the courage. When he went to school and found real comrades, the figure faded and was forgotten. Then he tells that he was shot and wounded in World War I. He fainted and came around after a time, bleeding and shivering and in a very bad state. And he saw a human figure bending over him, a red-haired man of thirty, and thinking it was somebody who had come to rescue him, he muttered, "Who are you?" The other whispered,

"Stepanek!" The next thing he remembered was that he was being treated in a hospital and slowly coming back to himself. He was very much puzzled about whether he had had a hallucination—whether he had projected something onto the man who had brought him in, who perhaps had been a black-haired Red Cross man. He tried to follow up the problem, asking the doctors and personnel at the hospital how he had arrived there, but nobody knew! The nurse knew he had been brought to the ward, and that he had been found on a stretcher in the hospital courtyard, but nobody knew who had brought him there, and he could never find out! He said that he didn't want to theorize about it, but that those were the facts. I have a rational explanation: As you see from the childhood story, Stepanek was his more ordinary and vital part, his inferior personality, the red-haired fellow who dared to do all the things he did not dare do. He himself was rather an introverted, sensitive kind of boy, and I think it quite likely that in the war situation, in a half-dazed way, he managed to drag himself to the hospital and was therefore literally saved by his inner instinctive personality—Stepanek. Then he broke down in the courtyard where he was found. His wound was not too bad. That seems to me the only possible explanation. The other possibility is that a man from the lazaret had picked him up and that, in his dazed condition, he had projected Stepanek onto him. Nobody knows!

This is only to illustrate the fact that the lonely child very often finds a companion in the unconscious other half and thereby experiences the unconscious. Normally, however, these shadow figures, and the other side, are projected onto other children, who take over the role of the "the other" at this age. It also shows the problem of a certain amount of personality dissociation, which comes up again in the rather exaggerated, romantic fit which the boys get at school when Otto von Lobe dies from the elixir. The fascination comes from the idea that the human individual, in its material shape, should be transformed and dematerialized and then become, as Melchior says when he has the discussion with his father, "a mirror of the stars." So, at bottom, the fascinating idea of an alchemical transformation haunts all those boys, and the accident happens through their attempt to put it into reality. There we see clearly that this double—the *puer-aeternus* boy—has to do with the Self, and that the realization of the Self, as it is presented in the alchemical process, is the real *fascinosum*. We also see how the two rhythms set in: the pull to death, expressed in Otto von Lobe, and the cynical pull towards reality, personified in Heinrich Wunderlich.

During Melchior's retirement into his dark room, a first meeting with the feminine principle takes place. Shut up in his room, having been expelled from school and quite under the shock of Otto von Lobe's death, he discovers Henriette Karlsen, who later dies from tuberculosis. He quarrels with her, as you remember, because she does not want to follow him into death. All the same, she dies afterwards. In anticipation of the story, I can tell you that the hero never unites with a woman in a real way. The marriage is nothing; rather than a relationship, there are complete hatred and disappointment on both sides. It is a complete fiasco. Thus, it is the same problem as in *The Little Prince*, for the contact with the anima does not work. Here is a different variation. You remember that in *The Little Prince*, the prince also quarrels and leaves the rose on the planet. There, the anima figure is not described as so aristocratic and lacking in vitality, but as rather childish, haughty and difficult to get along with. This girl, however, is more the aristocratic "broken-lily" type, a very attractive anima type. But how would you interpret it psychologically? The first love of a man is always very meaningful, for the girl is more the anima than she is real. Usually, these love affairs do not end in marriage; it is mostly an anima fascination linked up with the mother in this story—that she was a sad, suffering woman who sat reading the Bible—and obviously, Henriette Karlsen is a replica of the mother image. Sometimes men have different animae: one of them is like that, but there are others to compensate. If that is the dominant type, however, what conclusion would you draw? What does that predict?

Answer: That his vitality is feeble.

Not necessarily his vitality, but the feeling side; his Eros is weak. He himself is not necessarily weak, for Heinrich Wunderlich is a vital type, the one who becomes the cynical realist—so it could mean that it would still be possible for the ego to be quite realistic. What would you guess if you met someone between eighteen and twenty who had such an anima figure? What would he look like if you met him again at fifty? I would say that he has every chance of becoming either homosexual or remaining a bachelor. Those would be the two possibilities, because the whole relationship to the feminine side and to feeling—to Eros, relationship—is weak and very likely to die; that is, to fade away.

I have seen most cases like this among determined bachelors rather than homosexuals. I know of a man who got engaged three times to a dying girl and never understood that this must have something to do with him. After the third time, he thought he was just persecuted by fate and gave up. I knew him as a very old bachelor—a very nice man—but after the funeral of the third girl, he gave up, thinking a curse was on him. He never saw that his anima constellation made him choose such women and that he had a real instinct for picking out the doomed women. He always got engaged correctly and meant to marry, but the girl died, one from tuberculosis, and one in an accident, and the third, I don't remember how. What was so striking about this old man was the terrific sensitiveness which he covered up by his odd behavior and scurrility. He went about dirty and covered with tobacco; he lived in a flat that was more like a cave, decorated with beautiful things, but with ash and cigars covering everything. The mere mention of a charwoman put him into a rage, and he would shout about women—especially charwomen—who disturb everything. He was fantastically artistic and had a beautiful collection; he knew more about art, with feeling and understanding, than anybody I have met since. He was the type of the spiritually, highly cultivated, funny bachelor! You could see clearly that his anima was so sensitive that he could never get near a woman or make a friend of a woman, or even make male friends; his feeling was too delicate and too easily hurt. The only way he could survive was by keeping away from any close touch with other human beings. What saved him was his tremendous sense of humor; he always humored his own sensitiveness, covering it up with ironic remarks, a trick of many sensitive people; he always made fun of himself to keep his shell whole. That is the usual type when a man has this special predilection for dying girls. The other possibility is a relation to someone of the same sex, becoming homosexual, because there, a certain distance and delicacy of relationship can be imposed, and the snarls of passion and the realization of the marriage relationship with its disagreeable and wounding realities can be escaped. The similarity to *The Little Prince* is that the *puer-aeternus* problem is again connected with the problem of the weak anima figure and the weak Eros side, and relationship to the other sex is a problem.

Then there is a strange paradox: the girl Henriette, the only anima figure he meets before his wife, wants to prevent him from following the romantic pull from the Beyond, and then she herself dies. How would you interpret that? In a way, she does the right thing, for she warns him and tries to get him over onto this side and this life. But then she dies.

Remark: He has projected a sickly anima onto her.

Yes, and when she protests, the anima projection falls off. If she had joined in and walked into his romantic plans, then she would have carried out the role of the anima. By calling him away from those plans, however, she refuses to take on that role. The reason is not explained in the story, but at that moment, the anima projection falls off because for him to be able to continue his projection, she must cooperate in the pull toward death. Moreover, Melchior had chosen her because she was a dying person, which apparently the girl herself did not know and was consciously not attracted by death.

This also shows a typical tendency of young people which is indicative of a certain weakness: he belongs to the type of person who, when a projection falls off, does not carry on the relationship—another sign of his Eros weakness. Some people, when they notice that the other person is not what they had assumed, are pulled by natural curiosity to find out more about the matter. They think it odd that they were so attracted by a woman who ceased to attract when she proved to be quite different, and they try to find out what happened and why the attraction faded. In that way, there is a chance of realizing the projection, but the people who, as soon as they are disappointed, just end the relationship, always remain in the projection. If one is disappointed, that is just the time to follow the relationship, at least for awhile, to find out what happened. That is actually how Dr. Jung discovered the anima in himself. Being again disappointed in a woman, he asked himself why on earth he had expected anything else—what had made him expect something different? Through asking such questions and realizing an expectation which did not fit the outer figure, he discovered the image inside. It is therefore always helpful if a relationship—not only a heterosexual relationship—disappoints you, to ask yourself such questions: Why did I not see that before? What did I expect? Why did I have a different image of this person? Where did the error come from? For the error is something real, too. If one can do this, it indicates a desire to hold to the human relationship and to take back the illusion. When one holds onto the relationship and makes an effort to establish it on its own level, then the illusions must be investigated as something interesting. But people with weak feeling tend to break off the relationship as soon as the other person disappoints them. They just walk out because it is no longer interesting, and questions about why one had the wrong expectation and why one is hurt are not asked.

Question: But isn't there something in the other person which formed the hook for the projection?

Yes, but you can only discover that if you go on after the disappointment. At first, you think you know the other person, for when you project, you have the strong feeling of intimate knowledge. At the first meeting, there is no need to talk: you know everything about each other—that is a complete projection—the wonderful feeling of being one and having known each other for many ages. Then suddenly, the other behaves in an unexpected way and there is disappointment; you fall out of the clouds and feel that "this is not it." If you go on with the relationship, you must do two things, for now there is a double war: you must find out why you had such an illusion before, and you must find out who the other person is if he or she is not what you expected. Who is he or she in reality? That is a long job, and when you have done that—found the root of your own illusion and how the other person seems to be when looked at without projection—then you may ask why your illusion chose that person to fall upon. That is very difficult, for sometimes the hook is big, and sometimes very small, because the other person may have only few characteristics that fit the projection, so it may be more—or less—of an illusion. There are all degrees.

Obviously, Melchior is the type who leaves as soon as the projection falls off—as soon as the other person does not behave as expected. He even calls Henriette a coward; he insults her and leaves her. Subjectively, that shows the weakness of his dying Eros function. It is not even said that he was sorry or suffered from an unhappy love and disappointment afterwards. He writes the whole thing off, just like the little prince, only in a rather different form, for the prince leaves the planet and the rose, although she feels sorry and says, "Yes, yes, go, go!" Out of pride, she sends him away. If someone writes off his relationships so quickly, you may be sure that he will write himself off equally quickly. That is the suicidal type of person. Here is the weak anima, typical of a suicidal tendency in the unconscious.

That is how, to a certain extent, one can discover suicidal tendencies beforehand. I have met two types: one is not really suicidal, but could finish himself off in a rage—but that is a kind of accident. There are irascible people (really something of the murderer type) who get sudden fits of rage which may also go against themselves when they can kill themselves "by mistake." They lose their heads—and if they could have survived, they would be very sorry! That is not a genuine suicidal tendency; it is an inverted aggression. The aggressiveness is not integrated and may suddenly turn against the person himself, like the scorpion's sting. But Melchior's is the true suicidal type, and such people secretly, intellectually and coldly, write off those in their surroundings and write off themselves. They never really trust themselves or those around them—there are no real relationships, and that is something which goes through this whole book: there is no relatedness. That is the fatal element right from the beginning.

The quarrel between Melchior and his father occurs next, which is very important, because Melchior is still pursuing the idea of the transformation of the personality. His father is an astrologer, a magician, and is also interested in occult sciences, not, however, for the sake of the transformation of the personality, but rather out of curiosity or as a pseudo-scientific, occult occupation. The father and son clash emotionally and then write each other off again. It is another breaking-off reaction. This is so important, because it indicates the main problem: the enmity of Fo, the boy, and Ulrich von Spät, his adversary. At the beginning, von Spät pretended to be Fo's tutor; he wanted to catch him in some way and keep Melchior away from his influence. The boy, on the other hand, is afraid of von Spät and always runs away from him. He tries to bring Melchior under his own influence, and this battle continues. At one time, Melchior really loves Ulrich von Spät—that is the moment when he takes off his glove and shakes hands with him—while at other times, he hates him and wants to avoid him. We should go into this. Ulrich, "Late," is an allusion to the fact that he is the elder and would have the father role in relation to the boy. He pretends to be the spiritual mentor, or tutor, or father, so obviously this conflict is a further development of the one we already saw between father and son. If the son believes in the transformation of the personality—in a most unreal and fantastic way, admittedly, but still he believes in it—and if the father is also interested in magic and occult sciences, but not for the same reason, what two worlds would clash there?

Answer: The two generations.

Yes. The father refused transformation and wanted to keep the status quo, while the son wanted renewal. If you refer that to the idea of the transformation of the personality in alchemy, what then?

Answer: The material and the spiritual are separated. In writing off his father, he has written off the material side. Melchior is consciously searching on the spiritual level, but the material side then becomes the shadow.

Yes, but it is very subtle. In a way, the father is the material side—or which would you say he was?

Answer: He is both, for he is the wise old man and the magician!

You see, in a way, he *is* both! Because he studies the book, he is the spiritual side—he is mentally investigating this world—with a secret materialism. The other way around, you could say that the Fo archetype is a spiritual archetype; it is the *élan vital* the spiritual element. At the same time, that is also materialistic, because the boys wanted to transform the personality with real poison. That is materialism. So in both figures, spirit and matter fall apart. When the one adopts a materialistic trend, the other breaks up with the spiritual attitude; but when the other takes on the materialistic trend, then Fo pulls for the spiritual attitude. So I agree that spirit and matter have fallen apart in the wrong way—but in both! And what is lacking?

Answer: The anima.

Yes, the psyche, that which is between the two. That is why in both opposite positions, in both enemy positions, there is a separation of mind and matter. There is no *vinculum amoris* (bond of love) to unite them, for the anima is lacking. So the father has spiritual interests with a secret materialistic background, and the son has chemical-materialistic interests with a spiritual background. They clash and cannot understand each other. Presently, we have the same problem. Think of such movements as anthroposophy. For instance, in Los Angeles there is a new sect, founded by Manley Hall, whose members consider themselves to be something like the New Rosicrucians. There is a revival of interest in magic, in Freemasonry symbolism, in Rosicrucian symbolism, and in astrology and the occult sciences—and the followers of these movements all reject psychology. They want the Beyond to be called the spirit world, or they claim that an apparition of the animus is an angel from the Beyond, and they give these factors, which we try to name in a psychological way, old names which they take out of the old traditional books. In Basel, there is a man named Julius Schwabe, the founder of the annual Congresses on Symbolism. He invites people to report on symbolism and has professors from all schools. For instance, some talk on Tibetan medicine. He has also invited me to speak on Jungian psychology. As chairman, he summarizes in occult terminology and covers everything up by saying that such-and-such a thing is the old figure X of the Beyond, while the unconscious is called the "transcendental spirit world," and so on.

This is really Mr. von Spät (Mr. Late), because every one of his explanations is a backward pull. The explanations regress to medieval, and even to Sumerian and Babylonian, magical concepts. Or the speakers use concepts of the 16th century, or Paracelsus, and they are all nicely muddled! It is a beautiful potpourri of concepts from the past, pulled out of their context and used as a name for the phenomenon of what we call the unconscious, so that you feel as though it were all explained and quite clear, and that we just have to use the old names; i.e., stick the old names onto the phenomena. But behind that is a tremendous power gesture. For instance, Schwabe would say here, "Well, Fo is, for instance, the *Hermes infans, Mercurius infans*, the young Mercurius." And then one feels that something has been said! That is von Spät! The outer and inner realms fall apart in this way, as well as spirit and matter, and any other factor. If a man, for instance, has an obligation to his anima, and to the woman with whom he made friends or married, then he gets into a typical duality situation of life where one always has a real conflict, a double obligation, and where one is always torn between obligations to the outer and to the inner side of life. That would be the realization of the crucifixion, or of the basic truth of life! Life is double—it is a double obligation, it is a conflict in itself—because it always means the collision, or conflict, of two tendencies. But that is what makes up life! That realization escapes von Spät completely, or he escapes the realization! It does not even occur to him, and that is one more of those little, but fatal, turns in the story which point towards its tragic end.

CHAPTER TEN

At the last lecture, I tried to give you an outline of Ulrich von Spät, who is the great riddle in the book, and to show that the conflict between him and the boys mirrors, on a super-personal level, the conflict which has already begun on the personal level between Melchior and his father. Now the conflict appears on a much wider scale between the paternal protector and the runaway boy who gives the ring to Melchior, for von Spät alludes to the fact that he is chasing the boy to bring him under his power. But before we amplify these figures, I will present a few more chapters of the book.

You remember that, when Melchior has returned to his own home, suddenly the boy appears and warns him against von Spät, saying, "You belong to us, stay with us, and don't fall into the snares of von Spät. He has a secret with which he can petrify us." Melchior asks what the secret is, and the boys say that if they knew, they would be free. He takes away the ring he had given Melchior, saying it would only pull him into complete chaotic confusion. Then he disappears out of the window in a spark of light.

The next chapter begins with someone knocking at the door, but Melchior does not answer. The door opens carefully and his wife Sophie looks in. She is small and delicate-looking, with black hair, and her green eyes look at Melchior, her sensual and rather shapeless lips quivering a little.

"There you are again," she says, "alone in your cold room. Won't you come down? We are having such an interesting party."

"You know I don't want to have anything to do with those people," he answers bitterly. "Why didn't you have my room heated?" (He knows it was a trick to force him to join the party.)

"I am sorry. I forgot," says Sophie.

"You always forget when you have company," he replies. "You always want me to meet people who hold me back. I have no time for them."

"You have no time for me, either," says Sophie. "With those people I can talk in a human way, but that bores you."

"Yes, always talking and chewing over the same thing does bore me," says Melchior. "You sniff at everything, and it is always the same stuff."

A very angry expression crosses his wife's face, but she controls herself and answers quietly, "I like to feel myself among familiar things, but you can't bear them. You always want to make me and everybody else feel insecure, and you try to take the ground away from under our feet. People have become quite stupid after they have met you, and it is impossible to have any serious conversation with them; they always begin to talk nonsense."

"Yes, you can't understand me," says Melchior. "You always are so sure. I can only tell you that your security is complete illusion, just as the former security of your people was a self-deception. The smallest thing upsets them, for there is nothing either above or below. Only the person who has gone through complete dissolution and chaos can talk about security. I do not trust any solidity, or Gestalt, or permanence, or security."

Impatiently, Sophie says, "Well, our guests are waiting. Come along! Today it is absolute chaos, for someone has come who causes even more confusion than you, a new man who talks very strangely and pretends that he has only to command and an army of ghosts will obey him."

Melchior smiles and then says, "Does he talk about ghosts? You would rather believe in ghosts than in the spirituality of the world. Who is this ghost conjuror?"

"An old acquaintance of mine," says Sophie, "from my home town. We played together as children. But everybody always had to obey him, and we could never play as we wanted. He was small and weak, but nobody ever dared fight him. I left home very early and had never heard of him again. Now, after fifteen years, he has turned up unexpectedly, so I asked him to stay for tea."

"What is his name?"

"Ulrich von Spät!"

(So we discover that von Spät was a friend of Melchior's wife when she was a young girl.)

Melchior says, "Oh yes, he is staying at the Grand Hotel, isn't he?"

"How did you know that? Do you know him?"

"Oh, I just got to know him by chance a couple of hours ago, and now he has sneaked into our party on the excuse of knowing you." And he becomes very excited.

Sophies says mockingly, "Now, all of a sudden, you have become very lively. Now you are interested. I see now that I must just get crazy people to come to my party in order to get you interested."

Melchior interrupts her, saying, "Come on, let's go to the party."

When they near the room, von Spät can be heard saying, "Ladies and gentlemen, you laugh at what I say, but I can assure you that I can show you things like a fairy tale come to life. Everyone of you I can shut up in this little bottle which I hold in my hand."

As Melchior opens the door and comes in with his wife, there are shouts of laughter. He is immediately surrounded and notices that they all look excited and feverish, and he wonders whether von Spät is responsible for it all.

"Hullo, old man!" shouts the fat, vulgar art critic, Heinrich Trumpelsteg, patting him on the shoulder. "You have come just at the right time; your famous friend is about to show us a couple of tricks."

But Melchior's boss, Professor Cux, with his gold-rimmed spectacles, appears and introduces his wife, the dancer, a boyish-looking young girl, her face powdered green and her lips, violet. Melchior is amazed by the whole company and Professor Cux very tactlessly says, "Look at my wife! See how beautiful she is, and just look at these legs!" He lifts her skirts above the knees, and says, "And a further view is still more fascinating!"

Everybody laughs at this joke, Frau Cox loudest of all, and the women begin to lift up their skirts and show their calves, each saying that hers are the prettiest legs, so Trumpelsteg says, "All right, ladies, I suggest we have a beauty show. Take off your clothes and show yourselves in all your beauty, and we will decide who is the most beautiful. Like the Greeks, we want nothing but beauty, beauty!"

There are shouts of "hurrah" and a confusion of arms and legs and articles of clothing ensues; in a few minutes, all the women stand naked. Melchior looks across at his wife and sees that she, too, has undressed, and is looking at him mockingly.

"What on earth is happening here?" wonders Melchior. "It's like a madhouse. Mr. von Spät must have this strange effect. Do my ideas seem like that to people when they think about them?"

Mrs. Cux dances naked through the room, embracing everybody, and all the women follow suit, hitting, scratching, biting, and kissing each other, the men applauding violently. Melchior turns away and approaches von Spät, who comes towards him holding out his hand. "We meet sooner than we had expected," he says. "What a strange chance that just you should be the husband of the friend of my youth!"

"I don't believe in chance," answers Melchior, returning von Spät's glance. "In one way or another, we bring about chance."

It occurs to him that although that is a very banal way of talking, at this moment it has a real and definite meaning known only to him and von Spät.

Just then, Trumpelsteg comes along and, having heard the last words, says, "Hurrah for philosophy!" He speaks so loudly that everyone becomes silent and listens.

"Chance! Chance!" he goes on. "Naturally there is no such thing as chance for a magician like yourself. One makes chance! Mr. von Spät directs a whole orchestra of ghosts." And he laughs again.

Then Mr. Silverharness, the goggle-eyed parson who comes to study the disorientation of the modern soul, says, "Yes, Mr. von Spät convinces us of all the things you have spoken of. Don't only talk! We are enlightened present-day people, and we only submit to facts! Facts, Mr. von Spät!"

In a chorus, all the others scream out, "Yes, facts!"

"Facts!" says Schulze, the school professor, joining in. "Only facts convince us; we believe only in facts, as the great time in which we live has taught us!"

"Bravo!", shouts the chorus.

Trumpelsteg, no longer able to contain himself, jumps onto the table, and waving his ape-like arms, shouts, "But the arts, ladies and gentlemen. You forget the arts!" He then makes a long peroration and ends up by saying that they do *not* want facts. "Facts are mean. What we want is illusion! Let us be Knights of the Spirit!"

Everybody echoes, "Let's be Knights of Illusion!", clapping in accompaniment. Even Sophie, who was standing silently in her corner, begins to get excited, smacking her naked thighs and joining in the general laughter.

Melchior and von Spät look at each other, smiling. Melchior feels as if he is separated from the whole scene by a thin veil. The shrieks and all the noise don't seem so loud; everything seems farther off, more peculiar, and stranger. Only to von Spät does he feel himself closely connected.

In the next chapter, things begin to calm down and people sober up a little, but the atmosphere grows tense and people start whispering to each other. Ulrich von Spät leaves the room to return in a little while, opening the door and coming in slowly with his eyes half shut. He is surrounded by a bluish shimmering mist, out of which his white head appears. In one hand, he holds a wonderful little bottle and in the other, a shining knife. He seems to notice nobody. With stiff dancing steps, he goes up the two steps leading to the opposite corner, and the unfriendly looks which had hitherto fallen on Melchior are now directed towards him.

As he passes them, Trumpelsteg, the art critic, and Mrs. Cux, the dancer, who had made signs to each other, move out of the group and, holding something in their hands, cautiously follow him. Meanwhile, von Spät reaches the window, places his bottle on a little table beside him, and turns around, his white face looking like a sleepwalker's.

Suddenly a revolver appears in Trumpelsteg's hand; hoarse with anger, he stutters, "Stop! Stop! You mean to kill us all! It's not a joke any longer!"

Quickly, von Spät holds his own first finger over the bottle and lets a drop of blood fall in. In the same moment Trumpelsteg, small as a thumb, sits in the glass prison.

Mrs. Cux, horrified, springs at von Spät to knife him. But von Spät quickly holds his first finger over the bottle again, makes a cut with his knife, and lets fall a further drop of blood. Immediately, Mrs. Cux is transformed in the bottle.

At first, everybody is dumb with astonishment, but then come shouts of laughter from all except Professor Cux who, bellowing like a wounded animal, yells, "Give me back my wife or I'll fetch the police!" But he doesn't dare go near von Spät.

"Police! Police!" cry the others. "Where's the telephone?"

But Professor Schulze, the schoolmaster, runs from one group to another, whispering, "For God's sake, don't irritate him! He could put us all in the bottle, even the police, and what would we do then? Then we would be lost! Keep quiet!"

Petrified with horror, nobody knows what to do, but Sophie creeps around to her husband and, taking his hand, begs him to ask von Spät to free the prisoners. She tries to keep back her tears and says, "Why must I bear all this? What do you want of me, Melchior?"

Melchior doesn't even look at her, and only answers, "What do I want of you? Nothing! You made your decision long ago. We have nothing more to do with each other." Sophie drops to the floor, wringing her hands.

Then the parson, Mr. Silverharness, starts, "Dear brethren in Christ, this is the judgment of God. We, in our pride, doubted His almighty power, and now we are punished. Let us fall on our knees, and perhaps in His impenetrable goodness He will free us from the toils of Satan. Let us pray!" They all kneel down, but von Spät picks up the little bottle from the table and holds it up. Coming to look, they can all see how Trumpelsteg, completely naked, is beginning to get very fresh with Mrs. Cux in the bottle and how the two dance round and round, ever closer, until at last they sink together in a passionate embrace.

When the parson sees this, the prayer sticks in his throat and his eyes nearly fall out of his head. Everybody presses round von Spät to see what is happening in the bottle. Then some begin to laugh gently; in a few minutes, uncontrollable laughter breaks out and they fall into each other's arms, kissing and dancing. Exhausted with laughter, they look once more at the unconcerned, loving couple in the bottle, and burst out afresh.

Only Professor Cux is in a white-hot rage and wants to attack von Spät, but the others hold him back, tying him to an armchair with a rope so that he can't move. Von Spät places the little bottle on the table and claps his hands. A white mist forms in the room, and seven white-clad maidens appear and bow before him. Out of the ground comes the sound of dance music. Von Spät seizes the hand of one of the girls and opens his eyes for the first time, from which there comes a silver glow. When his eyes are wide open, he stands there, sevenfold, dancing with each of the maidens. When the dance is over, he shuts his eyes and is once more one person.

Afterwards, a great door in the wall of the room opens silently; in the next room stands a table covered with food and drink, and everybody is invited by a voice, which seems familiar to Melchior, telling them to come and eat. In the doorway stands the old apple woman of the station, throwing apples to the guests.

Laughing and talking, the naked women pair with the men; Sophie has slipped over beside Melchior, von Spät is with one of the white maidens, and Professor Cux is forgotten. Wonderful dainties and wine cover the table, and the old apple woman goes from one to the other, serving the guests. As she pours wine into Melchior's glass, she whispers, "You were a clever boy to know me at once, but you are not clever enough. Be careful! I wish you well, but you must be obedient!"

"Of whom should I beware?" asks Melchior, softly.

"You must know that yourself," whispers the old woman. "I can't say anything!"

Melchior takes her wrist and says he won't let her go; she must tell him more—she must tell him everything. But the old woman pulls away with unexpected strength and says,

Ring on the finger,
Faces at the window,
Ways cross,
Winds blow southwards.
Soon it will be time.
They're waiting! They're waiting!

Melchior silently repeats it all to himself. Great longing and restlessness surge through him, and his throat feels tight through the tears he is holding back. He manages to control himself and looks around at the guests, but nobody has been noticing except Sophie, who has overheard and looks at him sadly, thinking he will leave her.

The seven girls sit with their eyes shut, as though they have fallen into a sweet sleep. Von Spät also has his eyes shut; his head seems lifeless and made of stone. Melchior looks around excitedly and thinks, "Why do I hate and love him? Why do the boys run away from him? What is his power? What made him make such a demonstration of his power to these people? Did he want to tell me what I already know? Long ago, I overcame these people. Another company calls me. Why do I hesitate? The stranger keeps me bound. What does he want of me?" His glance falls on the window and sees Fo's face. For a minute it is there, and then it disappears again.

The other guests are still eating. Ulrich von Spät opens his eyes and immediately he is again sevenfold, sitting beside all seven girls at the same time. Suddenly Schulze, the schoolmaster, pushes back his chair, and tapping on his glass, begins to speak. "Ladies and gentlemen, even the most amazing miracles seem quite natural when one has grown used to them. Today, for a minute, we were shaken by unusual things which seemed like miracles to us. But now, think of it, there is imaginary food, people, wine, and so on, and we feel quite at home with it all! There are no miracles. There are only facts, and facts in themselves are always reasonable, so we don't need to get excited anymore. Ladies and gentlemen, we can just remain ourselves, what we always were. Let us raise our glasses and . . ."

A terrible shriek interrupts him. The seven forms of von Spät moan and shut their eyes. The seven girls dissolve into mist. In his usual form, von Spät lies unconscious on the ground.

Fo appears standing in the window corner and laughs. Twisting in pain, von Spät's blue eyes stare blindly up. His whole body seems wracked with unbearable agony.

"D'you feel it now? D'you feel it now?" yells Fo. "You overdid it. You wanted to rest for a minute and play, eh? For a minute, your power slept. D'you see now that you can never sleep? Now we are the masters!"

He dances round him with great bounds. His body is lit up. His hair is a dark flame. Quicker and quicker, he encircles von Spät with ringing cries.

Melchior looks at the face of the man lying on the floor. Horror and love battle within him. Almost unconsciously, he wants to throw himself at Fo and tell him to stop, but Fo whirls, glowing, to the window.

"Take him away, Melchior!" he cries. "We are in your debt. We give him to you! He is yours!" And he laughs once more, uncontrollably, but then, looking at Melchior, he says softly and urgently, "Melchior, we're waiting for you!", and disappears.

Gradually, von Spät's pain lessens. He begins to breathe more quietly and seems to be asleep. The blue mist has gone, and he lies naked on the floor. Melchior looks at his beautiful body for a minute, and before the others can approach, he snatches a cloth from the table and throws it over the sleeping man. Then he carries him and puts him on the couch in his study. He pushes his chair to the top of the couch and sits down, watching the still body. Sleep has removed the tension from the face, and now Melchior sees the real features which had hitherto been hidden from him by the everchanging expression. It is the face of a beautiful god, just slightly distorted. But after a few minutes, the features tense again and a movement goes through the body, and the sleeper, making an immense effort, opens his eyes, which are almost colorless and seem unable to see anything. After a bit he sits up and, noticing Melchior, lets himself fall back onto the cushions, and then says hoarsely, "I came too late. Fo is free again. You believe me to be your worst enemy. I came to your house to take the ring away, but sleep overcame me. Why did you protect me?"

"The sleeper was not my enemy," answers Melchior. "I realized that you were my brother."

Von Spät shoots up and cries, "I shall never sleep again!"

"Never sleep again?" asks Melchior, concerned. "What am I to understand by that? You cannot mean that literally."

"I shall never sleep again," answers von Spät, and his eyes open wide and become darker. "When I sleep, my enemies tear me to pieces. Everywhere, sleep lies in wait for me. I played for a minute, and for the last time he overpowered me. But I am his master. Our body is not earth. Our body is music, a mirroring of the stars."

Melchior lets his head sink and says gently, "I love the earth. I don't want to be the master. I want to give myself."

Impatiently, von Spät moves. "You speak like the boys," he says angrily.

"Who are the boys?" asks Melchior quickly. "Who is Fo?"

Von Spät hesitates and at last, almost unwillingly, says, "Nobody knows, nobody knows their true form. They approach you as wandering boys, as fleeting girls, as animals. They lure you away into chaos and darkness. Somewhere they have a kingdom, the entrance to which I cannot find (the title of the book *The Kingdom without Space*), but they are never there. They are always here. Perhaps they are here and there at the same time. They seduce everybody into an ecstatic dance. I must discover the way. I must destroy their kingdom. Those free, unbridled people must be brought into my service. They must all be mine. Fo has escaped me, the freest, the strongest, the boldest of them all. No darkness must surround them, no night, no refuge. They must be driven from the source of sleep. Nobody may sleep anymore!"

He has stood up. His body seems transparent; one can only see the gleaming outline. As he raises his face, the ceiling of the room disappears, and out of the darkness comes a face resembling his, looking down and dimly lit. "Who are you? Who are you?" cries Melchior, trembling. Von Spät's form rises to an immeasurable height, becoming more and more misty. Melchior's blood feels turned to ice, but he cannot turn away.

"Choose, Melchior!" cries von Spät, and his voice is like the distant ringing of glass bells. "If you want to join the boys, you only need to call and they will forget everything—what you were and what you are. If you want to come to us, just knock on the wall of this room and a door will open to you; a way will open to you to mastery in light. Think it over. The way to us is full of danger. You have to go through the horrors of the world. You are still free. When you have chosen, you will have made the decision for yourself. A return will mean destruction. We shall not protect you."

As he speaks, von Spät's form dissolves completely. The ceiling closes, the lamps burn again, the couch is empty. Melchior finds himself alone in his room.

The discussion between Melchior and his wife Sophie shows that their marriage is past repair: there is a complete split between the two; they do not understand and do not love each other anymore. Obviously, a terrific bitterness of disappointed love has piled up in Sophie, who feels that Melchior never takes part in her world and has never loved her, and, like so many women who feel unloved, she has, in her bitterness, sold herself completely to the animus. Instead of relating to Melchior, she tries to play tricks on him. For instance, in order to force him to join her parties, she does not have his room heated. She tries to catch and overcome him with tricks; therefore, love has turned into a fight for power. Eros has disappeared from their relationship. She also hates her husband because of his spiritual searching and the fact that he is not at one with the bourgeois world, but suffers restlessly from a conflict. He seeks something else, which upsets her need for peace and security. She wants to be the professor's wife—to have a nice circle around her and to play a certain role in it; and he, as she complains, destroys the security of the world she wants to build up. Therefore, they argue about security or insecurity in their marital quarrel. She accuses him of making everything insecure, of dissolving everything. And he, on the contrary, tries to show that the security of this bourgeois world is not real security; that only the people who can give themselves to the irrational adventure of life have genuine security. But the talk gets them nowhere, and so they break their discussion and join the party together.

It then turns out that von Spät has appeared and that he was a friend of Sophie's in her youth; that they had been boyfriend and girlfriend, and then he had disappeared. Last time, you will remember, we tried to describe von Spät as the father spirit, the spirit of tradition, which always comes from the paternal world. For a man, the father figure represents cultural tradition. Von Spät therefore personifies cultural tradition, which always comes late. It is that which is opposed to renewal; it is, as I tried to make clear to you, knowledge with its poisonous "We know it all." Every cultural condition contains a secret poison which consists of the pretension of knowing all the answers. On a primitive level, you see this in the initiation of young men when the old men of the tribe tell them the history of the universe: how the world was made, the origin of evil, of life after death, of the purpose of life, and so on. On this level, for instance, all such questions are answered by the mythological tribal or religious knowledge conveyed by the old to the young, and on that level, with the exception perhaps of a few creative personalities, this is swallowed whole. From then on, the young men know everything too: everything is settled, so that if a missionary tries to talk to these people, he is just informed of how things are: "Oh yes, we know, the world was made in such a way; evil comes from this and that; the purpose of life is so and so." We do exactly the same thing, except that in our case it is a bit more complex; basically, however, it is the same.

Ulrich von Spät represents the archetypal principle of handed-down traditional knowledge, and this eternally contends with the principle of the *puer aeternus*—the spirit of creating everything anew, again and again. Sophie Lindenhuis is secretly linked with von Spät, who turns out to be the boyfriend of her youth. Seen from the standpoint of her psychology, he would therefore represent the father animus. The pretension of knowing all the answers is exactly what the father animus produces in a woman: the assumption that everything is self-evident—the illusion of knowing it all. This attitude is what Jung is attacking when he speaks negatively about the animus: "everyone does that" and "everybody knows this"—the absolute conviction with which women hand out "wisdom." When one examines it closely, however, one sees that they have just picked up what the father (or someone else) said, without assimilating it themselves. The daughter tends to reproduce the knowledge of the past in the way she picked it up from her father. To hand on traditional knowledge—knowledge not worked on by the woman's individual consciousness and not assimilated—is dangerous and tends to be demonic.

It is also clear that von Spät's outstanding characteristic is a tremendous power complex. Sophie says that even as a child, he suffocated all creativeness and that the children had to play the way *he* wanted. The basis of von Spät is power, and power, in a wider sense, corresponds to the instinct of the self-preservation of the individual.

On the level of the animals, there are two basic, natural tendencies which, to a certain extent, contradict each other: the sexual drive with all its functions, including, for women, the bearing of children and upbringing of the young; and the drive toward self-preservation. These two drives are opposite, for procreation, giving birth, and bringing up the young often mean the death of the old generation. There are many animals among which the male dies after propagation has taken place. Or, for example, there are the spiders, where the male is eaten by the female after he has impregnated her and has fulfilled his function. He is no longer useful except in helping to feed the young by being eaten by the mother. That is an extreme case, but frequently older animals completely exhaust themselves for the sake of their young, even to the point of self-destruction. As hunters know, the sexual drive causes animals to forget self-protection entirely. They become blind to danger, and a roebuck pursuing a hind can run right into a man. If a buck is in that state, the hunter must hide behind a tree, for the shyest animal will be oblivious of his own security when sex is the important thing. Sex means the preservation of the species, and to it, therefore, the preservation of the individual is completely, or to a great extent, sacrificed. It is the species which is important—that life should go on. In the usual state, when sexuality is not constellated, then the self-preservation drive (which takes the form of either fighting or running away) is uppermost. The animal is occupied by eating and by keeping away from death; that is, by keeping alive as an individual creature.

These two drives, sex and self-preservation, are basic tendencies in animal life; in man, they reappear as two divine and contradictory powers: namely, love and power—love, including sexuality; and power, including self-preservation. Eros and power, therefore, as Jung always points out, are opposed to each other. You cannot have them together; they exclude each other. The marriage of Melchior and Sophie, for instance, has switched into a power game in which each tries to save his or her own world against the dangerous world of the other; the possibility of giving oneself, the generosity of letting the other's world penetrate one's own, is lost. Both partners fight for their lives. Since the wife has lost the capacity for love, she falls for the power drive and for von Spät. That is the backdoor by which he gets into the house, but von Spät is just as much the power drive of Melchior himself. Now how does the power drive react towards Eros, the other drive?

Answer: By ridiculing and exposing it.

Yes, in the bottle! And what is the bottle? He puts it in a bottle and then ridicules and exposes it, a classical illustration of the way in which the power drive deals with the other drive: he imprisons it! People imprison love and sex by behaving as though they were their owners, such as the woman who uses her beauty for making plots; she uses her beauty and her charm to catch a rich husband. That means she does not love him; she uses love, or what is supposed to be love, to make a career, to catch a rich husband, or whatever she may want. She behaves as if she were the owner, and she directs it. A woman who had fallen for von Spät would repress any spontaneous feeling of love. If she noticed that she was falling in love with a chimney sweep, she would repress her feeling *in statu nascendi* (nip it in the bud) because it would not suit her to love a social nobody. On the other hand, she would trick herself into believing that she loved the great Mr. X who had a lot of money. She would try to convince herself that she loved the man suitable to fit in with her ego and power plans, and any kind of spontaneous eruption of Eros would be repressed. So love generally degenerates into the most basic fact; namely, sexuality. It is reduced to its *prima materia*, so to speak, to physical sexuality, which is imprisoned in intellectual planning. Sexuality is used as a hook to catch a suitable partner for suitable reasons, and all real love, which generally dissolves the fetters and boundary lines and creates new life situations, is anxiously repressed.

Question: Isn't it important that it is a bottle rather than a box, or some other prison?

Yes. What is a glass bottle?

Answer: It could be used as a retort or something like that.

Naturally, the whole thing reminds one of the alchemical retort in which, naturally, the naked couple is together, but with a quite different meaning. Here obviously, it is misused: it is a kind of cynical misuse of the alchemical mystery.

Remark: It is the "nothing-but" attitude.

Yes. It is using an idea, or an intellectual system, with a "nothing-but" nuance: it is "nothing but sexual liberty," or "nothing but the body," or "nothing but me and Mr. So-and-So," and so on, thereby excluding any of the mystery. In general, glass is a substance which can be seen through, but which is a very bad conductor of warmth. One could say that it has to do with the intellect; that it represents an intellectual system which makes one able to see through something but which cuts off the feeling relationship. For instance, if Snow White is imprisoned in a glass coffin, she is shut off from life as far as feeling, but not as far as awareness, is concerned. If you are in a glass house, you can see and be aware of everything that goes on outside, but you are cut off from the smells, the temperature, the wind, and so on. All such perceptions are excluded, and therefore, so is the feeling relationship to the outer world or into the inner world. It is interesting that we put some animals in the zoo in glass cages, thus avoiding all of the reality-impact with danger; then we can study their behavior from an intellectual distance. In alchemy, as you know, the glass retort is even regarded as being identical with the philosopher's stone. The vessel is the feminine aspect of the philosopher's stone, which is the masculine aspect of the Self, but both are the same thing. In the present story, the glass is a mystical factor which is now in the hands of von Spät. What would that mean? What is the difference, psychologically, between the glass as a positive alchemical symbol and this mock alchemical vessel? The subtle difference can be discovered by first considering what the alchemical retort is in its positive form. What would that mean, putting everything into a retort?

Answer: Accepting the suffering of it.

That is part of it, but what does the retort represent psychologi-

cally? Most of you have read *Psychology and Alchemy*.[29] What does it mean if I have everything in the retort?
Answer: A transformation takes place.

Yes, the retort is a place of transformation. What is the precondition for any kind of psychological transformation? The precondition is looking at oneself, looking completely within. It means that instead of looking at the outer facts—at other people—I only look at my own psyche. That would be putting it into a glass. Suppose I am angry with somebody; if I turn away from that person and say, "Now let me look at my anger, what that means, and what is behind it," that would be putting my anger into the retort. So the retort represents an attitude that aims at self-knowledge—an attempt to become conscious of oneself instead of looking at other people. As far as the will is concerned, it requires determination; as far as intellectual activities are concerned, it means introversion, the search for inner self-knowledge at all costs, and objectively, not subjectively, musing about one's problems, making the effort to see oneself objectively. Nobody can find this attitude except by what one could call an act of grace. For instance, if somebody is either madly in love, or madly angry over some problem, perhaps a money problem, one always tries to get the person to look away from that particular question, whatever it may be, and try to be objective. One tries to get him to look at the dream—see how it looks from within, from the objective psyche—using the dream life as a mirror for the objective psychological situation. Again and again, unless something like a miraculous turn takes place, people cannot do that even if they want to. They begin again, "Yes, but you see tomorrow I have to decide with my banker; I have either to sell the stock or not." Yes, but let's turn away, let's look for a minute at the objective side, at what the objective psyche has to say about it! "No, you see I have to decide!" And then it is like a miracle if that person suddenly becomes quiet and objective, makes that turn, looks inside and says, "I will just abstain from looking at the emotions which flow toward it and try to be objective." That is a miracle, and it needs the intervention of the Self; something must happen in the person for him to be able to do it. One knows it oneself, for sometimes one wants to find that attitude again and cannot; one is

[29]Carl Gustav Jung, *Psychology and Alchemy*, vol. 11, *Collected Works* (Princeton: Princeton University Press, 1958; 2d ed., 1969).

pushed away from self-knowledge and cannot do it; and then suddenly this strange peace comes up within one, generally when one has suffered enough. Then one becomes quiet and silent, and the ego becomes objective and turns within and looks at the facts within, objectively, and stops the monkey dance of thinking about the situation. The monkey dance of ego self-assurance stops, and a kind of objectivity comes over the person. Then it is possible to look at oneself and to be open to the experience of the unconscious.

It can therefore be said that in a way, the alchemical vessel is a mysterious event in the psyche; it is an occurrence—something which takes place suddenly and which enables people to look at themselves objectively, using the dreams and other products of the unconscious as mirrors in which one can see oneself. Otherwise, one has no Archimedean point outside the ego by which to do it. That is why an awareness of the Self is necessary before one can look at oneself, and that is why people are often touched in the beginning of analysis by an experience of the Self. It is only that experience which enables them to strive towards looking at themselves in this objective way. That is what the alchemists meant by the vessel. It could also be said that the vessel symbolizes an attitude which is, for example, the prerequisite for doing active imagination, for you cannot do that except with the vessel. You can call active imagination itself a sort of vessel, for if I sit down and try to objectify my psychological situation in active imagination, that would be having it in a vessel. Again, this presupposes the attitude of ethical detachment, honesty, and objectivity, which is necessary to be able to look at oneself. That would be the vessel in a positive form.

With ego judgment, I quickly judge the unconscious; I put it in a vessel, too. But then it is the glass prison, the "nothing-but" attitude, which gives that prison a negative aspect. Then it is an intellectual system, and the living phenomenon of the psyche is imprisoned in any kind of intellectual system. The owner of it is power. This is very subtle. There are even people who are willing to look at themselves, but only in order to be stronger than the other person or to master a situation; they still retain an ego-power purpose and they even use the techniques of Jungian psychology—active imagination, for instance—but with their eyes fixed on power, on overcoming the difficulty, on being the big stag who *did* it. That gives the wrong twist; nothing comes out of it. Or there are others who honestly analyze themselves for a specific amount of time—but in order to become analysts and to have power over others. That is another snare of the same kind: only looking at oneself in order to exercise power over others; looking within not for its own sake—not just because one has the need to be more conscious. Thus, power sneaks into everything again and again, and turns that which has been a living spiritual manifestation into a trick, a technical trick in the possession of the ego. Ulrich von Spät is the demon of misusing everything, of making everything—even the highest spiritual powers —degenerate into such a technical trick.

I have been asked several questions. One of them is this: assuming that von Spät represents the misuse of intellect with the shade of "nothing-but" domination, what is the meaning of the miracle he performed? How would you interpret that? How can such an attitude produce miracles?

Question: Wouldn't the word "trick" be better than "miracle"?

Yes, one could also call it a collective-hallucination trick. Someone goes into a trance, and then a collective hallucination takes place, which vanishes when suddenly they all wake up and the dinner and everything else disappears. It was a trick of illusion, but how does that connect with the meaning we have so far established?

If we look at von Spät as being Sophie's animus, then he would be a father-animus image. And how does a father animus in a woman produce not only opinions but also magical tricks? I am reminded of the case of a woman who had a schizoid father; a rather cold, sadistic man who perpetually criticized his children, constantly telling them that they were nobodies and nothing and would never get anywhere. If they tried in school, he said that they would never succeed, or if they wanted to take up art, he told them they had no talent and would not make a success of it. There was always a negative attitude. He also had the habit, which drove the daughters mad, of cutting off the heads of flowers with a stick when they walked along in the fields. It was a *tic nerveux* (nervous habit) and was done in revenge, or out of bitterness over his own disappointed and destroyed feeling life. There is an inherited schizophrenia of many generations in this family, and here the father cut off his children's heads by his discouraging remarks, or he tried to do so, so that they should not grow up.

Now, this daughter picked up a series of lovers—old men, young men, artists, businessmen—the most apparently different kind of people, but always, when she had known them for more than a fortnight, they would start to torture her in a sadistic way by telling her that she was nobody and was disgusting; that she would never get anywhere. It was exactly her father's gramaphone-record kind of talk. I have never found out whether she made them do it, or if, by some divination of instinct, she always picked on such men. I never got to know most of them, except through what she said about them, but you could say that it was like black magic. In primitive language, I would say that there was a curse on that girl, and she always had to pick up critical, unloving, sadistic men who trampled on her feelings, which were already nearly destroyed anyway. In the dreams, it appeared that it was really the father. For instance, the night after one such quarrel with a lover who told her that she was no good and everything was wrong with her, and so on, she dreamt that her father always waited for her and beat her on the shinbone with a stick so that she would fall down. It is a well-known fact that the father animus, or the mother demon in a man, does not only act as an inner wrong fate, a distortion of the instincts in the choice of the partner and all these other things, but also is really like an outer fate, and can appear in synchronicities—in synchronistic miracles outside the personal life; in events for which we cannot make individuals responsible. I think it would be the wrong feeling-nuance to tell such a girl that she always fell for sadistic lovers because she had not overcome the sadistic father animus within her. There is quite a bit of truth in that, but it is not the whole truth. Later, when she is further along, one may have to try to get her to see that she has such a father demon and sadist within her, and that it attracts sadistic men. Sometimes, however, when one tries to deal with such a dark fate, one feels that one is up against a divine destructive power, so much so that one cannot make the individual responsible.

Question: Couldn't you say that she always had that thought in her head, and then it became a part of herself? To get those people into the bottle, von Spät always had to give a drop of blood, and it seems to me that the animus in a woman—that is, the thought in her head—gets right into her blood and actually becomes a part of her. Von Spät gave the whole of himself in making those tricks.

Yes, von Spät is naturally the secret-thought demon in a woman.

Remark: But he also gave his blood.

That is quite right, but there we have to go to another factor; namely, that when von Spät performs this magic, he becomes untrue to himself, which is why Fo catches him. It is very important to remember that if von Spät hadn't performed this magical plot or play, if he hadn't started to display magic, Fo would not have overcome him. "I'll never sleep again," von Spät said, after having been overcome by Fo. "When I sleep, my enemies get me; always sleep lies in wait for me. I played." So you see, he became untrue to himself because for a minute, he played: he forgot his power drive; he became amused in the magical performance. For a moment, he behaved like the Fo band, like the boys. He played: "and there he got me for the last time, but I am his master. Our body is not earth, our body is music, mirroring the stars." It is a true enantiodromia, and we must take von Spät as the spirit of intellectualism—thought power—power only as long as he does not play. When he begins to produce magic, he begins to turn towards the Fo principle. If you look at it as though there were two poles, one pole would be Fo and the other, von Spät. When von Spät is at his best and is himself, then he is awake: he does not sleep, he does not play, and he does not perform magic tricks. But he got drunk with his power, and displayed it more and more; he produced magic stuff to show off, and slowly, as he says, forgot himself for a minute. he went to sleep; he played. And then Fo got him! You could just as well say that he fell into Fo, for these two powers always fall into each other through an enantiodromia, as do all unconscious opposites; both are unconscious opposites because they are gods, which means basic archetypal drives in the psyche. It is a play of opposites in which Melchior is the suffering human, in the middle of the two, for von Spät and Fo both want to get his soul. When von Spät goes too far in his power play, he snaps into Fo, and you will see that when Fo goes too far into his other play, he snaps round into von Spät. So when von Spät begins to perform magic by cutting himself and using his blood, he is really verging slightly towards the Fo side; he is switching over into the other. Secretly, they are linked. You could say that they are two aspects of life, for both belong to life and you cannot live without either. But both claim to be the only one. They each have a total claim on the human being. Fo asks Melchior to give himself totally to him, von Spät asks the same thing, and, as we shall see at the end of the book, the tragedy is that Melchior cannot hold his own standpoint. Seen from the personal angle, this is the weakness of the ego, which is switched around between the opposites and which is their playball. He is between two gods or demons who both claim to be his unique owner, and what he cannot do is to keep his feet on the ground and say, "I will not obey either of you, but will live my human life." That is why he is caught up in this constant demonic play.

Miss Rump has discovered something very interesting about the word "Fo": namely, that its dominant meaning is "Buddha"; it is one of his designations. This makes sense, because it is said that Melchior had traveled in China and India, and Fo is the ruler of an invisible kingdom, which would be nirvana, as we shall see later. The decoration of the book cover is something like a Japanese *torii* on one side, which has a mystical meaning in the East—the door through which you go into the Beyond—and at the back of the book there is an eightfold star. These two designs are probably chosen consciously. Obviously, the author had read and was fascinated by Eastern material, as will become much more evident later, and he projects the *puer aeternus*—the creative demon and Eros demon—into the East. Von Spät, on the other hand, represents late Christianity. The Christian civilization is now old and worn out for us; it has lost the powerful *élan vital* that it had in the first centuries of its rising. We, the tired Western civilization, pretend that we know all the answers, but we are longing for a new genuine inner experience and are, to a great extent, turning to the East, expecting a renewal from there. (But this is obviously a projection.) That would be another aspect of von Spät, whose slightly morbid face suggests a beautiful, divine image, slightly oblong and sickly. Which god looks like that on many paintings? Christ. But von Spät is not Christ; it is only one image we have of him—a suffering, morbid god—something divine, but no longer capable of living.

At this point, much of the book does not need any comment. There is the journalist who just talks any kind of rot he thinks fitting at the moment, and the parson who pretends that he is studying the disorientation of modern life and then in the midst of his prayer just stops to stare at the sexual intercourse. The irony in all these things is transparent and comes out of the conscious layer of the author; therefore, no further psychological interpretation is needed. But the still unsolved problem is the role of the feminine. Women are described with the utmost scorn; there is not a single positive feminine figure in the book. The author ridicules them completely. There is no Eros in the book, and the only positive woman in the chapters we have read is the apple woman, who is a positive mother figure. She brings a message to Melchior when von Spät's power is at its height. When everybody is fascinated by his magic, the apple woman comes to the dinner party and whispers to Melchior, "Ring on the finger (the ring signified his betrothal, so to speak, with the boy), faces at the window, ways which cross each other, winds blowing southwards, soon the time will come, they're waiting, they're waiting," meaning that they are waiting for him. The message she transmits to Melchior is that he should not become untrue and disloyal to them. She is the only feminine figure on the side of the boys, and this makes a cluster which consists of a group of mother-bound boys whose feminine ruler is archetypal Mother Nature and, at the same time, the fat old woman who sells apples at the station.

That there is no young anima figure is typical for the German mentality. As Jung points out, on the other side of the Rhine, the anima has not been differentiated, but has remained completely within the mother complex. A man belonging to the Secret Service told me that when he wanted to loosen up young Nazi prisoners to get military information out of them, the leading—and practically always successful—question to put when they were determined not to tell the enemy anything, was (with a slightly sentimental quiver in the voice), "Is your mother still alive?" Usually then, they started to cry, and their tongues were loosened. He discovered that this was the key question with which to penetrate the armor of the hostile attitude in German youths. Naturally, such generalizations must be taken as such; they are only half-truths in individual cases, but if we may characterize national differences, there is still a lack of differentiation of the anima in Germans, compared with the more latin-influenced peoples. Germany itself also differs in the south, where there was a Roman occupation. There, the attitude is slightly different from that of the northern part, so the statement has to be taken with a grain of salt. This novel, however, shows clearly the state of complete undifferentiation of the anima, the only positive woman being this apple mother.

Sophia means wisdom; it is meaningful that Melchior's wife's name is Sophie, but she appears as a bitter, animus-possessed, socially ambitious, petty, unloving woman—the typical disappointed wife. Nevertheless, her name means wisdom, which shows how greatly the unloving attitude of the man has altered the feminine principle. Sophie could be Wisdom; she could incarnate the love for the human being—she could be all that the name includes—instead, she is changed into this destructive, small figure because Melchior has not known how to turn towards her and make her blossom with his love. She is negative wisdom, and she is bitter because he does not love human beings; she likes human contacts and he hates them; she wants to force him to make human contacts, but he remains in inhuman isolation. This is what they fight about. As you know, the Sophia is called "philanthropos"—"the one who loves man." She is an attitude of love toward mankind, which naturally means being a human being among human beings and loving other human beings. That is the highest form of Eros. As Jung sketches it in his paper on the transference, Sophia-wisdom is even higher than the highest love symbolized by the Virgin Mary because, as he says very meaningfully, "a little less is still more." This means that if I have an idealistic love for mankind, wanting to do only good, that is less than just being human among human beings. But all that is lacking at this party in which a completely barbaric animality breaks through with its egoism, its vulgarity, and its untruthfulness. This shows what happens if love for the human being is not present. It also shows what neglecting the Eros side produces: on top, a conventional layer of so-called spiritual civilization; underneath, the old animal and the old ape circus, which may break loose at any minute. As soon as the conventions are gone and the women have undressed, there is just the ape circus left, with a complete undifferentiation of anything human. This is what people look like when they have not developed the feeling function, except that, as a rule, they haven't the courage to reveal the ape circus which is lurking underneath. It takes a revolution, a Nazi movement or something of that sort, to bring it into the open, and then one is just amazed at what comes out. When the conventions are swept away, this ape circus appears.

Von Spät hates sleep. How would you interpret that? He is the enemy of sleep and says that when he has completely overcome his enemies, there will be no sleep, and his way to overcome the boys will be to cut them off from the source of sleep.

Answer: In sleep, there is no power drive.

Yes. In sleep, the power drive is knocked out, and we are completely helpless in the hands of our surroundings. It is a state in which power is knocked out and the unconscious comes up. So you think at first that he must represent consciousness, and Fo, the principle of unconsciousness. But if we look more closely, it is a bit different. Von Spät is something unconscious, too; namely, the unconscious demonic aspect of consciousness, when "it knows all the answers." Consciousness consists of something we think we know; it is an immediate awareness. Even though we do not know quite what it is, we have a subjective feeling that what consciousness is, is intimately known to us. But behind this conscious awareness lies unconsciousness; in other words, behind the I and the whole phenomenon of consciousness lies the shadow, the power drive, and something demonic. We must never forget that consciousness has a demonic aspect. We are beginning to be aware that the achievements of our consciousness—our technical achievements, for example— have destructive aspects. We are waking up to the fact that consciousness can be a disadvantage and that it is based on an unconsciousness. That which makes me so passionately want consciousness to dominate life is something unconscious. And we don't know what that is. The need, the urge and passion, for consciousness is something unconscious, as is what we know as conscious tradition. For example, to a primitive tribe its own tradition appears to it as consciousness. In an African tribe, if a novice, having been tortured and having his teeth knocked out, or whatever, is taught how the world was created, how evil comes about, that illness means a certain thing, that men must marry women of a certain clan for certain reasons—that to him is consciousness. To us, however, who have a different tradition, the mythological teachings that the young primitive absorbs seem purely unconscious. We even interpret such teachings as we do dreams, and that this is possible shows that what signifies collective consciousness to a primitive tribe is in reality full of unconscious symbolism.

I refer to other civilizations to illustrate my point, because one can observe another society *sine ira et studio*; i.e., dispassionately. But it is the same with our own religious tradition. We could say that Christian teaching is a content of our collective consciousness. If we look more closely, however, we see that it is based on symbols such as the crucified god, the Virgin Mary, and so on, and if we think about these, about what they mean and how to link them up with our actual life, we discover that we do not know because they are full of unconsciousness. We find that precisely those known aspects of our spiritual tradition are completely mysterious to us in many ways and that we can say very little about them. So consciousness contains a secret reverse side, which is unconsciousness. Just that is the demonic thing about von Spät; namely, that conscious views always behave as if they were the whole answer. One might say that perhaps it is now the task of psychology to uncover this secret, destructive aspect of consciousness.

I hope that we may get to the point where consciousness can function without the pretension of knowing everything and of having said the last word. If consciousness could be reduced to a *function*, a descriptive function, then people would cease to make final statements; instead, one would say that, from the known facts, it appears at the present time as if one could explain it in such-and-such a way. That would mean giving up the secret power premise that claims to have said all there is to be said, so that now we know all about it and it is *so*. It would be a big step if that false pretension could be eliminated. But that presupposes the integration of consciousness by our becoming aware of its relativity and its specific relation to the individual (I must know that I know and that I have especially that view). It is not enough to have a conscious viewpoint; one must know why one has it and what one's individual reasons for having it are. The average person is still possessed by collective consciousness and, under its influence, talks as if he knew all the answers. For example, people tend to regard a humanitarian attitude as being their own, forgetting that it is derived from the Christian *Weltanschauung*; they fail to realize that it is collective and that it is part of a *Weltanschauung* which they no longer share. Power is the hidden motivation behind such behavior. Knowledge is one of the greatest means of asserting power. Man has obtained power over nature and other human beings by brute force, but also by knowledge and intelligence. It is uncertain which is the stronger, for strength and intelligence are the two aspects of the power drive, and they account for the many primitive animal stories in which the witty, clever one outwits the stronger one: the hyena outwits the lion, and in South America, the little dwarf stag outwits even the tiger. This shows up in the power drive of the single individual; for instance, in the animus of women, either they trick their husbands or they make brutal scenes. Emotional brutality and cunning are the two manifestations of power.

Our consciousness is still secretly coupled with these two tendencies for domination, and knowledge is generally combined with them. You see this most irritatingly in the prestige drive of the academic world. it is a rare event in university life that a professor is interested in truth for its own sake; usually, he is more interested in his position and in being the first to have said something.

Remark: Les savants ne sont pas curieux, *as the French say.*

Yes, exactly! Which shows that the power which is contained in knowledge, the demonic drive to dominate through knowledge, is stronger than the objective interest in finding out any kind of truth. Ulrich von Spät symbolizes all these positive and negative aspects of a congealed, conscious tradition.

CHAPTER ELEVEN

Last time, we had reached that part of the story where von Spät suddenly wakes up. His magic is over because he slept or played, for a minute and was not quite alert enough, so the demonic boys caught him and overcame him. You remember that, at the dinner party which he had conjured up, von Spät had appeared with seven girls and sometimes he himself had multiplied so as to be the lover of all seven. He is seven men with seven girls, and then he is again one figure. At the moment when he wakes up, he is shocked out of his trance by the appearance of Fo. The seven girls and the magic dinner party disappear. How would you interpret the one magician and the seven girls?

Remark: With himself, it makes eight.

Yes, but when is there one with the seven? You must remember that the author had been interested in alchemy and had produced this alchemical pseudo-miracle of putting Trumpelsteg and Mrs. Cux in the bottle as a kind of mock representation of the alchemical *mysterium coniunctionis.*

In alchemy, especially in the later alchemical texts, which are probably the ones that our author knows, there are often representations of seven women sitting in an earth cave, and they are the seven planets or the seven metals, both representing the same thing. The idea was that every metal corresponded to a planet: gold-Sun, silver-Moon, copper-Venus, lead-Saturn, iron-Mars, tin-Jupiter, quick-silver-Mercury. The eighth figure among the seven women would represent the ruler of them all and would be either the sun god or Saturn, because Saturn was also represented as the old form of the sun. From his name ("late"), one can also conclude that von Spät probably represents the old sun god surrounded by the seven planets. We have interpreted von Spät as representing the principle of Christianity because he appears as an aristocratic, but rather morbid-looking, god. Now he appears as the old sun god, which would mean that it is not Christianity in itself—whatever that is, for nobody knows—but the old tired *Weltanschauung* of Christianity: that which has been realized and is therefore a habit of thought, but which is no longer vital—a kind of principle at the base of our social and religious institutions. In fairy tales, this corresponds to the old king who has lost the water of life and who needs to be renewed, or has to be dethroned, or must give up the throne to a follower; in other words, the *Weltanschauung*, having once again grown old, has become an aged ruler who is sterile and needs renewal.

There is a little incident which goes further, for at the end of the chapter I read to you, Melchior asks von Spät who the boys are. Von Spät says, "Nobody knows their real essence. They approach you like wandering boys, like animals, like girls. They seduce you into chaos and darkness. Somewhere they have a kingdom, but I cannot find the entrance. They are never there. They are always here. They are in several places at the same time. I must find the way. I must destroy the kingdom. Those free people must be subdued and the strongest and boldest one, Fo, must be subdued also. Their wild love must die. I will cut them off from the well of sleep. Nobody shall sleep anymore." At this moment, von Spät gets up and looks as if he were transparent. He lifts his head, and the ceiling opens; suddenly, a mirror-image, his double, looks down from above, shining. Melchior is frightened when he sees somebody looking down who looks exactly like von Spät and he cries out, "Who are you?" But von Spät disappears into a kind of cold mist, and then he calls down from far above, "You must choose, Melchior! If you want to go to the boys, you need only call them and they will seduce you into the sweet darkness, and if you choose their way, you will forget who you were and who you are. But, if you want to come to us, you must only knock on the wall of this room, and a door will open and the way towards the ruling of the light will come. Now think it over. The way towards us is full of danger, but you are still free. When you have chosen, you can't go back. If you want to go back, we will not spare you." After this, the figure of von

Spät disappears, and Melchior sees the lamp burning and the empty couch, and he is alone in his room.

How would you interpret this doubling of von Spät? The rest of what he says is more or less clear from what we said about him before, but how would you interpret the fact that he becomes double and then disappears into heaven—into the sky, the firmament —like mist?

Answer: Hasn't he been living as a human? He was living a human life, and now goes off into the god.

Yes, you could say that von Spät would be an incarnation of a divine principle and now he is again joining his eternal form. What would that mean for Melchior, practically, if he could draw conclusions from what he experiences? What does it mean if an unconscious figure doubles in a dream?

Answer: That something is on the border of consciousness.

Yes, and an indispensable condition of realizing consciously what a content means is realization of its inner opposite; that is, that it is this and not that. This is a table, which means that it is not a chair, and not something else. You cannot make a conscious statement without excluding all the other aspects. This is why, if a dream figure doubles, that always means it wants to become conscious— that it touches the threshold of consciousness and thereby reveals the double aspect. We have interpreted von Spät as the Christian *Weltanschauung*. What would it mean if that is doubled?

Remark: That the dark side of God is constellated at the same time.

Not necessarily. That is not in it at this point; that will come later. Here, the double is as light as von Spät. He is a kind of spirit magician.

Question: Would he be a pagan God?

Yes, that's closer! Do we, who belong to the Christian civilization, really know at bottom what it means? What archetype is behind the Christian civilization? Could we conscientiously pretend that we know what we mean when we say that we believe in a Trinitarian God and in Christ? Even the greatest theologian has never pretended to do so. Catholic theologians, for instance, speak of the mystery of each dogma. Some aspects can be put into words, but the nucleus is absolutely unknown to us. We would say that there was an archetypal content or an archetype behind it which, by definition, we do not know. One could therefore say that von Spät is that part which has entered human consciousness, which sounds familiar to us and which gives us that strange feeling of knowing what it means, of being aware and conscious of it. And then there is a whole other half which is completely unknown to us; that would be his other part. One might say that only after having realized the pagan opposite pole—which would be the world of Fo and the pagan mother goddess—could we become aware of the double aspect of Christianity, of its conscious and unconscious aspects. As long as we are in it, we cannot become aware of it, for we are, as it were, wrapped up in it; we need an Archimedean point outside to realize the specific nature of our own civilization. The pagan hole is projected onto the East, for the boy Fo has a name which points to Buddha, which means that the capacity for looking at our own cultural and religious background is only possible for us when we get into closer touch with other civilizations and their other religions. If, with a certain equanimity, you can accept the fact that the other person's religion contains some truth too, then you are able to become aware, objectively, of the specific character of our civilization. Detached awareness such as this is, of course, a modern development, and it has increased to such an extent that it is no longer possible for us to get stuck in the medieval prejudice that ours is the only true religion. Now that the world has shrunk and we are confronted with an infinite number of other civilizations, we have to ask ourselves what is specific and different in our attitudes and in our civilization from those of others. That question introduces a certain relativity which makes us realize how much von Spät, in some ways, represents something we consciously know and which we attempt to convey to others (for instance, in foreign missionary work), and how much there is an archetypal, unknown background; namely, the eternal aspect of von Spät, which is the image of something divine behind any specific form in which it may appear.

In a way, you find this development in the writings of Toynbee, who tries, with a kind of extroverted approach, to say that it is quite clear, now that we have come into closer contact with the East and other civilizations, that we shall simply have to adopt a kind of mixed religion. He proposes a new form of prayer which should begin: "Oh Thou, who are Buddha, Christ, Dionysus . . ." He suggests that we should just pray to a savior figure to whom one would ascribe all those names, and make a nice cocktail of all the essentials of all the religions, slightly blurring the not-too-important differences, to create a kind of generalized world religion where Buddhists and South African Negroes, and everybody, can join in and think what they like about these contents. This is the same reaction that we have already had on a smaller scale in the late Roman Empire. There, too, there were all those little local nations with their local creeds and folklore and religious teaching—the Celts, the Syrians, the Israelites, and so on—and then, when all this was put together in the Roman Empire, the Romans tried the same thing. They said that you just had to pray to Jupiter-Zeus-Amun, which was the highest god, and the underworld god would be Hades-Osiris, (in Egypt, Sarapis), and there you have a new cocktail religion where even the attributes of the gods were mixed! That would be as if we would now have new images of Christ, in which he would be represented as sitting in a Buddha position, with the *mudra* of pity, and somewhere the cross behind him in a decorative way. All that is possible—human naiveté is boundless!

This attempt at relativity—the typical development of von Spät, the late development of a tired civilization, of a worn-out and decaying *Weltanschauung*—has no chance of success because the very essence of religious experience is that it has an *absolute* character. If I say that my experience could, but just as well could not, be, or that I believe such-and-such but can quite understand another's believing something different, this indicates that my so-called religious experience is not genuine, because religious experience has a compelling and absolute character. One could say that this is the criterion of a religious experience. Consider someone who asserts that his experience has changed his whole life and that it will now pervade everything. If it really does apply to everything, and if it is a total experience, applicable to every field of activity, then you know that whatever it may seem, it is a truly religious experience. Otherwise, it is merely an intellectual experience, or a mood, which passes away or which is kept in one drawer for Sundays—taken out and put away again.

So we are in a terribly contradictory situation: to have a religious experience, one needs some kind of absolute obligation, yet this is irreconcilable with the reasonable fact that there are many religions and many religious experiences and that intolerance is really outdated and barbaric. The possible solution would be for each individual to keep to his own experience and take it as absolute, accepting the fact that others have different experiences, thus relating the necessary absoluteness only to oneself—to *me*, this is absolute (there is no relativity and no other possibility), but I must not extend the borders into the other person's field. And this is what we try to do. We try to let people keep a religious experience without collectivizing it and taking the wrong step of insisting that it must also be valid for others. It must be absolutely valid for *me*, but it is an error for me to think that the experience which I have to follow absolutely, has to be applied to others. We shall see that this becomes a crucial point in our novel. Here, however, we see that the breaking in of a new religious experience, which is represented by Fo, makes it possible to realize two layers of the late *Weltanschauung* of von Spät, who says "If you want to follow us (namely, von Spät) towards the kingdom of light, then just knock on this wall and a door will open."

The next part of the book is "The Open Door," so we must conclude (and we shall soon see that this is true) that at this moment, Melchior chooses the way of Von Spät and makes up his mind to leave Fo.

At the beginning of the chapter, Melchior meditates on what has happened, and then be becomes very excited, just as though he heard a bell ringing inside him. Suddenly he says, "I must find certainty," and he bangs on the wall with his fist. At that moment, he hears beautiful music and sees columns appearing; a big gate opens, and he sees the sea and the quiet waves. A great white bird spreads its wings and approaches him, and he sees a sailing boat coming in. Then everything becomes disagreeably quiet and dead. He shudders and is unable to move, and then he begins to delight in the stiffening which has taken possession of him. After some time, the clock in his room strikes, and his numbness disappears. Tears flow from his eyes. With widespread arms, he passes through the gateway and out into the night. After a few steps, he hears voices which he thinks are those of his wife, Trumpelsteg, and Cux. Dark figures appear from all sides. A muffled, bitter voice cries, "Seize him, seize him!" Somebody catches hold of him from behind, a black cloth is put over his face, and he faints. After some time, he regains consciousness and finds that he is lying bound on the deck of a little ship and that immovable figures are sitting beside him. A storm comes up, and they are tossed ceaselessly on the waves. Hours pass and no one speaks. Then a torch is lit, and in the forepart of the ship a huge man makes signals, swinging the torch above his head. In time, answering signals come from the opposite shore, and Melchior is relieved to be approaching land once more. Before landing, a black veil is again put over his face and his hands are again tied. He tries to cry out, but cannot, and faints. On land, he comes to and has to walk in the darkness with others beside him. After a time they come to endless passages, and sometimes he hears the sound of a door. He is astonished to feel ground under his feet, for he has had the feeling of walking on air. Someone bangs on metal. Then everything becomes still and dark, as before. In that moment, life returns to Melchior. He tries to fight, but he comes up against nothing but empty air. He is alone. Suddenly the darkness lifts, and a blaze of light stabs his eyes. He is in a big hall, decorated with red velvet, and behind a large table are enthroned three veiled people, dressed in red. Along the walls sit all the men and women whom he has known during his lifetime. They look at him severely, whispering among themselves.

The next chapter is "The Judgment." Melchior asks who tied him up and brought him there, but there is no answer. "I want an answer," he cries and bangs on the table, but a stern voice says, "You stand before your judges, Melchior!" Somebody then says that the accusers should come forward, and there is a lot of movement and whispering and murmuring in the hall. Melchior looks around and recognizes friends and enemies, relatives and neighbors, comrades, and the maidservants of his own house. All their faces are gray and covered with dust; their mouths, wide open and black; and their lips, bluish. Obviously, they are all dead and have come back from the tomb. He looks for his wife and sees her standing in the front row, staring at him with mad, demanding eyes. She says, "You never wore the slippers which I spent a whole year embroidering for you. You never loved me." Cux says, "You were never interested in my chemical discoveries, but were always only concerned with your own." Tumpelsteg says, "Always, when I had an idea, you picked my brains and used it yourself, and I was left empty." And Mrs. Cux says, "You never admired my beautiful legs and now they have become like sticks. You were heartless to me."

So, one after the other, they all accuse him. Now ghosts keep appearing around Melchior. He sees his mother's suffering face, his father's face, and then an old great-aunt turns up and says, "You always laughed when I wanted to read you the verses out of my album. I showed them to nobody but you, and you laughed at them. So everything I loved died with me." School friends turn up, and among them he sees Otto von Lobe (the one who committed suicide at the beginning of the book), Heinrich Wunderlich (the boy who became cynical), and Henriette Karlsen. He wants to walk up to her and say, "Are you here, too?" But others come between them. Then the old apple woman appears and accuses him, saying, "He always went away. I sat at the station. I saw it! I know, I know!" Then they all begin to murmur in a hostile way and the judge says, "You have heard the accusations. Do you admit your guilt?" Melchior says, "Yes, I am guilty. Every step I took, I did wrong. We kill while we live, but who wants to be the judge?"

There is silence and the judge's voice says, "You deserve the death sentence. You must die." The three mummies rise from their thrones. But Melchior says calmly that there is nobody who can judge him. He asks who those are who accuse him and then says they are just crazy shadows. The people are infuriated and say he must die. They call two wooden figures at the entrance, who seize him. He goes through a kind of nightmare of hell: there are fire and shut doors and doors which open and fall on him, and so on—just as it would be in a nightmare. In the end, they take a black coat and nail it on him so that he feels great pain from the nails entering his flesh. They lead him to a big marketplace in a little town, where all the houses are those in which he has lived all his life and the people standing around are those whom he knew in his lifetime. He must go up to put his head on the block, and there is great excitement, but just at the moment when his head should be cut off, he looks up and sees the white bird approaching. That gives him courage, and he seizes the sword and kills the executioner. A loud cry goes up from the people, but at the same moment the sea breaks in a great wave, bringing a horse which halts before him. He has just time to mount and ride away before everyone is engulfed by the sea, and he hears their cries as they drown.

The next chapter is "The Call." Melchior still has the sound of the cries of the drowning people in his ears. He goes up a mountain, where he finds a little river. He drinks from its cold water, after which he feels quieter, as though he has been freed from the nightmare. The horse has disappeared, but he sees a white bird again, and follows it. He still feels that there is an abyss behind, which seems to be following his every step, but it never quite reaches him. The night is cold. Suddenly, he hears a wolf barking.

How would you psychologically interpret the problem of the judgment? You see quite clearly that, from a literary standpoint, this is judgment after death. It gives the idea of what we think will take place after death. The people who appeared were people who were still living, like his wife and Mrs. Cux, who, we presume, are still alive. But there are also a number of dead people, so the living and dead are together, and they look like half-decayed corpses. What would that mean? What is now approaching? What is the accusation? This is a fatal turning point in the story, so it is very important that it should be realized.

Answer: That he has not been related to anybody.

Yes, exactly. Now the unconscious catches up with him and the general reproach is unrelatedness. He has not worn the slippers his wife embroidered; he has not looked at his colleague's work. It is complete, cold narcissism, which from the very beginning has been Melchior's disease; his absolute unrelatedness. We said before that with the lack of the differentiation of the anima and without any relationship to the feminine principle, there could be no Eros and no relatedness. The essence of the whole reproach is unrelatedness, but why are they all dead?

Answer: He did not keep them alive?

Yes, exactly. It is relatedness which gives life to things. If I am not related to someone, it is absolutely irrelevant if that person is alive or dead. A person to whom I am not related is as good as dead to me; there is no difference. All the people in his surroundings are dead. It is a whole dead world, so it can be said that they also represent his unlived life, for having escaped into complete intellectualism, he has not suffered in life. He has not lived a normal, human life, so that unlived life catches up with him. Going through the door is like going through to the unconscious, and the first thing which comes up is the realization of all the unlived life which he has not lived because he had no feeling. How would you therefore interpret the fact that he escapes his executioner?

Answer: It is a moment of realization and a determination to act for once.

You would evaluate it positively?

244

Answer: Well, he kills the executioner, doesn't he?
Yes, and do you think that is positive? What does execution by cutting off the head mean symbolically?
Answer: He could not think anymore.
Yes, it would mean cutting off the intellect. Do you think it would be a good thing that he escapes that?
Answer: It gives him another chance.
Answer: (from a different person): No, he should go through with it!
Yes, he should go through with it. What would the white bird be, therefore?
Answer: The spirit.
Yes, a spiritual attitude. That is the typical trick of the intellectual, onto whom all the unlived life and all the betrayed feeling relationships fasten, giving him a terrific sense of guilt; he then makes a clever *tour de passe-passe* with a spiritual or intellectual explanation—and escapes again. For example, he may say that these are mere feelings of inferiority or of guilt, which he must overcome. In fact, this is the explanation that von Spät gives. Melchior falls into the clutches of von Spät, who says, "Thank God you did not fall for those judges! Thank God you freed yourself from the wrong feelings of guilt." That is what the intellect calls it. We know that there are pathological and morbid feelings of guilt and that some-times one has to push them off. There is a kind of wrong conscience which tortures people to death; in women, it is generally the animus, and in men, the mother anima, that initiate such feelings. So it is a very mixed problem, because having the apple woman in it and all these feelings of guilt puts a little bit of the mother-anima poison in it. What would that mean? How does it look in practical life if people fall into that state? What does it mean if they suddenly realize their unrelatedness and the guilt they have piled up by unrelatedness, and then the apple woman comes in and it becomes so dramatic?
Answer: The anima does not want any further consciousness. She wants to keep him where he is.
Yes, and she does that by a terribly exaggerated emotional upsurge that bathes him in feelings of guilt. This is also illustrated by the red-velvet hangings and the childishly dramatic performance in which he is guilty of God knows what. That is the wrong kind of *mea culpa* (my guilt), combined with true guilt, making a mix-up of genuine guilt and a hysterical, exaggerated guilt realization, which is

just another kind of inflation of evil: "I am the greatest sinner. Nobody is as abject as I. I have done everything wrong in my life"—and so on. That is inflation; it is simply swinging over into the opposite. There is a beautiful hint of this inflation of guilt, or inflation of blackness, in the cloak which is nailed onto him. What does that remind you of?

Answer: The cross.

Yes. Before Christ was crucified, a royal-red garment was put on him because he was accused of pretending to be the King of the Jews; so they put a scarlet robe on him and a crown of thorns, and mocked him. That is a parallel. Only here, the garment is black and the execution is that of beheading, which is symbolic, because he had to be "de-intellectualized." The garment is not the realization of his royal nature but of his black nature. It is a kind of reversed crucifixion. But the destructive or poisonous aspect of it is the exaggeration; namely, the idea of feeling like a negative Christ: "I am the greatest sinner in the world and am now suffering for my sins." The royal garment of sin! There is the inflation. What about the nails in the flesh? They nailed the black cloak on him, and that causes the suffering.

Answer: It's like being nailed to the cross, isn't it?

Yes, it is an allusion to the crucifixion of Christ, but with a variation, for it is the wrong kind of identification. I can give you an interesting parallel in the dream of a woman who had tremendously impressive visions and because of that, was very much estranged from reality. She had an urge to exteriorize all this inner material by telling it, but afterwards, she had the experience, common to many people after telling their great inner experiences, of being empty, deflated—now I have told it all and am empty. This is because by telling the inner experience, one disidentifies, and just a miserable human being is left who says, "Yes, and now what?" As long as it remains an inner secret, one is filled with it. According to her dream, it was right for her to tell and to be separated from her visions, but then she dreamed that a monument was shown her— the figure of a naked man with an enormous nail going through his shoulder and coming out at the hip, and a voice said, "Lazarus was dead, and Lazarus is alive again." She asked me what this nail meant and I could not figure it out. I remembered vaguely something about the thorn in the flesh of St. Paul, but my knowledge of the Bible was not good enough to get it at once. So I said merely that in St. Paul there is something about a thorn in the flesh. I thought it a strange motif and looked it up in the Bible, and in *II Corinthians 12:7*, St. Paul says, "Because I have such great revelations I have this thorn in the flesh, so that I should not boast (I am putting it in ordinary language)—so that I should not boast of my revelations, God has put a thorn in my flesh and the angel of Satan is standing in front of me, beating me down." So, you see, the thorn in the flesh would be the reverse experience of being inflated. If I have great visions, if I have inner revelations and identify with them, then I get a thorn in the flesh to remind me constantly of my inferiority, my meanness and my human incompleteness. That is how St. Paul put it. With this woman, it was the same thing. Through her inner experience, she got a tremendous inflation, and this last dream was an effort to show her that the great inner experiences she had were, in another way, also a wound, a constant torture—something that made her incomplete and wounded. You could even say that those revelations *are* the thorns in her flesh.

Here we have the same motif, which again indicates that there is a tremendous inflation of the feeling of guilt. You know that when some people go off their heads, they say they are Christ, while others say that they caused the First World War. There is not much difference between the two! It is megalomania, this way or that, and sometimes it switches: one minute they will say that they caused the First World War; two minutes later, that they are the savior of the world. Once they have crossed the threshold, those two inflations are one and the same, and that is only the extreme case of something you always find on a minor scale when people have committed some sin. Either they pooh-pooh it intellectually or they bathe, in an emotional, childish way, in their sin—in order *not* to see their guilt—bathing with hysterical pleasure in one's sins and feeling so awful that everyone has to give comfort! That is a pathological reaction which is just an escape from the realization of the real guilt. Another aspect of the weakness of the feeling function in the author (or in Melchior) is this typical reaction of an intellectual when he is hit on his inferior feeling function, and because that becomes too painful and too insufferable, the white bird, a kind of spiritual elation, suddenly carries him out of himself by a trick.

Remark: I think it is so surprising that von Spät tells him to knock on the wall and Melchior naturally expects then to get to him, but instead . .

He does get to von Spät. You will see later that Melchior circles between the two worlds: the spirit world of von Spät and that of Fo—the world of the mother and the boys. This does not give the picture of a mandala but of an ellipse, because it is unbalanced, and the anima, which would make it round, is lacking. The mother would be an old figure like von Spät and the anima would be a young figure like Fo, and these two would make the circle complete. But these two poles are not there. Sometimes the apple woman turns up at one masculine pole and sometimes at the other, and the anima is not there at all. Together with the unrelatedness, this shows the complete deficiency of the feminine principle.

Von Spät says, "Knock on the wall!" He is always connected with the idea of stars, the firmament, music, spirituality, power and order. To von Spät belong: stars, firmament, music, spiritualization, ghosts, power and order. And to Fo belong: mother, trees, animals, and boys.

Melchior knocks on the wall and comes to the von Spät pole. He is first attacked by something else, and he always breaks away by means of the white bird. Then he comes to von Spät, who says, "You did very well, You broke through the feelings of guilt." so you see, the white bird is von Spät's messenger, and that would be the magic trick by which to get out of the feeling of guilt with a kind of false spirituality. You have just to do some yoga exercises or rebirthing, or something like that, and then you are free again. Von Spät is all for such tricks and compliments Melchior on his escape.

Remark: I don't see the importance of the slippers. I think the relationship might be under the slippers of one's wife!

To be sure, the slippers have a fatal implication, but on the other hand Sophie says, "I took a whole year to embroider them," which implies a lot of libido. Imagine embroidering for a whole year! It must have been *petit point* plus *petit point*, and she gave a lot of love to it. I don't see that Melchior would have been under the slipper, but simply to kick them away like that, after someone had worked a whole year for you, means being unrelated. If he had looked at the slippers, he would have said to himself that he must give some response to that feeling, but not get under her slipper. That would have created a conflict, because that is what women always do: they give genuine love and add a little power trap. That is exactly what the feminine problem is for man: usually there is a mixture of genuine love and devotion in women, and then a little left-handed power trick to put him in a box. His mistake is that he simply casts away the whole thing, and that is just what the *puer-aeternus* man often does. Because there is always a little power trick in the woman's love, he takes that as an excuse to reject the whole thing: all women are rotten—their love is nothing but putting one under the slipper, nothing but putting one into a box.

Cheap, sweeping statements such as these save the man the difficulty of asking every minute of the day, "Is this a trick or is it love?" Such statements show that the man is not up to that problem with women. If he is not conscious of his anima and his own Eros, he will always fall for tricks. For instance, he wants to go out, and his wife thinks that he might meet Mrs. So-and-So, in whom he is interested, so she pretends to have a headache and says, "Let's stay at home. I have a headache." But if he has a differentiated feeling function, he will sense that today this is a trick, and he therefore will say that *he* is going out, and that if she has a headache, *she* can stay at home. The next evening she has a real headache, and it is very unrelated if he says, "No, to hell with you, I am going out!" Only if a man has a differentiated Eros development can he find out whether a woman is playing a trick or whether it is the real thing, and that is exactly what men do not like to do. If a man takes a feeling problem seriously, he has to relate to what the woman does from minute to minute, and, on top of that, he must always be aware of whether it is power or real feeling, which are very close to each other in an unconscious woman.

If you are an analyst, the problem is the same: an analysand may bring you a tremendous amount of feeling, but, as Virgil says, "there is always a snake in the grass," which means that you are never quite sure what she is up to. But if you reject the whole transference on account of that, then you destroy the patient's feeling. If you cannot accept the real feeling in a transference, you are destructive to the analysand. On the other hand, if you fall for the transference, she or he will nicely put you in her or his pocket and make a fool of you. So whenever a man is confronted with the problem of relating to a woman, he has to perceive the difference between snake-in-the-grass tricks and genuine love, and he cannot discover that difference without possessing differentiated feeling. If he has that, he will smell a rat and know from the woman's voice that she is up to something, or from her eyes and her voice he will learn that it is feeling to which he must respond. But a man can learn that only by differentiating his anima for a long time, by dealing with her and with the problems of relationship. If he makes a principle of yes or no, then he is not capable of relating to women or of being an analyst.

Here, there is the either-or attitude. Melchior rejects women together with their slippers. Clearly, he is not a man who falls under the domination of his wife's slippers. He fought against that, and you remember the trick she played by not having his room heated so that he should be forced to come to her party. That is a typical feminine trick, but Melchior does not fall for it. He sees through such tricks, but he does not see that Sophie also loves him; he doesn't realize that, for a woman, the one does not exclude the other. For her, the two go together—she can love a man and yet play such tricks—and it is the man's task to discover from minute to minute which is which.

You will remember that Melchior, with the help of the white bird, escapes the big wave which drowns all his accusers and executioners. Then he walks up a mountain and slowly gets above the trees. Night comes, and he hears the howling of a wolf. In the light of the stars, he sees shadows; soon, a ring of wolves surrounds him. Terrified, he stops. Each time he moves, they snarl, but when he keeps perfectly still, they do not attack. So he sits there and does not know whether he has sat for hours or minutes. He looks towards the horizon where the sun is slowly rising up. At that moment, tears come to his eyes, and he sees the light coming and stretches out his arms towards it. The wolves disappear like clouds.

Towards midday, he walks into a fog that smells of mold and decay. He cannot see well, but he arrives at a kind of wooden fence. He goes into a courtyard overgrown with grass, in the middle of which is a tumbledown hut full of people with birdlike hooked noses and piercing eyes who are selling large, yellow mushrooms with green spots. The sun is shining on them, but a yellow mist rises from them and there is a strange smell. The little people say, "Please buy the mushrooms. They are the last. The earth is dissolving into mist, the sun rots. Buy mushrooms as long as there are any. The woods are dying, and the world is exploding. Bargains! Good bargains!" He turns faint in the mist and feels heavier and heavier. Still feeling the wounds from the black coat on his shoulders, he walks around among them. It looks as though the whole earth were covered with dirt and mold. He hears uncontrollable feminine laughter, and turns around and sees the old apple woman among the people, dancing completely naked and making indecent gestures. She too cries, "Buy mushrooms! Buy mushrooms! They are the last! Buy as long as there are any! The earth molds and the sun rots! The woods die! The world explodes! Bargains! Good bargains!" Then a handsome, sensuous-looking young woman who also makes indecent gestures and who is also quite naked, joins in. They surround Melchior more and more closely; he becomes terribly frightened and takes a knife and tries to kill them. But their blood changes into red mist, their wounds close, and they become alive again and laugh in a more and more cynical way. They seize him, and he shuts his eyes and sees a blue light within himself as if he had a vision of the cold sky with its stars and in the cold sky, an enormous body forming. He pulls himself out of the embrace of the women and tries to sing. His song is echoed a thousandfold until the music dies away. The lights go out and it is daytime again. He is standing in front of a glacier and sees a kind of crystalline building in the distance and von Spät standing in front of him. That whole hellish dream of the mushrooms has disappeared.

Von Spät says to him, "You have found the way. Now you are one of us. You have escaped the judgment of human beings. You have overcome the greed of the animals, and you have banished the vengeance of the decaying earth. Now you serve the stars, and you are master over human beings (the power principle), animals, and the earth. Come, and we will crown you as one of our brothers."

Instead of pleasure, Melchior feels as if something deadly cold were creeping toward him, but von Spät takes his hand and leads him away. "Night and chaos are overcome," says von Spät. "Sleep has no power anymore. It is daytime always and light all the time, except when you go down onto the earth to appear to sleeping people like a ghost." Then Melchior comes to a crystalline castle which is built like a mandala, with a round roof, but the cold is terrible. Von Spät tells him that he must wait until he is called and that his staff is there on the table beside him. (The staff is like a magician's wand and is decorated with pearls arranged as letters.) Melchior leans against a pillar and realizes it is made of ice. The room is empty. He takes the staff in his hand, and his clothes fall away from him. The wounds on his shoulders close and heal. He no longer notices the cold. A door opens slowly and he goes into a big open place filled with bright figures, their bodies like glass and their eyes like blue stones. On a big pedestal is a crown. Bells ring, and everything vibrates in harmonious music.

At one side he sees a group of petrified, immobilized boys, their heads hanging down. One of the glass people orders two of them to come forward, and with stiff movements they go up and take a shining crown, which they lift up in the light. Melchior moves toward them. The ringing of the bells ceases. At the moment, he feels lost and alone. Then the eyes of one of the boys meets his, and he gets a terrific shock, for they are the eyes of Fo. He then realizes that the boys belong to Fo's group. They have been caught by their enemy, Ulrich von Spät, and are immobilized and petrified. He thinks, "I am going to become as rigid as they! What have I done? I have betrayed those to whom I belong and for whom I have longed and waited all my life. They came to fetch me for their group, and now I have betrayed them to the enemy. I aɪ. [and this is the important sentence] shattering life. I am breaking life apart." With horror, he suddenly looks around while the two boys who have to offer him the crown approach him. He feels a terrible shudder go through him when they hold the crown towards him, and then he hears a soft voice whispering, "Don't you want to go away from here? Don't you want to run away?" It is Fo's voice. At this, Melchior comes alive again and thinks, "He is here! Fo is here!" For a moment, he hesitates, for von Spät is looking at him threateningly. But then he throws out his arms and says, "I want to go away, I want to go away." At the same moment, he feels the arms of the boys seizing him; somebody kisses him on the lips and everything vanishes. The wind blows warm. He feels as though he were sinking down in the warm air. He opens his eyes and comes back to consciousness in a meadow. The moon is shining and innumerable fireflies dance in the summer air. He sees Fo's face bending over him, and smiling, falls into a deep sleep.

After having fallen into the half-right, half-wrong feelings of guilt and then having pulled away from them into a kind of wrong spiritualization, he falls into the pack of wolves. How would you interpret this psychologically? First, the feeling of guilt because he missed the experience of love with the other sex and has missed life, and now the wolves.

Answer: The wolf is an attribute of the witch and in its negative aspect denotes the devouring mother.

Yes, in some variations of the fairy tale, Mother Holle has a wolf's head. Mother goddesses and witches often have a wolf's head of iron, and it does sometimes denote the devouring mother.

Question: This would be the opposite of the extreme spiritualization, wouldn't it? It would be the other side.

Yes. One could say that whenever a man escapes the whole problem of relationship by a wrong kind of spiritualization, he is still in the clutches of the devouring mother, and, what is much worse, he turns all the women in his surroundings into devouring mothers. What else can happen? If he doesn't relate, he can only be eaten! That is naturally the wrong thing, but it is a kind of involuntary and automatic reaction in a woman. The more the man refuses to accept relatedness, the more she feels that she has to imprison him, catch him, eat him up, forbid him to move around. So he calls up the devouring mother in every woman, and then it is a vicious circle. He is disappointed because every woman turns out to be a devouring wolf. Then he says, "There you are! That is what I always said," and walks out on the woman. Actually, his flightiness has constellated her devouring side, and for this reason he is caught in the vicious, destructive circle again. Because he does not relate, she comes with her trap and a box to put him in. Because he has no love, he summons her power complex.

So you can say that a man with that attitude towards feeling finds the devouring mother everywhere within and without. That would be the wolf. But beyond that, the wolf has not only feminine witch qualities in mythology. There are other aspects: for instance, in the Etruscan tombs, the god of death has a wolf's head or a wolf's cap. The Greek Hades was also very often represented with a cap on which was the head of a wolf, so it is also the abyss of death, thought of as being a kind of devouring jaw, eating people up. The wolf stands—not only in women but also in men—for this kind of drivenness in wanting to have things without any further purpose. Dr. Jung says that among the strongest drives with which we are confronted when we open the door of the unconscious are the power drive, the sex drive, and then something like a hunger which just wants to eat and assimilate everything without any reason or meaning. It is that which always wants more and more. If you invite such people to supper, they are not pleased but simply furious when you don't invite them again next week. If you give a tip, they are not grateful, for the next time if you don't give them more, they say, "What? only a franc?" The worst are those who in early childhood have been starved of love. They go about pale and bitter with a "nobody-loves-me" expression, but if one makes a kind gesture, there is no appreciation, only the desire for more, and if you don't give more, then they are furious and enraged. You could go on and on and pour the whole world into such an open mouth—and it wouldn't help. You could throw everything in; you could be up nursing them night and day, give them all your money, do anything you like—they would never find it enough. It is like the abyss of death: the mouth never shuts; there is only the demand for more. It is a kind of driven passion of eating and eating, and it generally results from an early childhood experience where the child was starved and deprived of love or of some other vital need on the psychological and physical level. One can only say no whenever such greed comes up, because there is no end to it. It is a divine-demonic quality. It is that thing which says, "More! Still more! Still more and more!"

The wolf, therefore, belongs also to Wotan in Germanic mythology. One of his names is "Isengrim" (iron grim), which really means iron head, but it has also been interpreted in folklore as "grim, cold rage," and the wolf very often stands for a kind of cold, hidden resentment. Most people who had a very unhappy childhood have something like this at the bottom of their souls. It never comes up. It is something absolutely frozen and cold, a form of petrified rage, and that is also behind the demand for more and more: "the others owe me everything." If one has to deal with orphans or children who have grown up in a "home" and have been beaten a lot, one can generally see the wolf very clearly. But naturally, it is not confined to them alone. Many others have this kind of wolf quality in them. Melchior has been frustrated from early childhood. We know that his mother was a weak, sickly woman, who did not look after him, that in early childhood he was so lonely that he saw his double at the window, and that he had to play alone. We know that he did not grow up in a warm, instinctually healthy atmosphere. So this is a typical case of such a situation, and in him there is this greed and the constant longing to have more.

After having overcome his half-right and half-wrong hysterical feeling of guilt, he nows fall into this new trap, and again, he gets out of it by longing for the light. When he stretches out his arms for the light, the wolves disappear, so he does not really deal with the problem; he falls into it, and then, by an enantiodromia, when the night turns again into day, comes out of it. He falls into that state without realizing what it means; by the grace of God, he gets out of it again. Naturally, nothing is worked out at all in such a case. It sinks again into the night, and the next situation in life will bring it up again. Some people who have this wolf problem have some conscious idea that this greed of wanting more and more and eating everybody and everything is mad and unreasonable, so they don't let it out. They behave very politely and never ask for more, but you always suspect that it is just correctness which keeps the starving wolf in a cage. Such people then suddenly fall into the wolf and come out with terrific and impossible demands which cannot be fulfilled. If you want to discuss it analytically, they will tell you of a very interesting dream instead, and the wolf side is just gone again. I may say, "Listen, I am sure you are furious because I could not do what you wanted when you rang me up, and I think we ought to talk about that." But they reply that that is quite all right, they quite understood. The wolf has gone into the woods again, although you know that nothing has been settled. It would be much better for that person to make a terrific scene, and then we could deal with it and talk about it. But it has all crumbled away, and if you then artificially, on account of the dream, say that now they should come out with it, you will get the reply, "But I know it is unreasonable. I know you have no time. I know I should not have asked it of you." So the wolf has disappeared, but without being transformed. That is what happens in the story. Melchior gets into and walks out of it, and the next step is the same thing with those moldy mushrooms and those sensuous women dancing around, saying that the earth is now being destroyed. How would you interpret this motif?

Answer: The Great Mother and her dactyls or Cabiri.

Yes, is the Great Mother with her primitive Cabiri adherents, but how would you interpret the mushrooms? They say the wood is decaying. The wood is a mother symbol, but what is this? You have the feeling that here is Great Mother Nature, but what about it?

Answer: She is not sane.

Yes, it is unhealthy nature, sickly nature. It is morbid, and there is also morbid sensuality.

Remark: It is very probable that the last thing we shall see on the earth is a mushroom!

That is quite possible. There is an area where the mushroom now plays a role that is invading our world; namely, in the new drugs, some of which are made from some kind of fungus. This is invading psychiatry, and it is now hoped that a chemical cure for schizophrenia will be found. It is indeed quite possible that this can be done, because any kind of over-emotional state causes intoxication. We believe that there is a certain condition of intoxication in schizophrenia, so naturally, you can eliminate these results with chemicals. The snag is, however, that if you analyze people after they have been treated with these drugs, you find that the psychological problem which brought about the schizophrenic episode is not removed. All the morbid emanations of the problem—that people behave in a mad way and rave, and other symptoms—these things you can stop with the drug, but analysis shows that the basic problem remains unchanged. If you do not use psychotherapy at this point, the patient is just headed for another episode and the drug will have to be given again. This process can be continued endlessly. After such a partial cure with drugs, a series of dreams will point out the danger of a counter-tendency—of saying that now I can continue with my wrong attitude, and the next time I go off my head, I will just ask for another pill. The worst thing about the drugs is that they even have a demoralizing effect with people of weak character. Such people do not want to change their attitude, for it is much easier to go on with it; if a psychotic episode occurs and they fall into the unconscious, they can have a drug to get out of it again—so it is all right! They do not want to return to psychotherapy because the other is the easy way, but it results in constant relapses and more drugs.

It is a shortcut to eliminate certain very dangerous conditions, but one pays for the shortcut, because it undermines the confidence of the patient in being able to pull out through his own moral effort. It undermines his belief in himself and naturally makes him forever dependent on the doctors who always have to give the pill at the right moment. Those are the pros and cons for using these remedies.

Remark: In my observation, there is something which goes dead in the personality. It's like a loss of soul.

Not always, if the drug has not been used over a long period. I have seen cases where that has not happened. Only belief and confidence have been lost, not the soul. It might go dead if the episode has already progressed very far and remedies have been used very much, but not necessarily. Confidence dies, however, and that is the danger.

Remark: We don't really know whether it might not, in some cases, be better in the long run for the person to go crazy.

That is naturally a question of the ultimate *Weltanschauung*, and there we come to the end of a discussion, for you have to make up your own mind as to whether you want to help people to become mad.

Remark: Nature brings it about.

Well, I think it is a dangerous attitude to say, "Oh well, there are people who are just good enough to go mad, so let them! That is how nature removes useless individuals." There you come just as well in physical medicine into the problem of euthanasia, where you say, "Oh well, let's kill off the old people and the morons," and so on.

Remark: I did not mean it quite so negatively as that, but I have seen one or two cases in which the patients were forced into a kind of sanity by these drugs to which I would think madness was preferable.

Yes, certainly, but that is not sanity. That is this kind of personal existence, like a whitened tomb, which simply enables people to be less socially disagreeable. In their social behavior they are more tolerable, except that nothing has been changed and they are just as mad as before. I have heard the confession of such a person. She had been changed into such a white persona, but later when her madness came back, and with it, her better part, she said, "I was mad all the time. It was only covered up. I had a pseudo-adapted behavior." That is not a cure, that is only banging people into socially adapted behavior, so that they may be less disturbing, which is naturally useful for the doctor. It is a self-defense mechanism of the doctor, really.

Remark: I think if we don't use the drugs too long that the effect is reversible. But also, what seems to be a loss of soul is really an abasement of the emotional level. When asked, they all say that the hallucinations and other experiences of the psychotic stage are still there, but that they do not experience the emotional part so strongly.

Yes. In a case where there was a lobotomy, the person told me that she always felt that the madness was still there. She used a metaphor and said, "It was in the cellar, but it could not come up the stairs anymore." She was carefully living in the upper story, and the madness was one story lower, which would be exactly what you describe. The emotional problem is not solved; it is only removed. There is a certain distance between it and the person, and in this case, the operation had the same effect; it simply means cutting off the overly strong emotion. If people fall into too strong an emotion, they generally switch to the opposite pole of being too reasonable afterwards. Then they have a secret homesickness for their former emotional madness, because to be emotional and mad is to experience the plenitude of life. You are never as fully alive as when you are mad. It is a kind of peak of life! If you are not mad enough to have experienced that, then just remember some time when you were absolutely madly in love, or in a mad rage. What a wonderful state of affairs that is! Instead of being that broken human being, always fighting between emotions and reason, you are for once whole! For instance, if you let out your rage, what a pleasure! "I told that person everything! I didn't keep back anything!" You feel so honest, and whole, for you haven't been polite; you've said everything! That is a divine state, absolutely divine, and it is a divine state to love in that way, where there is no doubt anymore. She—or he—is everything! Divine, complete trust! No safeguards against the failure of the other fellow human! None of that distrust that everybody has toward everybody else, but instead, "We are one! We are one! And the stars dance around us!" It is a state of totality. And the next morning, she has a pimple on her nose, and the whole thing collapses! You are out of the total state. But emotion creates the experience of being totally in something, whatever emotion it is. That is why if one makes people too normal, then they are adapted, but they do not feel total anymore and secretly, they long to return to their madness. So it is no solution, and then one has to swing back again into the emotion and try to get the two poles together. The reasonableness and the emotionality must both be lessened.

The opposites must unite, like the opposites in our book where pure emotion is represented by the boy Fo, and order and reason by von Spät. The author of the book is torn between these two. At one end, everything is order, but rigid; it is that over-adaptation you get from drugs. The excess of reasonableness that people have after an episode is a form of madness. It is mad to be as coldly reasonable as that, and the opposite is another form of madness. If you cannot keep in the middle between the two, you are lost, which is exactly the tragedy of the book. If you take it on a political level, you see

the same thing everywhere: mad mass-psychosis-emotional movements where people go around with either a Celtic cross or a
Swastika or whatever it may be, raving in emotion and feeling
whole. It is so wonderful to walk in thousands through the streets,
just howling, for then you feel whole and human. But then there are
the police and order, business order, the law, and all the rest, which
is von Spät. Then you regress into what is called the restitution
after revolutions, in which everything is in order, but power
dominates. People are deadly bored and think how nice it would be
if they could go back into the chaos of revolution, where at least life
flowed. You see more and more how nations switch between those
two poles, just as individuals do. Groups do the same everywhere,
and that is why we have to deal with the problem. It is urgent just
now. For instance, those people behind the barricades in Algeria[30]
with their Celtic mandala cross, have practically no plan! I am sure
that most of those young people just enjoy the plenitude of life,
feeling whole and heroic and themselves, without any further
thought. They look as though they were moved by a totality of
emotion of some kind, and then that switches to the boredom of
order. And what can you do with that? The order of von Spät is
cold!

[30]Lecture delivered February 17, 1960.--ED.

CHAPTER TWELVE

You will remember that von Spät nearly won out last time, and that Melchior was already in his glass-and-ice kingdom and on the point of being crowned when he suddenly realized that he was getting into a prison. Saying he wanted to go away, he broke his bond, thereby freeing Fo, who took him with them.

They come to a meadow lit by moonlight. It is warm and the atmosphere is beautiful. They dance around, singing, and one of the boys throws a spear at Fo, hitting him in the heart. Fo pulls it out of his chest, and from the open wound flows a great stream of water— not blood—from which all the boys drink. As the flow decreases, Fo becomes smaller and thinner, until he collapses. His whole body turns into a kind of mist which becomes transformed into waves of sound. The stream dries up; the exhausted boys sink back onto the grass and fall asleep with their eyes open. From their foreheads comes a glowing mist. The mist turns into circles which float higher and higher, eventually forming one great ball of mist which whirls round the moon in ever-narrowing rings, at last melting into it. The moon increases in size and, after a pause, sinks to the earth, splitting up into dustlike rays of light. Fo appears, coming out of the rays, and touches all the sleeping boys, who spring up, once more alive and laughing. They surround Melchior and welcome him to their group, but they tell him now he must be crucified. Unfrightened, he accepts the ultimatum. A crown of thorns is put on his head, from which he feels only a slight faintness but no pain. Then they crucify him. The nails in his hands and feet, the text says, feel like cold shadows, and his whole body, like a light shadow. He hangs. . .

"a shadow on the shadow of a cross, high between heaven and earth, his face turned towards the rising sun." But he sees nothing, for heaven and earth disappear. The first rays of the sun strike his chest and tear open his body, from which the blood rushes in a mighty stream, dividing into innumerable little rivers which lose themselves in the earth. He realizes that he is no longer hanging on the cross, but has become one with it, and that it has become an enormous tree. From his outstretched arms grow many branches; his hair waves in the wind, his head grows larger and larger, and his roots penetrate deep into the earth, from which flow springs of water. He hears the sound of a flute and sees Fo playing in the shade of the tree. The whole troupe dances around and fades away; already, some of the boys are flying, as big birds in the sunlight, and they nest in his hair. Many animals surround him, and more and more come: leopards, stags, wolves, bears, and foxes—they come from all parts of the forest.

A cry breaks from Melchior, and he becomes a boy like the others. Fo still plays the flute and together they sing, "All animals return to the Garden of Eden." As the song comes to an end, Fo puts aside his flute and takes Melchior's hand, saying, "You had a name. Do you still know it?" Melchior tries to think but he cannot remember, and he says he does not know. He asks if he had been asleep and has just forgotten his dream. Fo says that they all had other names before they were crucified, but now they will take him in their group and give him a new name; it will not be his true name, however, for that he will only hear when he comes to the kingdom.

"Which kingdom?" Melchior asks.

Fo answers, "Our kingdom! That's where we are at home. There, we play round the old fountains and drink of the holy waters, and there, in black mirrors, we see everything we have lived. From the dark surfaces (of the mirror) arise thousands of forms which we leave behind when we enter the kingdom and which we have to resume when we begin to wander again." (A very important remark!)

Melchior asks, "And why have we to wander about?" (Notice that this question is not answered.)

"Don't you want to be everywhere? To be the wind and the rain, the trees and the grass? Don't you want to be a part of the sunset and to melt into the moon? Don't you want to be every animal, and every human? To speak out of every mouth and see out of each eye? We escape into and out of every figure. Wherever we appear, everything changes into a whirlwind, and nothing is durable."

"But when do we get to the kingdom?" Melchior asks again.

"Today or tomorrow, or in innumerable years. What does time matter? We can suddenly stand at the crossroads, and one of the roads leads to the kingdom, or it stretches out into faraway golden shores beyond great waters. Or we open the door in a strange house—and have arrived. Everywhere, we can stand at its borders, but till then we must wander. If we stop, we shall never get there."

"And where are we going now?"

"On and on," says Fo, his eyes shining, "and immediately in front of us is a big city, and when we leave it, our group will have grown bigger. And in that city no one will know anymore . . . But you must have a name. Who should give it to you? He from whom you receive your name, he is your partner if the group scatters."

Melchior looks long at Fo and then asks, "Do you want to come with me?"

And Fo answers, "Yes, we have saved each other, so we will stay together."

He then beckons the boys who circle around and says solemnly, "You shall be called Li!"

"Li! Li! Li!" the boys cry.

This is the anticlimax. In the previous chapter, Melchior was almost completely caught in von Spät's kingdom, but with a tremendous enantiodromia, it turned into the opposite. Now he is in the kingdom of von Spät's enemy: Fo's kingdom. The first part of this chapter reveals who Fo is. We know that he is the leader of the boys and that his name points to Buddha; that Fo advocates eternal wandering in karmic incarnations, whereas Buddha teaches escape from the karma of incarnation, from the wheel of rebirth. Fo, on the other hand, considers endless incarnations a pleasure. Moreover, since he turns into the moon and then returns to earth after having been wounded, he is also a moon god—a moon god and the god of running water. When his chest is cut open, a spring of life flows, rather than blood; it is specifically stated that a white stream comes forth and that this water revivifies all those who drink it.

Earlier, we saw from an allusion that von Spät is associated with the old sun—Sol Niger, Saturn. In old sun-god mythology, he would correspond to the Greek Kronos; in medieval alchemical mythology, to Saturn. We deduced this from the fact that he danced with the seven girls, who would represent the seven planets surrounding the sun god. Fo, the opposite principle to the sun, is, logically, the moon god; the god of night, of sleep, of the irrational, of eternal change—naturally with a latent feminine tinge. And it must not be forgotten that in German, the moon is masculine (der Mond), while in Roman mythology, it was hermaphroditic and was worshipped as both a male and a female figure. This hermaphroditic aspect of the soul shows that the symbol of the Self and the symbol of the anima are not yet separated. Fo represents the unconscious in its feminine and masculine personifications. He is the principle of the night—the other side of the light of consciousness.

I have been asked to compare this book with Saint Exupéry's *The Little Prince* to show the difference between German and French mentality. Unfortunately, I can only do this very briefly, but one of the characteristics would be that on the other side of the Rhine—in Germany—the symbol of the anima is not as clearly differentiated. Practically the only feminine figures in this book are the apple woman (the Mother-Nature figure), Sophie, who is a very negative and also a rather maternal figure, and the pale anima girl, Henriette Karlsen, who dies almost before she appears on the scene. The powerful soul figure is a hermaphroditic being—namely, Fo, the moon god. If you compare him with the soul figure in Saint Exupéry's book—the couple on the asteroid, the rose and the little prince—the hermaphroditic aspect is at least differentiated into a couple, and the anima is differentiated one step further, although she is still a rather negative feminine figure, both haughty and hysterical. She has not progressed much, but at least she is separate from the symbol of the Self and appears as an independent being. The national differences are strongly contrasted in the two books. The German book gives the impression of a more archaic, more powerful symbolism and a much greater dynamism. The reader is pulled into an emotional, dynamic atmosphere with a hysterical, exaggerated tone which is not entirely agreeable. If we look at the negative factors, the French book is suffused with cruelty and childish sentimentality, in contrast to the dynamism and hysterical exaggeration of the German book.

Two assumptions can be made to account for this difference: first, that the pagan, pre-Christian layer in France is more Celtic; while in

Germany, it is Germanic (you can read about the difference between the Celtic and the Germanic character in Caesar and in Tacitus); and that—and perhaps this is even more important—France was thoroughly Romanized before it became Christian (as were southern Germany and Austria to some exent, and Switzerland too), whereas Germanic heathendom was directly covered over by Christian conversion along the line of the Main River. In the Mediterranean realm, Christianity was the end product of a long civilizing development, and therefore became a spiritual and differentiated religious form. On the basis of the Roman civilization, it was possible for people to understand the Christian symbolism; therefore, wherever Christianity was super-implanted on a Romanized background, the possibility of a transition existed, whereas in areas where Romanization was lacking, the historical continuity of evolution was interrupted and Christianity superseded something very different. Using a metaphor, you could say that north of the Main, people have "a hole in the staircase"—a lower story, an upper story, and in the middle, an open space. This situation is not only typical of Germany: it will arise soon (and it will be a much greater problem) in Christianized Africa, where it is already creating a terrific tension and restlessness, quite apart from the other cultural and economic problems. Africans who have been Christianized have the same hole in the stairs.

The problem also exists among the Americans who fell, when they went to the West as pioneers into a primitive civilization; namely, that of the American Indians. Survival in that primitive environment could only be achieved by becoming as tough and as primitive as the natives; on the other hand, the pioneers had a Victorian Christian past, and this explains why the North Americans have, in many way, the same hole in the stairs (or a variation of it) that the Germans have.

Such a hole is not only a disadvantage, however; the advantage it gives the personality is a tremendous dynamism and great efficiency. The inner polarity and the inner tension which such a cultural inner situation creates make people dynamic, efficient, and active. It can be said that if the electric plus and minus poles are very far apart and very strong, then the electricity is also much greater; it creates more dynamic and more active personalities, with the drawback of a certain tendency towards hysterical dissociation and a marked tendency to dissociate easily in mass movement, mass influences, and

264

so on, the nucleus of the personality and its balance being more easily disturbed. It is well known that in Africa, for instance, Christian converts among the Negroes are partly a very suspicious, unreliable, and unpredictable lot. Years ago—I don't know if it is now so—the whites in Africa always preferred to have unconverted heathen servants because they were much more solid and reliable people. The others had this strange kind of constellation of polarity between a kind of culturally highly developed consciousness and a very archaic, unconscious part of the personality, with all the problems that that creates.

Naturally, this hole in the stairs—now going back to a comparison of the French and German mentalities—is only relative, for the French have the same problem, but on a minor scale. It could be said to be only relatively different, and naturally when you make such sweeping statements about nations, there are innumerable exceptions; this is just an attempt to characterize it in a general way.

Question: Would the fact that the author comes from Riga and that he is a Latvian influence the whole concept?

The fact that he is from northern Germany, or a Latvian, would make it even worse, since it would mean having no home, but rather having widespread Roman (underground), Russian and Slavonic influences. In northern Germany there is already a strong Slavonic influence, which is why there is a kind of secret hostility between north and south.

The crucifixion of Melchior is very revealing. One sees that Fo really represents the return of the archetypal figure, which is also behind the figure of Christ, in an older form. If we try to compare Fo with other gods, one could say that he was closer to Dionysus. Wherever Fo appears in the book, roses and grapes are mentioned, so he is a kind of return to Dionysus. This crucifixion in which the crucified person turns into a tree reminds us of Attis, who was turned into the maternal tree. One could therefore say that in giving himself to Fo, Melchior becomes "attified" or turned into an Attis; since all the others had gone through the same fate, they seem to consist of people who had first lived an earthly life and then were crucified and turned into those eternally wandering boys. The myth of Attis is repeated in each one of them. As we know, Dionysus and Attis represented the early-dying son god, the son of the mother, the god who dies in the spring. The date of the Feast of Easter has been taken over from the Feast of Attis, and mosaics were executed in ancient Rome with the cross with grapes around it and an invocation, "O thou, Dionysus, Jesus Christ," so that at the beginning, at least, there was considerable doubt as to whether Christianity did not mean a repetition of Dionysus—or of Attis—but in another form. The Church fathers tried to make a definite cut to establish Christianity, hoping in this way to prevent the new symbol from being sucked back again into a past (which would have implied a victory for von Spät). To make sure of its creative *élan*, the newly converted Christians were emphatic in contending that Christianity was entirely different from the cult of Dionysus, but the similarity of the archetypal figure was so striking that everyone felt very doubtful, which accounts for such stress being laid on the fact that Jesus Christ was a historical personality, in contrast to the archetypal god figure.

To return to the cultural problem: if, therefore, Fo returns in the form of Attis or Dionysus, he could be said to represent an attempt by the unconscious to create an archetypal experience which would bridge the gulf created by this sudden Christianization. One might think that, having passed through this experience, the author might now really understand what the figure of Christ means. If you sweep away all the accumulated historical dust, you see that this is a return to the original experience of what it means to take the cross upon oneself; to carry it and be crucified with Christ—only there is a different shade of something more ecstatic and more dynamic and, in an archaic way, vital. It is an attempt of the unconscious to recreate the Christian symbol and to revive it in a form in which it is linked again with the deeper layers of the personality. How widespread and how vital this problem is can be seen by the fact that the one finds the same attempt of the unconscious in a completely different sphere. Those among you who heard my lecture on Niklaus von der Flüe will remember that there, Christ appears with a bearskin—as a Berserk—and there too, it is an attempt not to abolish the symbol of Christ, but to reinterpret it, linking it with the archaic layers of the instinctive psyche. Only if we understand it in this more complete form can the symbol of Christ survive, for if it is not anchored in the depths of the soul, it will be cast off, and there will be a return to atheism and neo-paganism in some form.

The same thing can be seen in Negro spirituals, which give a parallel phenomenon. In them can be found a pagan layer of the psyche, with its symbolic expressions and religious emotions. Upon that is put a Christian doctrine—just a lacquer which any kind of movement or antipropaganda would remove, unless the main archetype of this Christian doctrine, which in our civilization is called Christ, calls up a similar archetypal symbol, constellates it, and links with the whole emotional personality. Then it becomes a living faith, which means that people can only understand from within what Christ means in them personally. Otherwise, it is purely intellectual; there is the hole in the staircase and below, one still prays to Dionysus, or here, Wotan, because the one who is speared and who hangs on the world tree is Wotan.

In this book, the archetype constellated below is Wotan, as is naturally the case in a Germanic civilization. In France and those countries with a Celtic background, the archetype called up in this form is Mercurius-Kerunnus, a stag god. This is a god who is transformed and crucified, and who is the sacrificed sun god—the spring god and the resurrected god. In Celtic countries, it is the archetype of Kerunnus which is constellated behind the figure of Christ. In medieval legends—the legend of the Holy Grail and Celtic material in England, Ireland, and Wales—it is the archetype of Mercurius-Kerunnus, and in all those cases there is an attempt to link these superimposed figures of God with the old roots of the archaic and genuine inner experience of those people.

There are other motifs in the description of the kingdom of Fo, for he says, "We play around old fountains (which reminds one of the Germanic fountain of Urd at the base of the world tree) and we drink of the holy water. (If you drink from the fountain of Urd, you become a seer. The shamans and the medicine men drink from that fountain.) In black mirrors, we see what we were." Here, an Eastern influence is introduced which we already noticed before: the idea that in this kingdom you can mirror all former incarnations. We shall see later that the author believes in reincarnation, something he has taken over from his Eastern studies and blended into this German material. Since the Germanic races were, in general, on the introverted side, pre-Christian Germanic civilization was introverted and had an affinity with the Chinese and with Eastern spiritual life. There, Germanic runes (which we now believe to be the letters of the Germanic alphabet) were originally used as an oracle, as are the sticks of the *I Ching*; even later, they were still used in this way. For instance, when the Germans took prisoners, a certain number were slaughtered in honor of Wotan, for which purpose the captors "threw" the runes; that is, they took sticks on which they carved different runes, and if the specifically marked death rune lay on top, then that particular prisoner was one of those to be slaughtered or sacrificed, while the others were kept as servants or slaves. According to the myth, this technique of divination was invented by Wotan when he was speared—we do not know whether by himself or by another, but we must also remember the spear of Longinus in the case of Christ—and here, Fo is speared. Wotan then hung nine days and nine nights on the world tree, *Yggdrasil*, after which he discovered the runes at his feet as he bowed down. Therefore, one could say that the creative product of the long crucifixion was the discovery of the runes—a new manifestation of cultural consciousness which originally consisted in reading the moment of Fate. This also underlies the ideas at the back of the Chinese oracle, the *I Ching*, which is a way of exploring the way of Tao, a method of divination based on the principle of synchronicity.

Even nowadays, many people who have a Germanic racial background display a great affinity for the Eastern world; at present, there seems to be quite a widespread tendency in Germans to seek the healing of their problem—the wounds caused by the war—by turning to Eastern philosophy. This would mean finding a sufficiently introverted attitude with which to work out the problem from within, instead of from without. Naturally, the big economic boom now being experienced is very unfavorable for this, but all those who try to work out such problems turn to introversion and cling mostly to Eastern philosophy to help get into this attitude.

I once suggested to one of my analysands, a man from north Germany who was in the habit of consulting the *I Ching*, that he look at this problem in these forms. The night after I told him what I am now telling you, he dreamed that he was in front of Prussian military barracks. At the entrance was a shield with writing on it in Chinese signs and in Germanic runes, which shows that the unconscious at once picked up the suggestion as something very relevant. In Scandinavian mythology, the Trolls are also regarded as a manifestation of the principle of synchronicity. I do not want to go into that, but I would say that, from the north of the river Main, people, if they are creative, are more introverted and, like Eastern people, are more interested in synchronistic phenomena than in rational causality, as is the case with Western people. North of

Germany, there is a tendency, which you see more clearly in Russia, towards the great problem of uniting the Eastern and Western minds in a middle attitude. You know that in the so-called Pan-Slavonic movement, to which Dostoyevsky belonged, it was claimed that Russia was the chosen country which one day would be able to unite the introversion of the East with the efficiency and extroversion of the West. Just now, they have departed from that idea by becoming completely extroverted.

The kingdom is characterized here in a strange way, for it is partly the Garden of Eden, to which all the animals return, and partly the old paradise of the Germans, the fountain of Urd under the world tree; but it is also clearly influenced by Eastern ideas of the nirvana, where one finally escapes the eternal wandering from one reincarnation to another, except—which is interesting—that Fo and his band have not reached the kingdom and that they see a meaning in wandering, which is opposed to the Buddhist teaching, according to which one should escape the karmic wheel of reincarnation. This is a more Western tendency, and a rather fatal one; namely, the glorification of dynamic movement in itself, even if it has no goal. The exaltation of feeling psychologically alive and being in a creative movement with neither result nor goal is a dangerous, demonic aspect.

You will remember that I spoke of von Spät as being at one pole and Fo, at the other, with Melchior in the center. At first, von Spät was successful; then, with Fo and the crucifixion, came the enanti-odromia which is really Fo's victory, and later it turns the other way once more. Von Spät is fatal, because things are absolutely static at his pole, for once you are in the glass palace—in the spirit kingdom—nothing happens anymore. Everything becomes clear, glasslike, transparent and rigid. At Fo's end, however, there is an absolute glorification of the creative movement and ecstasy in itself, with the idea that creative ectasy has a meaning in itself, irrespective of whether there is any result. What is being taught is a constant continuation of emotion and creative ecstasy. We find this expressed in rock-and-roll dancing, which represents the enjoyment of psychic and physical dynamism and musical rhythm, with no further goal. When it is over, you are tired, and the next evening you start again, and that is, in itself, satisfactory. On von Spät's side is result without life movement, and at Fo's end, eternal movement without result. It is another extreme one-sidedness, with no union of the opposites. It is simply being torn between them.

von Spät Reason without life	Melchior (ego)	Fo Eternal movement without result
ice-north	Li (consciousness)	south

Healing could only occur if two other feminine poles had developed, because in a man's psychology the feminine, the anima principle, is the principle of reality and is also realization. That is lacking in this constellation.

I will now condense the middle part of the book.

Fo, his eyes shining, says that now they are going towards a city, and then he turns to give a name to Melchior (the name is "Li"— pattern, order, principle, consciousness—the thing that Melchior should provide). What follows is easy to understand and not very symbolic. It tells of the mischievous deeds of Fo and his band.

The story is that there was a town called Stuhlbrestenburg. *Bresten* is an old German word for disease, and *Stuhl* means either chair or excrement; here, it obviously means the latter, so it would mean "Excrement-Disease Town." In this town, it is said that there was once a big fire which practically destroyed it. The king of this town, who was of a whimsical turn of mind, had thought that the old walls should not be pulled down but that the burnt-out houses should be cut off at a certain level and left completely black as when they were burned; over them, a new town should be built on the foundations of the old one, but carried out in a very light and elegant rococo architecture. The king, Walter II, thought this very amusing, but the bad part of it was that in the subterranean area, a criminal world collected and connected all the cellars, one with another, so that the whole criminal underworld could communicate. From time to time, these people made a raid and robbed banks, etc., and then they hid again in the burnt-out black cellars. The police could never completely exterminate them, so that the bourgeoisie in the upper stories of the houses were constantly threatened by the others. The situation became aggravated when the police caught one of the chief criminals, who divulged information concerning the geographical network of the underworld, with the result that the police decided on a big coup to clean up the whole gangster setup. Of the townspeople, it was said that they worked hard, but that they lived at a terrific pace, both violently and greedily. Their factories, churches and pleasure houses—brothels and so on—were full of life, but the atmosphere was hot and a bit unclean; a kind of miasma rose up perpetually from the black walls below.

Trouble arose in the neighboring town of Rattenhausen (Rats-home) when a school teacher who had once done some wrong to a pupil, a romantic boy of the type of Otto von Lobe, suddenly had the hallucination that one of the boys in his class was this same boy whom he had wronged twenty years earlier, and the teacher fell on his knees in front of the boys, begging for pardon. It turned out that the boy, Ranke, of whom he was supposed to have begged forgiveness, was at this time at home in bed and had not been at school. The headmaster himself went to the boy's home and verified the fact. There was a great fuss and the teacher lost his job; the next morning, more than half the boys did not turn up in school and could not be found. The second result, which occurred practically at the same time, was that a very honorable banker, Mr. Rotbuch, was seized by a crazy idea at midday when the rest of the staff was absent. He opened a window on the first floor of the bank and threw all the money out onto the crowded marketplace, resulting in an indescribable tumult in which two people were killed and many were severely injured.

The banker was arrested and put in a lunatic asylum. When he regained control of himself, he said he did not know what had come over him, but he had seen two boys wearing turned-up collars and leather caps; they had come to him and told him to do this, and he had acted under a kind of compulsion. On the same day, the doors of the prison were found open, the wardens tied up in the henhouse, and the director of the prison, dressed in full uniform, was discovered flailing around with his arms and crowing like a cock. All the prisoners had disappeared and it was supposed that they had fled to Stuhlbrestenburg and joined the underground gangsters.

In the *Rattenhuser Bote*, a leading article appeared explaining the whole thing as a mass psychosis; saying that a group of shameless teenagers who had probably read too many stories by Sherlock Holmes, Karl Marx, and Alexander Dumas, had been poisoned in that way and had tried to seduce the people into following impossible ideas. It was all, it was said, the result of the haste and greed for new sensations which belonged to present-day life—what was a miracle yesterday was a daily event today—so that even sober people were no longer able to discriminate between the possible and the impossible. In such stormy times, the article continued, when everything is topsy-turvy, we can only advise our worthy fellow citizens to believe only in things which are officially confirmed, for we need something solid by which we can stand, and the only thing which remains firm is official sanction—*Sigillum Signum veri* (the seal of the State stands for truth). The principal officials recommended searching for the evildoers so that they might not bring about more harm and confusion, and the people should follow the Government's lead. *Caveant consules.* A psychiatrist, Mr. Hinkeldey, wrote another article on mass psychosis and warned against overwork, too much introversion, and too many fantasies. He recommended cold footbaths before going to bed and rubbing the whole body with a damp cloth on getting up in the morning!

In the next chapter, the same boys, wearing the turned-up collars and leather caps, appeared in the cathedral. People outside heard beautiful music, went in, and found the place full of people, the altar candles burning. Dance music was being played, which infected everybody to such an extent that they forgot where they were and danced round madly. The music got wilder and wilder, with drums, violins, and trumpets, and when the organ joined with the thunder of the underworld, people could stand it no longer. The teacher, the district court judge, and the public prosecutor jumped about like goats, together with the market women. When the music ceased, Pistorius, an old member of the consistory, appeared in all his vestments, and the people were suddenly silent and fell on their knees, begging for pardon as he went up to the pulpit. But from the pulpit came loud, continuous laughter; Pistorius's full, red face became smaller and whiter; for a minute he looked like a half-grown boy. Then there appeared, standing up in the pulpit, his shaggy front legs supported on the reading desk, a bleating, white he-goat. It was a mass hallucination in which they were all caught, all except Flamm, the teacher, who began to speak until hundreds of boys descended on him from the organ and clapped and mocked him. Then a naked youth appeared at the altar and played on his flute, whereupon the choir appeared as dogs among the people. Those who were frightened tried to escape, but the doors were shut, so they climbed up on the benches and tried to get out by the windows. When the flute fell silent, the youth, the boys and the roses all disappeared and the doors stood open. No one dared say a word, and they slunk out onto the street.

The judge, who had been in the cathedral, went across to the court, where a man was to be tried for a sex murder. The public prosecutor stood up to speak and opened and shut his mouth for an hour, getting more and more excited, but not a word was audible. When he dropped, white and exhausted, onto his seat, a woman dressed in white applauded. The defendant's lawyer then got up to speak, but before he could begin, his exact double appeared before him and accused him of being a fraud. He was so horrified that he could only stammer a few words, whereupon the other accused him of being unable to say anything in his defense. With difficulty, the uproar in the court was quelled. Then the fraudulent lawyer began a long speech in which he said that after all, the accused was only seeking his own pleasure, just as others seek their pleasure in judging. What was the difference? Some took pleasure in morality and others, in immorality: some, in murdering people and others, in following the law. He turned everything upside down, and there was such confusion of the just and the unjust that everyone was exposed in his apelike greed and amorality. In place of the counselor, the naked boy who had played his flute in the cathedral appeared, and a woman dressed in white then intimated that she and the counselor had spent half an hour together in the next room, where she had been quite irresistible, and that he had stuck a paper knife into her breast when, in his arms, she had first turned into a boy and then a sow. The ivory handle of the paper knife was still visible in her breast. The boy took hold of the counselor's hand and said, "See, it is full of blood," and as the blood ran onto the ground, the accused came up and good-naturedly asked the counselor for a kiss, saying that they were brothers. The accused was then declared innocent; the boy and the woman in white clapped their hands and cried out, "And now, kiss each other!" Once more, there was a terrific scene in which everybody embraced and kissed—anyone and everywhere. Outside, all the bells of the town began to ring, and everybody questioned everybody else—contended, contradicted, fought, screamed, and raged—until the police came with their swords.

While all this was happening in the law courts, the king was in the theater. (He was a romantic young man and sick of ruling. Actually, he appeared very much to resemble Ludwig II of Bavaria, the artist king.) He was deadly bored with his duties as king and, sitting in his royal box, was filled with romantic ideas and melancholy, and was bored with the play. In the principal scene, there was a discussion between the hero of the play, the director of some electricity works, and his stepbrother. The director made a long speech in favor of materialism, of himself and of his like, saying that with them, the gold is in the good hands of practical idealists. But then two boys appeared on the stage, and once more there was chaos. The director was transformed into a ball, which was first tossed from one boy to another and then to the king, who caught it and threw it back, whereupon it burst with a loud bang. The king clapped delightedly, and two more boys appeared, putting a crown on his head, a scepter and an orb into his hands, and an ermine cloak around his shoulders. The boys took him by the hand and led him down a ladder of flowers which had appeared between the box and the floor of the theater. The audience stared in dumb horror. The court marshal tried to save the situation by shouting "Hurrah!" and some began to sing the national anthem; the crown fell from the king's head and proved to be made of paper. Smoke began to rise from the corners of the house. The king and boys disappeared, the doors burst open and dark figures appeared with hatchets and pistols, and the audience shrieked, saying that these were the people of the underworld. People were shot or killed by the swords and hatchets of the intruders; the smoke increased and the building burst apart, burying the people underneath it.

Throughout the town, a terrific battle was going on, and nobody knew who was fighting whom. A dark figure had swung himself onto the top of a stationary tram in the marketplace, and, standing in the glow of the burning theater, he cried out, "Friends! Stop! Be reasonable! It is only because you are afraid of each other that you are murdering each other. The old order makes enemies of you. Create a new order! Do not forget who are your real enemies. They are the boys! They hide everywhere and in every form. Who are they? Who knows them? Where do they come from? Wherever they appear, everything becomes chaotic. If you follow them, you will have no peace. The ground will shake under your feet. All life and order will vanish. A whirlwind will seize you, and madness will tear you apart in horror!"

For a minute, the people remained motionless, but their uneasiness grew. Cries, oaths, and questions broke out: "The boys! The boys! The boys! Where are they? Look for the boys! Kill them! No, kill that man, he is a traitor!"

Again, the speaker stretched out his hands. "My friends," he began, "you are searching for God, the new God, to be created by your own will, your longing, and your work. (The God whom the ego has created! What nonsense!) You want your life to have a new form; you want a holy order, the holy order of your work. It lies within you, this holy order and longing. I will show it to you. I will teach you about that which you feel within you. I will give you the laws you can follow. We (the ghost world of von Spät) want to heal and to serve you!"

The moonlight fell on the figure, and a crowd of people surged around him, begging him to teach them and to stay with them.

"We want to help you," answered the figure, his voice sounding like a bell. "Do not dive again into the old dark well! Do not hunger for an eternity that does not exist!"

Again, the crowd cried out for the boys, saying they would kill them. The figure warned against touching them, but nobody listened. In the middle of the square a flame shot up, and a group of naked boys appeared in its red light. In a second, there was a deadly silence. A boy moved forward and spoke, "Come to us, those of you who are free. Let the others build towers up to heaven! Let them petrify in their order, work, and happiness! Let those who love the flame and eternal transformation come to us—into our night when their day suffocates you—into our kingdom when theirs is destroyed!"

A song broke out from the naked group, and a shudder went through the crowd. But then a new song joined in, for the glassy men were also singing. The crowd seized rifles and made a dash for the boys, but a gust of wind changed into the sails of an immense fireboat which lifted the singing group above their heads. There were shouts of "Shoot them down! Don't let them escape!" The guns took aim, the fireboat in which the boys were collected dispersed in sparks. Millions of roses were scattered all over the square, filling the air with sweet, breath-taking scent.

From the boat (clearly the Thespis boat car of Dionysus) and the roses, it becomes more and more evident that this is an apparition of the old archetypal figure of Dionysus in a new form; from the two speeches I have given you, it is clear who von Spät and Fo are, for the polarity is obvious.

The contents of the book speak for themselves. It is amazing to think that the book was written about fifty years ago and that we have passed through all that was predicted—which shows how prophetic art can be. Even the burning of the Reichstag came about, and there is no need to make any further interpretation. But the strange and uncanny thing is the motif of the burned town, upon which the light-hearted and thin, upper architecture is constructed. That shows if there is such a hole in the staircase—such a blatant contrast between the lower, emotional, archaic parts of the psyche, with its pagan outlook on life, and an upper layer of higher civilization—then, if the problem is not made conscious and faced, it continually creates general catastrophes such as wars and revolutions, followed by a kind of repressive reconstruction on top of the debris, the old rubbish not having been cleared away.

It is frightening that just this is happening again in Germany, for the Germans are creating a big economic boom, with great *élan*, upon the burnt-out ruins of the world wars, and the one thing which you cannot presently discuss with the Germans is what really happened. Most people in Germany do not want to face that particular question—it is all past, it was horrible, and "I disapprove of what took place, but let us not look at it anymore. Let us quickly build up again a new form of life"—which means that nothing has been cleaned up. Now that things have quieted down, they do not say, "Let us look back and ask ourselves what really happend, psychologically," for it would now be the moment for reflection. Instead, a subterranean world is built up once more, teeming with revolution which is already showing itself.

It is as if people break down neurotically and pick up again with the help of a drug, and then go on in the same old way, instead of turning to the unconscious and asking what was at the bottom of it. In a breakdown, there is always something positive which wants to come through and which creates the breakdown; if the person does not turn and do as Cinderella did—discriminate between the good and the bad corn—that person not only loses connection with the positive values of the unconscious. The same is true of National

Socialism, which was a distorted impulse towards renewal and creativeness. If this archetypal figure, Fo—who is clearly a kind of new form of the archetypal savior figure—had been realized by the Germans, not in this political Führer craze, but subjectively or inwardly, it would have been the beginning of a great, creative dynamism. Instead, it was externalized and mixed up with political propaganda and a fatal power drive which culminated in the catastrophe which we have all seen and from which we have all suffered.

On a large scale, we see a development absolutely parallel to the development of the neurotic individual, for what is constellated in a neurosis is really something creative which, if not recognized, will work towards a breakdown. If one turns towards it, that which makes one sick is also that which heals. It is clear from this book that the romantic, religious *élan vital* of National Socialism might have brought about a tremendous cultural renewal of the German people and great progress in consciousness, but because of the wrong twist, the dynamic energy got into extroverted political aims instead, and the opposite came about with the terrible catastrophe. There is another reason why I lecture on this book (I speak of the Germans because the book came out of Germany, but the problem is widespread): the same situation exists in America, especially among teenagers and juvenile delinquents. In different countries there is a different tinge, but it is the modern problem and not just the German problem, although Germany was the first, the *locus minoris resistentiae* (place of lesser resistance) where the disease showed itself. But we all suffer from it in different variations.

If this breakthrough of the new God had been realized inwardly, it would have led to the discovery of the unconscious and the necessity of turning creatively towards one's own unconscious. But von Spät, who represents the eternal seduction to turn the unique inner experience into an outer collective order, got the Germans into this fatal vicious circle. What is more terrifying is that the Germans are building a light rococo architecture again, all rosy and white, on top of the burnt-out ruins. They are therefore moving toward another catastrophe—unless for once a few people notice what they (and we) are moving into.

Question: Are there any large groups in our society which do not have what you describe as "a hole in the staircase"?

I would say that the problem exists least in Italy and in the

Mediterranean countries, but they have it too, because naturally this wind blows everywhere, even over the Alps. The book says it: "Winds blow southwards."

I will now give a short resume of the rest of the book, but first I want to say what Miss Rump has found out about the name "Li." With "Fo," it is clear that the author means Buddha, but "Li" is a very great problem because there are innumerable "Li's" in the Chinese dictionary, and it is not clear which the author means. The most probable would seem to be "reason and reasonableness, order," because, you remember, Melchior represents the ego-figure torn between those two opposites, so that Li—reason—would fit best with the ego. Moreover, Melchior is a chemist, a scientist, and until the time when he became torn between those two powers, he might really have been called the cultivated, reasonable scientist. So he is reason, or consciousness, torn between the opposites. Miss Rump also informs me that the original meaning is quite interesting: namely, the secret tracings which one finds in precious stones, the tracings and patterns such as those found in an opal or an onyx, in which there are frequently dark, interior patterns. But how does such a secret pattern become the basis for the word "Li"— "reason"? One must naturally think in Chinese terms. You know that all the cultural patterns in China were obtained, according to the myth, from the meandering of the big Chinese rivers. They sketched the map, and these patterns stand for the cultivated surface of the Chinese earth. So for China, consciousness would be an awareness of the secret pattern of nature.

The Chinese, the Eastern peoples—and, strangely enough, to a certain extent, the Germanic people—are not interested in causal rationalism; instead, the natural tendency is towards becoming aware of the patterns of Tao, an awareness created by divination, and, through that, an awareness of synchronicity and of image analogies. Within this mentality the secret patterns in a stone correspond to reason; in the book, however, there is a fatal association because Fo and Li connect, and if you write them together, you arrive at "foli(e)." Since the outbreak of the whole mass psychosis is predicted in this book, it is possible that the author thought of this connection.

The next chapter is called "The Transformation of Love." Melchior (now called Li) walks over the sunburnt earth. Bushes are in flower, and under his feet he feels the burning soil. He feels elated as he walks through nature; every bush reaches out to him and he feels completely relaxed. The waves of the river follow along beside him, and as the sun sinks slowly, the river increases in size, as does the noise of the waves, until they take hold of him, pressing on his feverish skin and lifting him off the earth. Suddenly, he hears a cry from the earth, and falls. Lips search for his mouth, and he realizes that he is embracing a delicate human being. He feels the pressure of lips on his mouth and enfolding arms. He feels skin against his own and hears the beating of a heart, and realizes that he is embracing a woman.

"Who are you? And where do you come from?" he asks.

Their embraces become more and more passionate. He feels as if a white hall with columns in it rises around them, but the columns dissolve in a blaze of scent, and there are dark walls which glitter fleetingly.

His body changes and is transformed, and he realizes that he has a woman's body and is in a Lesbian embrace with another woman who, in turn, changes into a bronze giant with a broad chest and strong, bony arms, whose white teeth gleam between black lips and whose eyes are unfathomable. One change follows another, for the giant has changed into a being with a brown face and thick, laughing lips, the long fingers of whose hands caress him. Afterwards there is a Negress, then an Indian, and then a dark girl. In every-changing embraces, he knows himself to be in new rooms and with different bodies. Sometimes he is a slave, kissed by an emperor; sometimes a whore, together with soldiers who smell of blood; sometimes a priest, in the scented bed of a delicate woman. Everything becomes dark, and he can no longer distinguish anything. Then he finds himself between temple walls, beside which stand motionless, slit-eyed priests, while he himself, a black-haired peasant, is tied together with a peasant woman on an altar, looking around with tortured, animal eyes and bleeding from many wounds. The priests surround him, their swords raised; Li cries out in nameless terror and the swords strike. Li sees his blood spurt and everything becomes a red mist. Out of the mountain rises a primeval forest with giant trees and man-high bushes. The roars of tigers come out of the bushes. A panther digs his claws into Li's flesh, and he himself is a wild, spitting cat. Millions of gay-colored birds scream overhead, and Li dissolves in emptiness and knows no more.

He falls and falls. In one second, he falls through all the rooms through which he has passed. He hears music. Through the endless forests of pillars move crowds of dancers. A tremendous light breaks and sunlight bursts through circles of blue. He awakes on cushions of clouds to find Fo sleeping beside him, breathing quietly. From his face comes a light, and his lips twitch now and again as though in slight pain. His body lies clear and white in the morning light and is of such grace and charm that tears flow from Li's eyes. Fo opens his eyes and sees Li. Taking his face between his hands, he kisses him on the brow. They look around and see their comrades awakening in the new dawn.

Here you can see that the kingdom and the power of Fo become as dominating, strong, and absolute as was the power of von Spät, for now Li is drawn into the earth and the principle of eternal transformation, whose main drive is Eros, or even sexuality in all its different forms.

The next chapter is entitled "Downfall." The boys raise their hands to the light in greeting, but there is a rushing in the air and they cry that the storm is coming. "The storm, the storm!" they cry. "The kingdom is approaching! We're home!"

"We are home!" repeats Fo. "We are diving into the black springs to bloom afresh in the world!" Then they sing a refrain which comes again and again in the book: "Time sinks, Space disperses, Gestalt is obliterated."

The boys surround Fo, trembling. Fo lets his arms sink and his limbs begin to shiver in pain, and soon the whole group is shaken with pain. Their faces suddenly seem age-old and faded, their eyes blind, their skin flabby, and their hands thin and clawlike. All look at Fo, who appears bent under a heavy burden. As in a fog, figures stream out of him. They flutter around and disappear into emptiness. Out of all the others also, who are twisting in pain, come many figures: girls, old people, ghosts, angels, wings, men in all kinds of dress, and soldiers in full uniform. Li sees hundreds of faces. He is plagued by dreadful pain; he cries out and hears how the others also cry. Their groans are mixed with the sound of the forms in the air and the rising storm.

With every shadow that separates from the boys, their bodies become more ethereal, their movements become weaker, and their cries, softer. They begin to glow with a soft, inner light, but the train of forms never comes to an end because they have to let out all those formations with themselves—the eternal incarnations in their different forms—before they can enter the kingdom. The boys grow weaker and weaker, but their suffering is voluntary, because it means the approach of the kingdom. Their eyes fixed on Fo, they do not notice how the far-away lights of their home become covered with mist and disappear; they do not feel the unfriendly air which surround them. They are lamed by their own heaviness. Who had them in his power? Who has approached to seize the defenseless blind? A roll of thunder gives them a terrible shock. The clouds in which they had floated disappear and earth appears beneath them. They want to cry out, but they cannot. Almost soundlessly, the words drop from Fo's lips: "That . . . is . . . not . . . the . . . kingdom."

With all their strength, they try to pull themselves together before the last of the forms can leave them, but the swamp fastens on them and swallows them. Fo's eyelids droop over his eyes. Li sees how Fo falls to the ground, but he is unable to move to help him. Many-colored birds circle around, fluttering hither and thither, and strange figures appear in the middle of the group. Silently, they approach the stiffened figures and lay their arms around the necks of the boys to kiss them.

In the eyes of the some of the boys appears a nameless horror. Fear gives new power to their limbs, and they thrust the strangers away, but the others let themselves be kissed. As one of the strangers approaches Fo, Li cries, "Wake up! Wake up!"

But Fo does not hear, and the stranger bends over him. Scarcely had he touched him when Fo springs up, crying, "Hold back! Stop! Save yourselves! Hold back!" The few boys who had defended themselves, with Fo's eyes on them, make a terrific effort and recover. "To me! To me!" cries Fo to the others, but it is too late. The sacrifices, sunk in a deathlike sleep, do not hear, and the strangers breathe upon the floating, released shadows, which dissolve in the air. Without looking around, the strangers go, carrying their prisoners with them, and as they move off, their bodies are transparent as glass.

Li finds himself on a wide, icy surface. "What is happening?" he asks himself. "Since the enemy barred the way to the kingdom, something has happened to us. We are losing ourselves hopelessly in a maze. We don't know each other anymore. Our group is becoming scattered."

The sun shines red. A gust of wind sweeps away the snow. The ice is like a mirror, and Li feels the freezing cold.

Here we have the other enantiodromia. Just as when Li was crowned and had cried out that he wanted to go away and the boys had carried him back, so now, when they are near the kingdom and detaching from all projections—in the Eastern sense of the word, getting free from karmic projections, from involvement in the world, and turning positively to the kingdom, discovering the Self—then at this moment the other pole again interferes and the swing is back again. They have missed the turning point. Once more, it is a meaningless enantiodromia.

Practically, this is best illustrated in the alternating states of schizophrenic people, for there are moments when they are filled completely with the collective unconscious in the form of constant transformation, and they even say that they are God, or Jesus, or the tree of life, or the gold-and-silver island. They may say, "I and Naples have to give macaroni to the whole world," for that is the kind of speech which is made at such a time. In that form, the person is caught in the collective unconscious, in eternal transformation. But if it is a schizophrenic episode that has something fatal in it, there is fragmented rationalism in the material, for just as they say, "I am Jesus Christ, I am the World Tree," which is understandable, they go on, "I and Naples must provide the world with macaroni," which brings in absolute banality, a fragmented part of the banal outer-ordinary, which disturbs the harmony of this manifestation of the collective unconscious and by which schizophrenic material can at once be recognized, for fragments of intellectual banalities are inseminated in most important material. You could say that in such material there are von Spät fragments; that the glass kingdom is broken up and ground in with the collective unconscious material. To say, "I and Naples must provide the world with macaroni" is complete nonsense, but to say "I am Christ and the World Tree" is quite meaningful, because we have a divine source in the Self, and every Christian mystic must accept that with a grain of salt. If one could sort out the material, the illness would not be fatal, but if the individual pulls out of it with drugs and without sorting the grains, then he falls into the rigid normality which is typical for the post-psychotic state. Then people are rigid, normal, and highly intellectual, and they totally condemn everything they had experienced, saying that they do not want to talk about it. They completely repress it and carry on in the rigid normality of established reason, which is generally the standard of the collective conscious, and intellectually, something very cheap.

In both cases, two things are lacking: first, the possibility of realizing the reality of the psyche, for the schizophrenic takes the archetypes and the inner world as being completely real when he is in this state, which is why he thinks he is Jesus Christ. But he does not say that with the nuance of the mystic; he means it quite literally, for he will say that he is Jesus Christ and therefore is not going to his office tomorrow, which shows that he does not understand it on the level of the soul, or the inner plane, but takes it literally and concretely. In my experience, the greatest fight one has in getting a schizophrenic out is to make him understand the symbolic level of interpretation, for he insists on the thing being concrete, and in that way, he introduces a strange rationalism and materialism into his madness. He does not see that there is a reality of the psyche. He cannot accept the hypothesis of psychic reality as opposed to outer physical reality; he mixes the two, which accounts for the nonsense. When such people snap into the von Spät state, they are rational, but again they do not recognize the reality of the psyche.

The other thing which is lacking is the feeling function; that is, the possibility of assessing values correctly. Dr. Jung tells the story of a schizophrenic patient of his who stopped to listen to something from time to time. He had great difficulty in finding out what she was doing when she broke off like that, but finally she confessed that she was telephoning the Virgin Mary—just quickly getting her opinion! At such times, the patient was inaccessible because there was someone else on the line with whom to speak! Now, if you had a mystical experience of the Virgin Mary such as a Christian mystic might have, then you would be completely overwhelmed. People who have had such inner experiences remain shaken for days afterwards, which is an adequate reaction to an overwhelming religious experience. But it is typical for a schizophrenic to say, "Hullo! Oh, yes! The Virgin Mary? Okay," so that either you believe nothing of it, or you are horribly shocked. In that case, the values are lacking. If people are raving, everything is said in the same tone, whether they are Jesus Christ, or delivering macaroni. The cheapest banalities and the deepest religious material are interspersed without any evaluation.

For this reason, the fairy-tale motif is very meaningful where the figure of Psyche, in the famous tale of "Amor and Psyche," has, like Cinderella, to discriminate between the different grains, separating the good from the bad, which means that it is a function of the psyche to discriminate values. If the anima is lost out of sight, feeling is lost, and that happens often in schizophrenia. As soon as feeling and contact with the anima in a man have gone, then there is this picture, and many get into such a state that a mass psychosis arises, just as we have already had and as we may possibly have again.

Now Li is caught in the ice and finds himself among the ghosts of the dead. He sees his dead father, Henriette Karlsen, and Otto von Lobe once more. He feels cold and lost. He wanders about, and we see that he is slowly moving back again to the north and to the ice pole of von Spät. You know that von Spät is associated with ice and the north and that when the wind blows southward, Fo is approaching. Here, naturally, the cold belongs to the land of the dead. (We have to skip some of the book.) He sees a horse, a white bird, and Fo beside him, and says to Fo, "Now let's go." They jump onto a black horse and ride off, but part of him feels doubtful and cheated—something is uncanny—but Fo hurries him on and they get into a boat. In the same moment, with no preceding dawn, the sun rises. Li looks into the eyes of the steersman and sees von Spät. He gives a cry and everything goes dark. Von Spät had taken on the appearance of Fo and had gotten him into the boat by trickery. It is again an enantiodromia, but this time, one factor comes near consciousness; namely, that von Spät and Fo are two semblances, or aspects, of the same thing—each is secretly the other—which is something which one always find in extreme psychological opposites, for at the turning point, the two are one. It is the Tai-gi-tu of Chinese philosophy: the germ of the opposite is always in the black or in the white.

The next chapter is called "The Return." It opens in a lunatic asylum where people walk up and down in a garden. One of the women has the beard of her late husband in a glass frame, and she asks the warden and everybody else to bring him back to life.

Among the madmen is a sad-looking old man whom we can recognize as Melchior. When he went to the boat, Melchior probably died, and in a reincarnation, arrived in a lunatic asylum. There is a description of the way the people in the asylum sing and fight with each other, all of which we have to skip. Another old man, a bald-headed paranoic, walks up to Melchior and says, "Listen quietly to me for once. We must not continue to misunderstand each other. Why do you always spy on me? That is senseless!"

"I don't," says the other.

"Yes, you do. I can feel it. You have done so from the first day you came here, but let's not speak of that. I am the emperor, as you know, but I don't want to be acknowledged as such. I live in a thousand forms, but you knew me at once. I also know who you are. You are a great man, a great master. I will not mention names, but I know you. Why should we live in enmity? We could unite. Let's divide up; you take the south and I will take the northern part of the earth (the two poles). I am even ready to give you a part of my share, for I will admit that in the south, the people are less intelligent, but that part is easier to rule. Let us join up! I will accept any proposition you care to make. Or, perhaps, you would like the north? Take it! I will take the south. I don't mind! The south is quite enough for me; that doesn't matter. The main thing is that you don't persecute me anymore! Let's unite! It is high time, for otherwise everything will grow over our heads. We must destroy mankind before there are too many, and we must do it quickly before they notice anything, for otherwise they will stop us. We want to bring paradise on earth again, for the world has become too ugly. We will save a few women so that by them we can generate new human beings. But be careful, for God's sake! Tell nobody! We must keep it all a secret."

He stretches out his hand, but the other old man, Melchior, answers, "I don't know what you mean!"

The bald-headed man says, "Don't you want to do it? Do you want it all for yourself? Ah! Now I know! You want to kill me! But look out for yourself! I am watching! I know! I know!" He looks round everywhere and sees a white figure in the distance. He runs away, screaming.

The white figure, who is the doctor, approaches Melchior and asks how he is. Melchior asks to be set free. The doctor answers that he knows he is completely cured, that the wonderful chemical experiments he has performed there fully established that. "And I shall not try to rid you of your fixed idea that you are the Dr. Melchior von Lindenhuis of Schimmelberg, who disappeared a hundred years ago. I think it is impossible to get you away from that idea, but the wild fantasies you had a year ago when you were found in a boat, drifting about on the open sea, have left you. However, you still cannot remember your real name, so in order to make it easy for you with the authorities, I will request that you be allowed to use that name, and then you can continue your courses at the University and live a normal life again."

Three days later, Melchior is set free.

This is a fatal turn, because, though veiled with madness, the other half—the shadow, the bald-headed, old man—has tried to unite the opposites. It is a last-minute attempt in the lunatic asylum to unite them, to bring together the two sides—the southern and the northern half of the world, Fo and von Spät—to recognize the opposites and realize that they are two aspects of the same thing, but then it is mixed up with megalomanic ideas of destroying the whole world and creating a new race. As you know, the *Herrenrasse* (the sovereign race) was one of the fantasies of the Nazi regime: all other people were to be destroyed quickly because of overpopulation (a part of the trouble that we face in the present), and a new race was to be created. The proposition of the bald-headed man shows a strange mixture of constructive tendencies (the union of the opposites) and of megalomanic, destructive fantasies. The union of the opposites does not succeed, and Melchior regresses into rational normality once more. If we refer it to the author, he must have been near complete madness, in which he could have realized the problem of the opposites, but instead he switches into the one-sidedness of his conscious standpoint. So Melchior is released from the asylum, becomes a professor at the university, and is once more successful in a boring way, just as at the beginning of the book.

On his way home one afternoon, he sees a young man in the street who has the typical beauty of the ephebi and whose whole appearance attracts him. As he passes, he looks at the man and then lifts his hat and introduces himself. The young man looks astonished, but says he is Walter Mahr (The "Mar," i.e., nightmare, and "mare," the female horse). Melchior explains that he had the impression that he had seen him somewhere before, but the young man replies that he does not know how that could be; that he was born and grew up in that town from which he has never been away; and that Melchior has only lived there for three years. But they are standing at the door of Melchior's flat, and he begs the young man to come in for a few minutes. There, Mahr confesses that, as a boy, he had often dreamed of a face like Melchior's, though much younger. "Yes," Melchior interrupts. "One dreams many things, and I may well have dreamed of you."

"I dreamed," Mahr continues, "that the face looked in at the window and called me in a voice that was also like yours. And once, another sat on the edge of my bed and said I should follow him and let myself be crucified."

Melchior's excitement grows as Mahr talks, and he says that everything has become confused to him and that he cannot remember. He mutters to himself about the cross and streaming blood, and then he tries to fire Mahr with the idea of their going off together. Mahr looks at him and then seizes his hand, kisses it and says he will come. Melchior tells him to go now, but to come again tomorrow and to get ready to wander.

When Mahr has gone, Melchior sits thinking for a while; then he undresses and looks in the mirror at the young beauty of his body and wonders what his bald head is doing on such a body. Then he dresses again and sits down at his desk to write, but it occurs to him that there is no sense in doing that work anymore. For the first time, he goes out into the street and into a coffeehouse, where he meets a friend. They talk of the fête being held in commemoration of the big revolution of one-hundred years earlier in Stuhlbrestenburg, and of the scenes in the street and the killing of the king in the theater. But Melchior interrupts, saying he is tired and must go home.

In the street, he thinks he hears steps. The streets, lamps, the heavens, and the stars, all seem strange, and he hears steps keeping pace with his own. Without noticing it, he breaks into song in which he is joined by an invisible choir. The singing gets louder; pipes, drums, and cymbals play a march, and he sees himself entering a lighted city, riding a white horse. At the windows and on the balconies of the palace are veiled women and girls, and as he reaches the middle of the square, they let their veils fall and stand there naked, throwing roses. A door opens before Melchior, boys hold the bridle of the horse, and Melchior gets down—and finds himself in an empty street standing in front of his own door.

He cannot take another step; his knees give way, and he falls down. Lying there in the snow, he cries until he cannot cry anymore. He gets up and goes up the steps to the door, but he shrinks back as he puts the key in the door; it is as though the door were warning him. He hesitates and thinks of going back to the coffeehouse to wait there for morning, but when he remembers all the empty streets and his tiredness, he cannot, so he overcomes his horror. On the stair, he stands in the dark, listening, and before his own door he almost turns away again—it seems so strange and frightening. In his flat he hurries to his room, strikes a light, and lets the match fall, feeling that a stranger is there. He clearly hears the breathing of the sleeper and thinks he recognizes it. At last, he lights a candle and sees a sleeping man with fair, wavy locks in the armchair by the fireplace. Melchior looks at the sleeper and recognizes von Spät. In the same moment, the fog in his memory leaves him and he remembers everything that happened.

"Now," he thinks, "now I have him in my power, now I am the master. I am awake and he believes me to be powerless. Now I shall call the boys and they shall tie him up." He looks at von Spät and sees the morbid, divine face, which fascinates him again, but he shakes off the temptation and cries out, "I want to go away!"

Nothing happens. He raises his arms and cries again, "I want to go away!" But still there is silence and nobody comes. For a third time he cries out, but it is useless. He lets his arms drop and knows that he is alone and that the boys are in the power of the stranger.

"It is all over," thinks Melchior, and feels terribly tired. He looks at von Spät again, who is still sleeping. He is afraid to look at his eyes and hear him speak. Carefully, without undressing, he lies down on his bed and immediately falls asleep.

He dreams that the glass men have overcome everything and that the boys are destroyed. It is a long dream, and at the end of it, he hears his name called and comes face-to-face with von Spät. He draws his knife and dashes at him; like a flash, he carves a cross on his breast. Von Spät cries out, "Melchior!" And Melchior wakes up and sees von Spät standing there, a lighted candle in his hand, and it is still night.

"The world is mine," says von Spät. "It was useless to call the boys. They could not hear you. They are only reflections in a mirror."

"I do not belong to you!" cries Melchior. "My will is my own!"

"I will break it, as I have broken others," says von Spät, calmly. "Come with me, and I will show you the last act."

"The game never ends," says Melchior.

"Come with me," repeats von Spät, "and look!"

Out on the street, the snowstorm has intensified. They walk for over an hour, the snow blowing in their faces, but at last they come to a dark alley and a dilapidated house where an oil lantern burns. Von Spät halts. Over the entrance are the words: "World Stage Radium."

"We have arrived," says von Spät, who had not spoken all the way, and he knocks with his stick three times on the door. A dwarf looks out.

"You are late," the dwarf says. "The audience has all gone. Nobody wants to see it, but we are continuing to play to the end. The last act is just about to begin." He leads them through old passages, with cracks in the walls, until they come to a door in the wall through which he begs them enter and enjoy themselves. They sit down and look into the empty auditorium. It is dark, except for an occasional lantern in whose light a couple of forms move about.

"It's a good place," says von Spät. "One can see the actors from an angle which prevents one from taking the play too tragically."

"What does it matter to us? What shall I see here?" asks Melchior.

"The last act," repeats von Spät.

A bell rings and curtain flies up. Melchior sees the boys and von Spät, doubled on the stage. He sees the same streets that he had seen in a dream an hour or two before, the transparent inhabitants, the immovable inhabitants, and the immovable faces. And this time he knows who they are, for he recognizes the boys.

Von Spät gets up and then sits down on a rather high chair behind Melchior. He pulls out some large opera glasses and, supporting his elbows on Melchior's shoulders, looks at the stage over Melchior's head. The boys dance round von Spät's mirrored form, singing, "Time sinks away, Space vanishes, Gestalt disappears." It is Fo's voice. Melchior wants to jump up, but von Spät's elbows press heavily on his shoulders and hold him down. The dancing boys separate into pairs. An immense gateway rises up in the background. The last smile is stiffening on the boys' lips, their eyes are shut in deep sleep, and the eyes of von Spät's double also close slowly.

Melchior feels the pressure of von Spät's elbows lessen. He turns and sees that he has fallen asleep. He shakes off his elbows and forces away the sleep he feels creeping over him. Strange words pour from his lips and re-echo in the place.

Then he sees a new figure on the stage and recognizes himself. He sees the figure hurry to Fo and shake him, and he sees how Fo slowly opens his eyes and springs up. He hears himself cry, "He is asleep! Now is the time!" They dash at von Spät's image with shining knives. At the same instant von Spät sitting in the box falls lifeless to the ground. Melchior sees himself on the stage with Fo and sees how they hurry away.

The wind seizes Melchior and carries him. Snowflakes fall on his face, a pale light is dawning. He is alone on the snowy streets. Gradually the snowstorm diminishes and the sun tries to break through the clouds. Melchior feels his strength leaving him. He is so weak he can hardly move. Powerless, he drops in the snow and looks into the distance. "The circles are closing," he whispers. "Everything is fulfilled. My shadow has freed your shadow. The enemy is destroyed. Where on the wide earth are you? Beyond the great seas which divide us I hear your voice. Day and night, night and day, you wander over the plains and climb the high mountains. Golden ships with red sails carry you across the sea. Swarms of birds surround your head. Over wild roads you come nearer and nearer. In time it will be morning, and you will appear before me naked and glowing, stars in your hair, and your cool lips will kiss my beating heart. The earth will no longer be dumb. Your words will call to all life, your breath come from everybody, your love blossoms from every heart. The cross will be raised. The awoken will shed their blood into the veins of the world and will transform from one form into another. The new play begins. Grapes darken and await you. See, how we rest, breathing in happiness. Everything is still. Come to us in the foliage of night in naked conflagration, young flame, singing flame, singing flame, Master and Child."

At the end of this hymnlike prayer, he gets up and stretches his limbs. He stumbles through the snow and then thinks he sees a drop of blood in the snow. He looks closer and sees that it is a rose petal. A few steps further on are another and another; the whole way is strewn with them, and in the snow is the trace of delicate, bare feet. He follows the footprints, which lead higher and higher. The fog thickens round him; the earth disappears. Everything is white and grows whiter and whiter; only the rose petals glow, blood red, and draw him on. Far ahead in the fog he sees the back of a figure. His weakness disappears. He feels nothing and knows nothing but the form in front of him.

The sun comes out; the fog suddenly lifts. On a peak, Fo stands in a glow of light, roses in his hair, and spreads his flaming arms.

The tired wanderer falls on his knees. "The kindgom!" he stammers. "The kingdom without space!" and dies.

Again, there was an enantiodromia. Von Spät had won out again by taking Melchior in the boat; a hundred years later, Melchior is in the lunatic asylum, because as soon as you are in the kingdom of intellectual reason, anything experienced at the opposite end—in Fo's realm—seems to be sheer madness. Melchior escapes from the asylum. On the stage, when they stab von Spät, Fo wins again, this time in this world. Fo remains victorious: he finds the kingdom at last, but he leaves his body behind; von Spät gets the body. He himself is a dead old man, which means that the problem is not solved but is again postponed, because if a solution is described as taking place after death, it means that conscious means for realization have not yet been found in this reality. That is why, in Christianity, victory over evil and the union of the opposites are projected into the time after the Day of Judgment. Paradise comes after death. In *Faust*, Faust finds redemption after death, and in *The Kingdom Without Space*, the solution is again projected into after death. Here it is clear that the bridge to realization has not been found because the reality of the psyche is not realized in this fight. It is all fought in the projection—intellect against the archaic reality of the unconscious—but having no name for it and not seeing its reality, the author mixes psychic reality with concrete reality. This is also the ominous background of our present-day problem, in connection with which I would like to quote a saying of Rabelais to which Dr. Jung drew my attention: *La verite dans sa forme brute est plus fausse que la faux.* (Truth in its *prima materia*, in its first appearance, is falser than falseness itself.) And that is very true for what we have just experienced. In spite of it all, these are attempts to bring forth a new creative, religious attitude and a renewal of cultural creativeness

—which can only be a psychological and individual form—but it comes up with such a disgustingly false, political twist that it is falser than wrong itself. In spite of this, however, we must turn towards it and discriminate the seeds in it. Otherwise, we are stuck and are forever building light, "rose-colored" buildings upon burnt-out ruins.

In his life and art, Bruno Goetz himself has gone beyond this unsolved problem. In a poem called *The Fool and the Snake*,[31] he describes the divine *puer* as a symbol which first overcomes, then purifies, and finally unites with, the great snake (Saint Exupéry's boa). The destructive aspect is overcome and the opposites unite in a sacred marriage; let us hope that in the collective development this, too, will follow.

If we compare the two *puer* figures—the little prince and Fo— you see that they have the romantic outlook on life in common, and both are opposed to senex (old man) figures such as the king, the vain man, etc. (in Saint Exupéry) or to von Spät (in Goetz). In both cases, they represent a possibility of an inner creative renewal, of a first realization of the Self, but because of a certain weakness of the ego and an insufficient or lacking differentiation of the anima, these *puer* figures become a lure into death or madness, or both.

An American version giving form to the *puer* image would be Richard Bach's *Jonathan Livingston Seagull*.[32] But Bach's book has a positive end: it is the *love* for his fellow birds which induces Jonathan to return to his flock to teach them to fly. Also, Jonathan is a bird, not a human being, so it is right for him to remain in the air. But there is a dangerous lure for a *puer* to identify with Jonathan and become a "misunderstood genius"—but it can be also rightly understood and then bring a healing message of love, freedom, and devotion to one's task.

In the German version of the novel by Bruno Goetz, it becomes very clear that the *puer-aeternus* problem is not only a personal one, but a problem of our times. The senex, the old man, is characterized as a worn-out image of God and world order, and the *puer*, Fo, is a new God image, which, in the novel, does not succeed to incarnate in man (in Melchior). If the new God image cannot be born in the soul of man, it remains an archetypal unconscious figure, which has dissolving and destructive effects. We are moving towards a "father-

---

[31] Bruno Goetz, *Der Gott und die Schlange* (Zurich: Balladen, Bellerive, 1949).

[32] Richard Bach, *Jonathan Livingston Seagull* (New York: The Macmillan Company, 1970).

less society"[33] and the "son" is not yet born, i.e., realized consciously in our psyches. This inner birth could only take place with the help of the feminine principle. That is why the collective attention has turned now to the latter. If the bitter and intriguing Sophie could become again what she was—Sophia, Divine Wisdom —this could be achieved.[34] Then the *puer* could become what he was meant to be: a symbol of renewal and of the total inner man for whom the neurotic *pueri aeterni* of our days are unknowingly searching.

[33] Alexander Mitscherlich, *Society Without the Father: A Contribution to Social Psychology*, trans. Eric Mosbacher (New York: Schucken Book, Inc., n.d.).

[34] Jung, *Psychology and Religion*, "Answer to Job," pars. 609ff.

BIBLIOGRAPHY

Adler, Gerhard and Jaffé, Aniela, eds. *C. G. Jung: Letters.* 2 vols. Princeton: Princeton University Press, 1973.

Bach, Richard. *Jonathan Livingston Seagull.* New York: The Macmillan Company, 1970.

Cate, Curtis. *Antoine de Saint-Exupéry, His Life and Times.* New York: G. P. Putnam's Sons, 1970.

Eaton, Frank. *Der Deihter Bruno Goetz.* Ria University Studies. Vol. 57, no. 4, 1972.

Goetz, Bruno. *Der Gott und die Schlange.* Zürich: Balladen, Bellerive, 1949.

Hannah, Barbara. *Jung, His Life and Work. A Biographical Memoir.* New York: G. P. Putnam's Sons, 1976.

Hoffmann, Ernst Theodor Amadeus. *Tales of Hoffmann.* New York: Dodd, Mead & Co., Inc., 1932.

Jung, Carl Gustav. *Aion: Research into the Phenomenology of Self.* Vol. 9, part ii. *Collected Works.* Princeton: Princeton University Press, 1959; 2d ed., 1968.

—."Answer to Job." In *Collected Works,* vol. 11.

—.*The Archetypes and the Collective Unconscious.* Vol. 9, part i, *Collected Works.* Princeton: Princeton University Press, 1959; 2d ed. 1968.

—.*The Structure and Dynamics of the Psyche.* Vol. 8, *Collected Works.* Princeton: Princeton University Press, 1960; 2d ed., 1969.

—.*Symbols of Transformation.* Vol. 5, *Collected Works.* Princeton: Princeton University Press, 1956; 2d ed., 1967.

—.*Two Essays on Analytical Psychology.* Vol. 7, *Collected Works.* Princeton: Princeton University Press, 1953; 2d ed. 1966.

—."The Psychology of the Child Archetype." In *Collected Works,* vol. 9, part i.

—.*The Practice of Psychotherapy.* Vol. 16, *Collected Works.* Princeton: Princeton University Press, 2d ed., 1966.

—and Kerenyi, Carl. *Essays on a Science of Mythology.* Trans. R.F.C. Hull. Princeton: Princeton University Press, 1949.

Kubin, Alfred. *The Other Side.* Trans. Denver Lindley. New York: Crown Publishers, Inc., 1967.

Mitscherlich, Alexander. *Society Without the Father: A Contribution to Social Psychology.* Trans. Eric Mosbacher. New York: Schucken Book, Inc., n.d.

Magee, John Gillespie, Jr. "High Flight," in P. Edward Ernest, ed. *The Family Album of Favorite Poems.* New York: Grosset & Dunlap, 1959.

Ovid, *Metamorphoses.* With an English translation by James Justus Miller. (Loeb Classical Library.) 2 vols. London and Cambridge, Mass., 1946.

SIGO PRESS

SIGO PRESS is a publishing firm specializing in Jungian related works with an appreciation for its content and its audience.

OTHER BOOKS AVAILABLE

SANDPLAY: A Psychotherapeutic Approach to
the Psyche   Dora M. Kalff

An excellent tool for anyone working with or interested in art therapy, play therapy and early childhood development.

**ENCOUNTERS WITH THE SOUL: Active Imagination
as Developed by C. G. Jung**   Barbara Hannah

Active Imagination is thought to be *the* most powerful tool in Jungian psychology for achieving wholeness. Barbara Hannah in her book *Encounters With the Soul* illustrates step by step this important method of reaching the unconscious.